THE TESTAMENT OF OUR LORD

THE TESTAMENT OF OUR LORD

*Translated into English from the Syriac
With Introduction and Notes*

BY

JAMES COOPER, D.D.
PROFESSOR OF ECCLESIASTICAL HISTORY IN THE
UNIVERSITY OF GLASGOW

AND

ARTHUR JOHN MACLEAN, M.A., F.R.G.S.
SOMETIME DEAN OF ARGYLL AND THE ISLES

WIPF & STOCK · Eugene, Oregon

Wipf and Stock Publishers
199 W 8th Ave, Suite 3
Eugene, OR 97401

The Testament of Our Lord
Translated into English form the Syriac with Introduction and Notes
By Cooper, James and Maclean, Arthur John
ISBN 13: 978-1-60608-350-5
Publication date 12/19/2008
Previously published by T & T Clark, 1902

PREFACE

IN submitting this TRANSLATION to the Public, I may be permitted to say, in the first place, a few words as to the *Testament* itself, and the principles which have guided its present Translators; and I feel bound, in the second place, to indicate the respective parts which Canon Maclean and I, while jointly responsible for the work as a whole, have taken in producing it.

The *Testament* is one, and not the least interesting, of a series of writings, whereof the *Didaché* or *Teaching of the Twelve Apostles* is the first, and the so-called *Apostolic Constitutions* one of the last, whose aim seems to have been to provide the clergy of the Early Church with a manual of their duties, and especially with directions for the proper fulfilment of the offices of Public Worship. None of these books is authoritative in the sense of having been issued by those who had public authority given them in the Church to do so, nor did any of them succeed by their own merits in obtaining such acceptance as was won by the Great Liturgies. But they certainly helped to prepare the way for the Great Liturgies, and the *Testament* in particular became influential in the process which led to the formation of the Ethiopic and Coptic service books. The fact that they were not themselves accepted is proof sufficient that they never *quite* represented the mind or embodied the ideals of the Church, or of any considerable local section of it. They are coloured, no doubt, by the private idiosyncrasies of their unknown authors. But at least they exhibit to us ideas that were entertained among Christians at the time when they were severally written, and they show how, in the formative period of the Church's worship, the minds of those professionally interested in the subject were working.

The *Testament* possesses the special interest of being the production of the very period—the very moment, we may say—when the great transition in the Church's fortunes, from Imperial persecution to Imperial favour, was leading to the inevitable transformation of her buildings and her services to suit her altered circumstances. She was not going to break with the past: far from it. There was a great deal still in the Empire—in the Government offices, in the Army, in society, that rendered it spiritually unsafe for her members to have much to do with them; and made it needful for her still to take precautions against casting her pearls before swine. There might even be, if Julian's reign was to be prolonged, a recrudescence of pagan persecution. All the same, the Church breathed more freely. She could build for herself churches, baptisteries, clergy-houses, hospices, according to her own ideas of what these ought to be; and she could so order her services, that if those who were not Christians attended them, they might be impressed by their dignity and holiness. At the same time, it was eminently needful that the discipline and order of the Church should be preserved, and that there should be no lowering of the spiritual tone of her ministers and office-bearers.

The *Testament* reflects this state of things as in a mirror. It vibrates, moreover, with the pulsation of the great controversies—Arian, Macedonian, Apollinarian—through which the Church was passing, or into which she was just about to pass. The volume is thus far more than a mere antiquarian curiosity. It had a message to its own time: it has a message to all time, and very distinctly to the time now present. In this light, even its Apocalyptic Prelude—bold as it is, to the verge of profanity—has nevertheless this measure of apology, that our Lord is, in point of fact, no mere figure of the past, but the Living Head of His Church, from whom each of His ministers in succession derives his charge, in and by whom alone he lives, and to whom he must answer at the last.

Probably enough the Compiler meant, by prefixing his startling Prelude, to claim for his work the authority of an undefiled tradition, in which were gathered up those counsels of the Great Forty Days during which the Risen Saviour spake to His disciples the *things concerning the Kingdom of God* (Acts i. 3); but beyond that, there may well have been in his mind the thought now indicated, of the abiding relation between Christ and His Church. That relation, at least, is no pretence, however crude or objectionable the form may be by which the Compiler endeavoured to express it.

Apart from this, the *Testament* is a veritable mine at once of devotional expression and liturgical lore; while its witness to the state of doctrine and the ecclesiastical order and organisation in Eastern Christendom in the middle or third quarter of the fourth century, is of surpassing value.

On account of its devotional merit, my first thought was to render it, or at least its prayers, in such a form as might most easily be used for purposes of worship; but that is a task which the reader who desires thus to use the book may perform for himself. More and more did it become clear both to Canon Maclean and to myself that our business was to give it as literally as possible, so that the English reader might come as near as might be to the sense and feeling of the Syriac. Perhaps this may be found to be best even for him who may search the book for the making of prayers: it is certainly what the student of history, of dogma, and of the usages of the Ancient Church is entitled to look for at our hands.

The full Syriac text of the *Testament* was published, along with a Latin translation, by the Patriarch Ignatius Ephraem II. Rahmani, at Mainz in 1899. In January 1900 his work was put into my hands by the late learned Rev. Professor Dickson, D.D. of this University. A first cursory perusal sufficed to show me something of its historical and liturgical importance, and my impression was deepened when I set myself to make an English translation, for my own use, of Rahmani's Latin rendering. I felt that the

Testament deserved a place in the *Ante-Nicene Library* of Messrs. T. & T. Clark, even if its date might turn out to be somewhat later than that of the First General Council of the Church. I communicated my views to Messrs. Clark, was encouraged by them to go on with the translation I had begun, and I wrote to the Patriarch requesting his permission to issue this; but it very soon became evident that what was really needed was a critical examination and independent rendering of the Syriac text. This I was not competent to supply; and I should have given up the attempt altogether, had I not, very fortunately, been able to secure the collaboration of the Rev. Canon Maclean, whose long residence in the East, on the staff of the Archbishop of Canterbury's Mission to the Assyrian Christians, his knowledge of Syriac, and his experience as the Editor of the Syrian *Liturgy of Adai and Mari*, combined to give him special fitness for the task. He has performed by far the greater part of it. He has collated the Syriac text. His is the translation: his, in great part, the Introduction, the Notes, the Appendices, and even the Index. It is he, not I, that the English reader has to thank, should this book prove of the use we hope it will to the student of the thought and worship of the Church in the fourth century.

It remains only that we acknowledge the kind interest taken in this work by such friends as the Right Rev. the Lord Bishop of Salisbury, and the help derived from the books of the writers whose names are mentioned in the table printed below.

JAMES COOPER.

8 THE COLLEGE, GLASGOW.
September 1902.

CONTENTS

INTRODUCTION—
SEC.   PAGE
- i. Scope of the Work 3
- ii. The Manuscripts 5
- iii. The Parallel Literature 7
- iv. Question of a Montanist Original 15
- v. Theology and Characteristics 16
- vi. Date 25
- vii. Place of Writing 42

THE TESTAMENT OF OUR LORD—
- I. 1–18. Prelude, etc. 49
- 19. The Church Buildings 62
- 20–22. The Bishop 64
- 23–27. The Eucharist 69
- 28. The Mystagogia 84
- 29–32. Presbyters 90
- 33–38. Deacons 97
- 39. Confessors 105
- 40–43. Widows 105
- 44. Subdeacons 111
- 45. Readers 112
- 46. Virgins 112
- 47. Charismata 114
- II. 1–7. Catechumens 115
- 8, 9. Baptism and Confirmation . . . 124
- 10. Baptismal Eucharist 128
- 11, 12. Maundy Thursday, Pentecost, etc. . . 129
- 13. The Agapé 130
- 14. First Fruits 131
- 15. Property 131
- 16. First Fruits 132
- 17. Christian Meals 133

CONTENTS

THE TESTAMENT OF OUR LORD—*contd.* PAGE

II. 18-20. Paschal Solemnities 133
    21. Visiting the Sick 135
    22. The Psalms 135
    23. Burials 135
    24. Hours of Prayer 136
  25-27. Conclusion 137

APPENDED NOTES to Book I. 141

APPENDED NOTES to Book II. 207

APPENDIX I. The Abyssinian Anaphora of our Lord . 245

APPENDIX II. The Mystagogia of the Arabic Didascalia . 252

INDEX OF QUOTATIONS FROM AND REFERENCES TO THE BIBLE . 255

INDEX OF SUBJECTS AND AUTHORS 258

PRINCIPAL MODERN AUTHORITIES CITED

ACHELIS, *Die Canones Hippolyti* in Texte und Untersuchungen (Leipzig: Hinrich, 1891).

ARENDZEN, Articles on the *Apocalyptic Prelude* of the Testament in Journal of Theological Studies, vol. ii., and on the *Apostolic Church Order* in J.T.S., vol. iii. (London: Macmillan, 1901).

BRIGHTMAN, *Liturgies, Eastern and Western*, vol. i., Eastern Liturgies (Oxford University Press, 1896).

—— *The Sacramentary of Serapion of Thmuis* in J.T.S., vol. i. (1900).

BUNSEN, *Analecta antenicaena*, vol. ii. [=*Christianity and Mankind* (in English), vol. vi.], the portion cited here by de Lagarde (London, 1854).

DE LAGARDE (formerly Bötticher), *Constitutiones Apostolorum* (Leipzig: Teubner; London: Williams & Norgate, 1862).

—— *Reliquiae juris ecclesiastici antiquissimae* (Leipzig, 1856).

—— *Aegyptiaca* (Göttingen, 1883).

—— *Didascalia Apostolorum Syriace* (Leipzig, 1854).

DUCHESNE, *Origines du culte chrétien* (Paris: Thorin, 1889, 1st edition; 1898, 2nd edition), for the Pilgrimage of Silvia.

FUNK, *Die Apostolischen Konstitutionen* (Rottenburg, 1891).

HAMMOND, *Liturgies, Eastern and Western* (Oxford University Press, 1878, old edition of Brightman), for the Western Liturgies.

HAULER, *Didascaliae Apostolorum Fragmenta Veronensia Latina*, vol. i. (Leipzig: Teubner, 1900).

HEFELE (Bishop of Rottenburg), *Conciliengeschichte* (*A History of the Christian Councils from the Original Documents*), vols. i., ii., English translation (Edinburgh: T. & T. Clark, 1872, 1876).

JAMES, *Apocrypha Anecdota* in Texts and Studies (Cambridge University Press, 1893).

LUDOLF, *Ad suam historiam aethiopicam commentarius* (Frankfort-on-Main, 1691).

PAYNE-SMITH, *Thesaurus Syriacus*, 2 vols. (Oxford University Press, 1870–1901).

PLATT, *The Ethiopic Didascalia*, with English translation (London, 1834).

RAHMANI (Uniat Syrian Patriarch of Antioch), *Testamentum Domini nostri Jesu Christi* (Mainz : Kirkheim, 1899).

SMITH AND CHEETHAM, *Dictionary of Christian Antiquities*, 2 vols. (London : Murray, 1875, 1880).

SMITH AND WACE, *Dictionary of Christian Biography*, 4 vols. (London : Murray, 1877–1887).

TATTAM, *The Apostolical Constitutions or Canons of the Apostles in Coptic, with an English Translation* (London : W. H. Allen & Co., 1848).

WORDSWORTH, J. (Bishop of Salisbury), *The Ministry of Grace* (London : Longmans, Green, & Co., 1901).

—— Two Articles on *The Testament of our Lord* in Church Quarterly Review for January and April 1900 (London : Spottiswoode & Co.).

—— Article on *The Testament of our Lord* in Revue internationale de théologie for 1900 (vol. 31).

—— *Bishop Sarapion's Prayer-Book* (London : S.P.C.K., 1899).

In the quotations from the above dictionaries and magazines, from Brightman's *Liturgies*, Lagarde's *Constitutions*, Hauler's *Fragments*, Ludolf's *Commentary*, and Wordsworth's *Ministry of Grace*, the numbers denote the pages or columns. Superior numbers, when given, denote the lines on the page.

ABBREVIATIONS

Test.	Testament of our Lord.
C.H.	Canons of Hippolytus.
Const. H.	Constitutiones per Hippolytum.
Eg. C.O.	Egyptian Church Order.
Eth. C.O.	Ethiopic Church Order.
H.	Hauler's Verona Latin fragments.
Copto-arab.	Translation of Testament into Arabic from Coptic.
Ap. C.O.	The Apostolic Church Order.
Ar. D.	The Arabic Didascalia.
Cyr. Jer. (Cat. Lect.)	St. Cyril of Jerusalem's Catechetical Lectures.
A.C.	The Apostolic Constitutions.
Ap. Can.	The Apostolic Canons.
J.T.S.	Journal of Theological Studies.
Dict. Chr. Biog.	Smith and Wace, Dictionary of Christian Biography.
Dict. Chr. Ant.	Smith and Cheetham, Dictionary of Christian Antiquities.
C.Q.R.	Church Quarterly Review.

Words in the Translation enclosed by square brackets are not in the Syriac text.

MANUSCRIPTS OF THE TESTAMENT.

M.	Codex Mosulanus.
B.	Codex Borgianus.
S.	Codex Sangermanensis.
C.	Codex Cantabrigiensis.

ADDITIONS AND CORRECTIONS

Page 40, line 10.—*Add:* "The complete cycle of the festivals in the *Pilgrimage of Silvia* is : Epiphany (*i.e.* the Nativity) with octaves ; the Presentation of our Lord in the temple, forty days later ; Palm Sunday ; Easter, with octaves ; the fortieth day after Easter ; Pentecost ; the Dedication (Holy Cross Day). The commemoration on the fortieth day after Easter seems *not* to have been of the Ascension, which was commemorated at Pentecost together with the descent of the Holy Ghost (so in the *Testament* the Passion and Resurrection were probably commemorated together, p. 39). Possibly there was a Martyrs' festival in Silvia, but the manuscript breaks off at this point."

Page 152, line 22.—*Delete:* "The use of the name. . . . p. 135*b*." *Add:* "Perhaps the earliest use of the name 'archdeacon' is found in the *Pilgrimage of Silvia*, though it there does not, apparently, represent in any way a separate office, but the principal deacon, whose duty it is to call people to prayer, is so called."

Page 159, line 37.—*Add:* "The idea so strikingly brought out in the *Prayer for the Laying on of Hands on a Bishop*, of the Holy Angels as the prelates and priests of God's upper sanctuary, finds a curious illustration in the armorial bearings of the Scottish burgh of Dumfries, in which the Archangel Michael appears mitred and habited as a Western mediaeval bishop, and pierces the Dragon with his pastoral staff instead of a sword or spear. (See also *Dict. Chr. Ant.* i. 87)."

INTRODUCTION

THE TESTAMENT OF OUR LORD

INTRODUCTION

§ i. The Scope and Character of the Book

THE *Testament of our Lord*, of which an English translation is here offered to the reader, is an apocryphal work of uncertain date, which professes to give us the words of our Lord Himself, and to tell what He said to the disciples after His resurrection and before His ascension. It is supposed to be the last Will or Testament which He gave them, and to provide them with rules for the conduct of their work. It professes, in fact, to give in detail "the things" which He spake "pertaining to the kingdom of God" (Acts i. 3). The First Book begins with a preface and an introductory chapter, and then proceeds to an apocalyptic discourse about the end of the world (I. 2–14). Then come four chapters which join on that discourse to the "Church Order" which follows. This "Church Order," of which we find several parallel forms elsewhere, contains minute regulations as to the Church, its buildings, and its organisation, with ordination prayers and a liturgy complete. The Church buildings are first described (I. 19); then the qualifications, ordination, and duties of a bishop (I. 20–22); then the Eucharistic Liturgy, with its pre-anaphoral prayers (I. 23–27); then a "mystagogic" instruction for festivals—that is, the teaching of the mysteries of the Christian faith to the baptized (I. 28); then the qualifications, ordination, duties, and daily prayers of a presbyter (I. 29–32); then the qualifications and duties of a deacon, the Eucharistic Litany said by him, and his ordination (I. 33–38); regulations as to confessors in persecution (I. 39); rules about the order of widows and their prayers (I. 40–43); about subdeacons, readers, virgins, and gifts of healing, etc. (I. 44–47). The Second Book deals first with baptism; it decides who are to be admitted as catechumens, who rejected (II. 1, 2); it gives rules about the instruction (II. 3–5), exorcism (II. 6, 7), baptism (II. 8), confirmation (II. 9), and communion (II. 10) of the candidates. It then passes to the fast before, and ceremonies of, Easter (II. 11, 12, 18–21), the agapé or love-feast (II. 13), offering of first fruits (II. 14, 16), rules for burial and property (II. 15, 23), grace before meals (II. 17), methods of singing (II. 22), hours of prayer (II. 24), and concludes with a return to the pretence of a "Testament."

This work, which is undoubtedly Greek in origin, is only known in translations into Syriac, Ethiopic, and Arabic. Selections from it were first published by Lagarde in Syriac from the Codex Sangermanensis 38, and the same editor attempted a restoration of the underlying Greek of those selections in 1856 in the *Reliquiae juris ecclesiastici antiquissimae*, pp. 80–89. But although complete copies of the work were on the shelves of several European libraries—at Cambridge, Rome, and Florence—no European scholar seems to have thought it worth while to read, or at any rate to make known, the whole book. The credit of publishing this most interesting and curious composition is due to Mgr. Ignatius Ephraem II. Rahmani, the Uniat Syrian Patriarch of Antioch, who published it at Maintz in 1899, using all the manuscripts which are mentioned in the next section, with the exception there noted. Mgr. Rahmani has added prolegomena and dissertations which are mentioned several times in the following pages. If we cannot in all cases agree with

§§ i., ii.] SCOPE OF THE BOOK 5

the views of his Holiness, his work is always suggestive and stimulating.

The *Testament* was translated from Greek into Syriac, as its subscription testifies, by the celebrated James of Edessa in the seventh century; and it is this translation which makes the work known to us. But there are other translations, not yet published, into Ethiopic and Arabic, the latter at least having been very freely altered in its course through Coptic into its present form. There is much evidence that the book was greatly valued, especially in Monophysite circles, and it has left very distinct traces of its influence on the liturgies and ordinals of later times, particularly on those of the Abyssinians and Copts. A short notice of James of Edessa will be found in the Notes to II. 27.

It may here be stated that the aim of this volume is to elucidate the meaning of the *Testament*, and to investigate the customs of the Early Church as they really were, without any consideration of their bearing on modern controversies. It may be further premised, that in this volume the name "Testament Compiler" is used for the writer who put the book, either exactly or approximately, into its present shape. The date of his work of compilation will be discussed below, in § vi.

§ ii. THE MANUSCRIPTS

The following are the Syriac manuscripts used by Rahmani:—

(1) A codex now in the library of the Uniat [Western] Syrian Metropolitan of Mosul, on the Tigris. This contains the Bible and the "Syrian Octateuch" (see below, § iii.), the first two books of which are our *Testament*. This codex was written by one Behnam in the monastery of the Syrian saint of that name, near Mardin in Mesopotamia, in the year 1654 A.D. (or 1652 ?). This codex is called "M." in these pages.

(2) A codex now in the Borgian Museum at Rome, but coming from Mount Lebanon, and dated A.D. 1576. It contains the whole "Syrian Octateuch," and is noted here as "B."

(3) The St. Germain manuscript (Codex Sangermanensis 38), mentioned in § i. as having been used by Lagarde, and noted here as "S." It is much more ancient than the above manuscripts, being referred to the eighth century. It contains extracts only from the *Testament*, but those extracts are taken from all parts of the book, and it is clear that the translation of James of Edessa lay complete before the scribe, with the probable exception of our I. 32 (see Note to I. 33). This codex does not contain the liturgical portions of the *Testament*, and is professedly very fragmentary in the second book. A few additions to Rahmani's collation of Lagarde's edition will be found in this volume.

In addition to these three Syriac manuscripts, Rahmani has used a translation made through Coptic into Arabic, the manuscript of which is in the Borgian Museum at Rome; he promises also to publish this translation, and to his present book the notices of it in this volume are entirely due. The date of the translation into Arabic is the year "643 of the martyrs, which agrees with the year 313 of the Hegira."

Besides these authorities used by Rahmani, there are Syriac texts in the Malabar Bible of the University of Cambridge, and in a book of Church Ordinances in the Laurentian Library at Florence; and there are two copies of an Ethiopic translation of uncertain age, perhaps made from the Coptic or from the Arabic, in the British Museum. But none of these are published.

There is a very short fragment of the apocalyptic prelude in a Latin translation in a manuscript at Trèves (Codex Treverensis 36). This fragment has been published by Dr. M. R. James in *Apocrypha Anecdota*, pp. 151–154 (Cambridge

Texts and Studies, ii. 3, 1893). This has been taken to be the original form of the prelude, but the evidence is not conclusive, and some reasons are given in the Appended Note at the beginning of Book I. for supposing that it is at least possible that it may be an abbreviation of our prelude, and even that it may be translated not from the Greek, but from a Syriac version.

Very important for our purpose is an independent Syriac version of the prelude in a Cambridge manuscript (Cod. Cantab. Add. 2919), published by Dr. Arendzen in the *Journal of Theological Studies* for April 1901 (J.T.S. ii. 401 ff.), and therefore after the publication of Rahmani's work. This manuscript contains I. 2–14*a*; it is headed, "From the Book of Clement on the End"; it professes to give our Lord's own words, but it is only an extract from a longer work, and omits expressly our I. 10. Dr. Arendzen supposes that this translation was made later than that of James of Edessa, but that in some cases it may represent the Greek more faithfully. The chief differences are given in the footnotes, and there is some discussion of them in the Appended Notes, where the question is raised whether this Cambridge manuscript (here called "C.") does not represent a Greek text of the prelude even independent of and prior to the Testament Compiler himself. There is something to be said on both sides of this last question; but if it should prove that C. gives us the prelude as it was before our Testament Compiler inserted it into his work, it would follow that he got his whole idea, if not the name, of a "Testament" from the original of C. This Cambridge manuscript is dated A.D. 1218.

§ iii. THE PARALLEL LITERATURE

1. CHURCH ORDERS OF THE SAME FORM. It has already been mentioned that the *Testament* is one out of many

"Church Orders" which are replicas of one original, with highly interesting variations indeed, but all reproducing the same general outline, and built on the same framework. For a full, yet compendious, description of them—the best that has yet appeared—reference may be made to the newly published *Ministry of Grace* by the Bishop of Salisbury (Dr. John Wordsworth), who in his Introduction gives an admirable account not only of these parallel Church Orders, but of a large mass of other illustrative literature. Only the shortest summary is made here; but it is necessary that the reader should have a conspectus of the Orders before him, or he will be unable to unravel their undoubted intricacies. The contents of these Orders, where they illustrate the *Testament* (and it is often only by a reference to them that we can make any sense out of our book), is discussed and summarised in the Appended Notes; their approximate date is shortly spoken of below in § vi. Here a list of them is given, with a note of the books in which they may conveniently be found.

(α) We must, probably, postulate a "*Lost Church Order*" as the original of the rest. By extracting the common parts of the others, we might restore conjecturally a considerable portion of this original. It has been thought, with much probability, to represent the usage of the Early Roman Church, though, as Dr. Wordsworth points out, it might have been brought to Rome from the outside.

(β) *The Canons of Hippolytus* ("C.H."), which represent perhaps the Roman Church Order of the first part of the third century, are now only known in an Arabic version—a version of a version—and in what is clearly a later form. Their date will be very shortly discussed in § vi.; here it may suffice to say that if Professor Achelis' supposition is correct, they are an interpolated form of a third century book. It might be thought that they represent the original of the other Church Orders, and that we need not postulate a

"Lost Church Order." But they contain so much of which there is no trace in the parallel, or rather later, Orders, that we must look on them rather as a collateral than as an ancestor.[1] They were edited in Arabic with a Latin translation in 1870 by D. B. von Haneberg. But the most convenient form of them for most readers will be that published by Professor Hans Achelis. He gives a Latin translation of the Arabic, with parallels from the Egyptian and Ethiopic Church Orders, the "Constitutions through Hippolytus," and the Apostolic Constitutions, for all of which see below. The sections of C.H. used in this volume are those of Achelis. These Canons do not contain a Liturgy, but they have full Ordination prayers.

(γ) *The Egyptian Church Order* ("Eg. C.O.") forms the second book of the Egyptian Heptateuch (see below). It does not contain a Liturgy or Ordination prayers, and is very much shorter than the *Testament*, with the general outline of which it agrees. The most convenient form of this Order for the English reader will be found in Archdeacon Tattam's *The Apostolical Constitutions or Canons of the Apostles in Coptic*, which gives the Coptic and English side by side. But this book is scarce. Achelis prints a German translation (see β), and Lagarde gives the text in his *Aegyptiaca*, pp. 248-266.

(δ) *The Ethiopic Church Order* ("Eth. C.O.") forms part of the "Ethiopic Statutes" (Stat. 21 ff.). A portion only of them has been published, namely, by Job Ludolf (Leutholf) in his *Ad suam historiam aethiopicam Commentarius*. This book is also very scarce. Ludolf, who gives the Ethiopic text with a Latin translation, publishes first the "Apostolic Church Order" (see 2, below), which takes up Stat. 1-20 incl.,

[1] The following sections of C.H. are wholly wanting in the *Testament*: 1-6, 55-58, 81-90, 93-96, 100, 154-163, 169, 178-185, 195, 196, 201-204, 206-214, 216-219, 222, 226-232, 239-241, 243, 245, 247-261, also some parts of the Ordination prayer in C.H. for a bishop, etc.

and then, in Statutes 21, 22, 23 (pp. 323–328) gives the first part of the Ethiopic Church Order, with Ordination prayers for bishops and presbyters, and an Eucharistic Liturgy. But he unfortunately leaves off just before the Ordination prayer for a deacon. Achelis gives a German translation in his parallels (see β), and an edition of the whole of the Statutes is promised by the Rev. George Horner.

(ϵ) *The Verona fragments*, published by Hauler ("H."), are scattered portions of a compilation in Latin containing the Didascalia, Apostolic Church Order (for which see 2 β, 3, 4 γ, below), and a Church Order which is another form of that we are now considering. The last is of the greatest interest for our purpose, as it forms a connecting link between the *Testament* and the rest, and with some confidence we may consider it to be a direct source of the former. It contains Ordination prayers for a bishop and presbyter, and (in part) for a deacon, an Eucharistic Anaphora, part of a description of baptism, rules for the agapé, etc. Only the first volume of Dr. Hauler's work has been published, the Commentary not yet having been brought out.

(ζ) *The Testament of our Lord* is the form of the "Church Order" which is the subject of this volume.

(η) *The Arabic Didascalia*, §§ 35–39 incl. ("Ar. D."), also contains a portion of a similar Church Order. It is obviously either the immediate source, or the immediate descendant, of the parallel portions of the *Testament*. Reasons are given in the Notes (I. 19–28) for believing it to be derived from the latter. These chapters (only) are published by Dr. F. X. Funk in his work, *Die Apostolischen Konstitutionen*, in a German translation (pp. 226–236).

(θ) *The Constitutions through Hippolytus* ("Const. H."), so called, are usually thought to be a first draft of part of the eighth book of the Apostolic Constitutions, and reproduce part of the "Lost Church Order." A portion is given by Achelis (see β); the text may be conveniently seen in Lagarde's *Reliquiae*, pp. 1–18 (see above, § i.). For a brief discussion of this work and an excellent summary of the parallel literature, see Brightman's *Liturgies Eastern and Western* (" L. E. W."), pp. xvii.–xxiv.

(ι) *The Apostolic Constitutions* (" A.C."), in book viii., also reproduce large portions of the Lost Church Order. See on " Compilations" below (4 δ). The so-called " Clementine Liturgy" is part of this book.

2. OTHER CHURCH ORDERS. (*a*) The well-known *Didaché* or *Teaching of the Apostles*, first published by Bryennios, may be called an elementary " Church Order." It contains moral discourses on the "Two Ways," and rules concerning baptism, the Eucharist, fasting, etc. It probably dates from the first quarter of the second century. It may be conveniently seen in Bishop Lightfoot's posthumous *Apostolic Fathers* (London, 1891), where it appears with Greek text, a short introduction, and an English translation.

(β) *The Apostolic Church Order* (also called " Canones ecclesiastici sanctorum apostolorum ") is a short work which takes the discourse of the "Two Ways" from the Didaché, divided so that a portion is put into the mouth of each of the twelve Apostles, who are enumerated somewhat curiously, Peter and Cephas appearing as different Apostles. It is found in six different languages, and the English reader may study it in Tattam (see iii. 1 γ, above), or in the English version of Bunsen's *Analecta Antenicaena*, or more conveniently, and with some important variations, in Dr. Arendzen's article in the *Journal of Theological Studies* for October 1901 (J.T.S. iii. 59 ff.). Dr. Arendzen has published for the first time a complete Syriac text, from the Cambridge Malabar Bible, and from the Mosul Codex used by Mgr. Rahmani for the *Testament* (see ii. 1, above). This " Apostolic Church Order " has had a considerable influence on the *Testament*. [See Notes on

I. Preface, 16, 19 (division of the presbyters), 20 (marriage of bishops), 40 (widows), all portions which we must probably ascribe to the pen of the Testament Compiler himself.] The date of this work in its present form has been argued to be about 300 A.D., though it must reproduce a Church Order of an age earlier than Tertullian, as it places readers before deacons. Its Montanistic features, and the chief place it ascribes to St. John, will lead us probably to fix on Asia Minor as its place of origin.

3. THE DIDASCALIA does not immediately affect us in the present investigation, though it is of considerable use for illustration. It is supposed to be originally a work of the third century, and is extant in several forms. Lagarde has published it in Syriac (Leipzig, 1854), and has restored the Greek in Bunsen's *Analecta* (see 2 β, above). This is the earliest form known. It reappears in Latin in Hauler's Verona fragments (see 1 ϵ and 4 γ), in the Arabic Didascalia, §§ 1–34 incl. (not published), in the Ethiopic Didascalia, published in Ethiopic and English by Platt (London, 1834), and in a much enlarged form in the first six books of the Apostolic Constitutions (see below). The Didascalia consists of moral instructions with ecclesiastical regulations interspersed, and, in some forms, with a certain amount of liturgical matter.

4. COMPILATIONS. From the above and other material several compilations have been made.

(*a*) *The Syrian Octateuch.* The first two books consist of our *Testament;* the third book, of the Apostolic Church Order; the other five correspond to the eighth book of the Apostolic Constitutions and to the Apostolic Canons; these last five have not been published.

(β) *The Egyptian Heptateuch,* or "Sahidic Ecclesiastical Canons." The first book contains the Apostolic Church Order; the second, the Egyptian Church Order (1 γ); the last five correspond generally to the eighth book of the

Apostolic Constitutions and the Apostolic Canons. The Heptateuch may be read in English (and Coptic) in Tattam (*op. cit.*, see 1 γ, above). Both the Syrian Octateuch and the Egyptian Heptateuch are probably derived from the Apostolic Constitutions, and so treat the matter dealt with in the "Testament" and "Egyptian Church Order" respectively twice over, though in different ways; in their early books giving those works, and in the later reproducing the divergent treatment of the same material in A.C. viii.

(γ) *Hauler's Verona Latin fragments* are a compilation containing (first) the Didascalia, (second) the Apostolic Church Order, and (third) the form of the Church Order parallel to our *Testament* (see 1 ϵ, above). It is this last part which is of supreme importance for our present purpose. For the interesting connecting link in Hauler, see Note to Test. I. 15.

(δ) *The Apostolic Constitutions* (Greek). These eight books are so well known that the briefest description here will suffice. The first six books are an enlargement of the Didascalia. The seventh reproduces the Didaché with variations, and contains liturgical matter, on baptism, etc., of which the source is not known. The eighth book begins with a Hippolytean treatise *On Spiritual Gifts* (which also appears in Const. H.), and then proceeds to a "Church Order" parallel to our *Testament* (see 1 ι, above). In the manuscripts, the so-called *Apostolic Canons* (which are later than the Apostolic Constitutions, and perhaps date in their present form from 400 A.D.) follow the eighth book. For an excellent account in English of the Apostolic Constitutions, see Brightman, L.E.W. xvii.–xlvii.; the most complete work on the subject is that (in German) of Dr. Funk (see 1η, above). The Greek text has been published by Lagarde, as also by Ültzen and others; the sections used in this volume are those of Lagarde. There is an English translation in the *Ante-Nicene Christian Library*

(Edinburgh: T. & T. Clark). The Apostolic Canons are given in Hefele's *Councils* (at the end of vol. i., Eng. trans.). The compiler of the Apostolic Constitutions has been with' the greatest probability identified with the interpolator of the Ignatian Epistles.

5. OTHER ILLUSTRATIVE LITERATURE. Of a large mass of early Christian books, the following may be specially mentioned as throwing light on the subjects dealt with in the Testament of our Lord.

(*a*) *Sarapion's Prayer Book*. Sarapion (or Serapion) was Bishop of Thmuis in the Nile Delta in the middle of the fourth century, a great friend of St. Athanasius, and an opponent of the Arian party. His Prayer Book has been published in Greek, with full notes, by Mr. Brightman (J.T.S. i. 88 ff., 247 ff.), and in English by the Bishop of Salisbury. It contains Ordination prayers, a Liturgy, etc., but only the bishop's part is given. The date is about 350 A.D.

(β) *The Pilgrimage of Silvia* (so called) is an account of a journey made at the end of the fourth century by an anonymous lady from Gaul to Jerusalem, in order to visit the Holy Places. She describes fully the services at Jerusalem, and her account is therefore most valuable for our purpose. The book was discovered by Gamurrini in 1884, and first edited by him in 1888; it has since been published by Geyer in *Itinera Hierosolymitana* (Vienna, 1898), and (in English) by Dr. Bernard (London, 1891).

(γ) *The Catechetical Lectures* of St. Cyril of Jerusalem (English translation in the Oxford *Library of Fathers*).

For an account of other literature, especially of the *Statuta ecclesiae antiqua* (conveniently called by Dr. Wordsworth the "*Gallican Statutes*") and the *Edessene Canons*, the reader may be referred to Bishop J. Wordsworth's *Ministry of Grace*.

§ iv. A Supposed Montanistic Original of the Testament

Several features of the *Testament* have led to the conjecture that it was once a Montanist Church Order, or, to put it more accurately, that the work we know is derived from such a source. Dom Morin of Maredsous first called attention in the *Revue Bénédictine* for January 1900 to this subject. The following have been noted as Montanistic features. The dislike of digamy (I. 20 Note), revelations and gifts (I. 29 Note, 23, 47), the mention of the prophets [1] as continuing, and the frequent references to prophets and prophetic utterances (I. 19*, 22*, 23* deacon's admonition, 26*, 27*, 28*, 31*, 35*, 38*, 43*; II. 1*, 9*, 24, etc.), the mention of the Paraclete in the prayer over the oil (I. 24*; but only there,[2] and then in connection with the Constantinopolitan "the Lord"), presbyteresses (I. 35*, 43*; II. 19*), the college of clergy (I. 19*), the frequent references to the Apocalypse, the absence of Phrygia in I. 10 (but this is in the probably independent Apocalyptic Prelude, see Appended Note), the passage about the Souls in I. 40* which recalls Tertullian (but only distantly), the alleged ascetic tone (but on this see § v.), the frequent references to works of the Spirit, also to the bearing of the Cross (*e.g.* I. 13 [but this is the prelude], 18*, 23* deacon's admonition, 26*, 28*, 40*, 46*; II. 7*), to children of the light (§ v.), etc. But of these passages, those marked with an asterisk are found, by comparison with the parallels, to be not improbably the Compiler's own work, or at least the Compiler's interpolations in his sources.

On the other hand, there are non-Montanistic features.

---

[1] But the absence of the prophets in the quotation of Eph. ii. 20 (I. 35) is remarkable.

[2] The name is several times found in A.C., etc.

There are no prophetesses, widows are ordered to be silent in the church (I. 40*), virgins are not bidden to be veiled ordinarily (I. 46*), and there is no reference to general fasts except the two days before Easter and the ordinary weekly ones (these are not explicitly fixed). The "monarchical episcopate" (I. 21*) has also been noted as a non-Montanist feature; but the *Testament* has "monarchical Church," not "monarchical episcopate."

On reviewing these instances which have been alleged, we are struck by the fact that some of these "Montanistic" features occur in the Prelude, for the joining of which on to the supposed Montanistic Church Order there is no evidence, and also by the fact that some of them occur in passages interpolated into sources such as Hauler's Verona fragments, and therefore can hardly have occurred in the supposed Montanist Church Order. On the whole, while the evidence is not strong enough to say positively that such an Order existed, we may at least conclude that the *Testament*, both in its Prelude and in the ecclesiastical part, shows distinct traces of Montanistic influence, as also does the Apostolic Church Order. It would seem, however, to be an over-statement of the case to look on the *Testament* as a Montanist Church Order merely edited or touched up by a later hand. The evidence rather points to the work of a later compiler who used earlier, and probably Montanistic, material.

§ v. THEOLOGY AND CHARACTERISTICS OF THE TESTAMENT

1. THEOLOGY. From its theological side the *Testament* may be regarded as a strong protest against Arianism and undue subordinationism. Starting from this point of view, Bishop J. Wordsworth has written an article in the *Church Quarterly Review* for April 1900, with the thesis that the *Testament* sprang from the school of Apollinarius of Laodicea (in Syria). Apollinarius (or Apollinaris) the Younger was long recognised

as orthodox, and was admired by St. Athanasius and St. Basil for his classical learning, and especially for his opposition to Arianism. But he fell into error on the other side, and late in life he propounded a heresy which, while upholding the true divinity of our Lord, did not recognise His true humanity. Dividing man (with Plato) into body (σῶμα), soul (ψυχή), and spirit (πνεῦμα), he ascribed to Christ a true body and a true "soul"—*i.e.* that soul which man has in common with an animal (ψυχὴ ἄλογος, *anima animans*)—but denied that He had a rational spirit (ψυχὴ λογική or πνεῦμα, *anima rationalis*), saying that the divine Word or Logos took the place of it. In this way, by denying the real humanity of our Lord, he paved the way for the Monophysitism of the next century. He said that Christ was not complete (ὅλος) man nor God, but a mixture of God and man. For further particulars, reference may be made to Dr. Schaff's article in Smith and Wace's *Dictionary of Christian Biography* (i. 134). Apollinarius seceded from the Church in 375, and died about 392. After his death his disciples early perverted and exaggerated his doctrine, and the school of Apollinarius soon became famous for their pseudepigraphic writings. We must notice that the Arians also put the Logos in the place of our Lord's human spirit, but they asserted His changeableness (τρεπτότης), while Apollinarius strongly maintained with the Church the contrary (Schaff, *ubi supra*).

The passages of the *Testament* which Bishop Wordsworth marks as Apollinarian (C.Q.R., April 1900) are chiefly in the Mystagogia[1] (I. 28*). Notably the reference to our Lord *in His soul* (= ἔμψυχος ?) going down to Hades, the division of man into flesh, soul, and spirit, the ascription of the saving work of our Lord to His Spirit, the "indivisible mind" "incomprehensible," "passible yet not passible" (but see Note on

[1] In what follows an asterisk is affixed to the passages which are probably the *Testament* Compiler's own work.

I. 28), "in all its kinds," and the conclusion about the Spirit and the Voice of God through whom our Lord praised the Father. Dr. Wordsworth finds these or similar phrases in Apollinarius' writings. He also finds a parallel to the interpolation in the Baptismal Creed ("who came from the Father, who is of old with the Father," II. 8*), which is peculiar to the *Testament* Creed, in the words "who is ever with the Father" (ἀεὶ συνόντα τῷ πατρί) of the "Detailed Creed" (κατὰ μέρος πίστις), which is ascribed to Apollinarius, and was perhaps written about 375. The "Detailed Creed" also speaks of the "consubstantiality" of the Holy Ghost, as Test. I. 41* (see Note there and at II. 8, where it is remarked that in Eg. C.O. we have the expression "the consubstantial Trinity"). Bishop Wordsworth's other quotations are more doubtful for our purpose, and can hardly be relied on.

We note in these instances the phenomenon that the *Testament* and Apollinarius agree in certain striking phrases, especially if the "Detailed Creed" be the work of Apollinarius. We may equally suppose that the *Testament* borrows from Apollinarius, or *vice versâ*; or we may suppose that the phrases common to both were current in extreme anti-Arian circles in the fourth century. Dr. Wordsworth somewhat rashly assumes that the *Testament* must borrow from Apollinarius. But here the curious fact is to be noticed, that in spite of this connection with Apollinarius there is no actual heresy in the *Testament*; and this will be a very important factor in determining its date (§ vi.). If the *Testament* was written after Apollinarius had separated from the Church, the writer would either have agreed with the heresiarch, or have disagreed: if the former, he would have quoted his heresy; if the latter, he would not have quoted his writings at all. There is a similarity in phrases, not in heresy. This consideration points either to a date before the secession of Apollinarius, or—but other things make this alternative unlikely—to a date when the heresy was long past. Thus Dr. Wordsworth hardly seems to have proved his thesis, but his calling attention to the undoubted connection between the two writers is invaluable. We may notice in passing the absence from Test. of such characteristic phrases of Apollinarius as the "incarnate mind" ($\nu o\hat{v}\varsigma$ $\check{\epsilon}\nu\sigma a\rho\kappa o\varsigma$) in Christ, or that He "passed through the Virgin Mary."

Let us ask, however, what is the theological "tendency" of the *Testament*? Bishop Wordsworth (*ubi supra*) suggests that it is a polemic against the writer of the Apostolic Constitutions, and that the latter is the "adversary" of the *Testament* Prelude. Now, putting aside the question of the priority and independence of the Prelude, it must be remarked that the A.C. writer was not an Arian, although he had leanings towards that heresy, and that he probably denied our Lord's human soul (cf. Brightman, L.E.W., p. xxviii.). He says that "some of (the heretics) impiously pretend that Christ is bare man ($\psi \iota \lambda \grave{o} \nu$ $\check{a}\nu\theta\rho\omega\pi o\nu$), thinking He is of a soul and body," and the interpolations in the Ignatian Epistles more strongly deny His human soul than A.C. itself does. Thus a writer with Arian leanings makes a strange statement which causes Funk (though Lightfoot does not agree with this) to think that he was an Apollinarian. The safer conclusion to draw from the facts is that very loose theological ideas on this point were current in the fourth century in widely different schools of thought; and perhaps the quasi-Apollinarian phrases of the *Testament* are merely other instances of the same fact.

We must certainly conclude that the *Testament* writer had a dislike of an exaggerated "subordination" of the Son, such, for instance, as we see in A.C. ii. 30, 44, viii. 12 (Lagarde, 59^4 ff., 73^4, 254^{10}): the order of the Persons of the Holy Trinity in the Invocation in the Liturgy (I. 23*), where the Son precedes the Father, would be enough to show this. The

Test. writer shows a great fondness of prayers to the Son (*e.g.* I. 26*), and in several prayers there is a confusion of the Persons addressed (*e.g.* I. 23* oblation and concluding thanksgiving, 30*, 43*, II. 7*; in the conclusion of I. 23* the confusion is much worse in the derived Anaphora of our Lord; see Appendix I.). The Compiler had also a firm hold on the personality of the Holy Spirit, especially, for example, as compared with Sarapion (cf. I. 41*). He dwells on the work of the Holy Spirit (*e.g.* I. 28*, II. 9*, 10*). He ascribes to the Holy Ghost the Constantinopolitan phrases "the Lord" (I. 24*) and "Maker of life" (I. 41*), unless these are later additions. He calls the Holy Spirit consubstantial with the Father (I. 41). He uses the name "Trinity" in I. 19*, 21* (see Note), 23* (thrice), II. 7*.

One reservation must possibly be made. It is just possible that the Mystagogia (I. 28), which hangs very loosely on to the rest, is an addition by an editor later than the Compiler.

2. OTHER CHARACTERISTICS. It will be useful here to keep in mind the portions of the *Testament* which are either the Compiler's own work, or at least are not to be found in any of the earlier parallels. The following include the principal of these portions, though there is besides scattered over the whole work a multiplicity of phrases and sentences interpolated by the Compiler:—in Book I., the Preface, §§ 1, 15–18, large parts of 21 (especially the formula said by all the bishops, the first part of the Ordination prayer and other interpolations in the same), 22, large interpolations in the Eucharistic prayer, concluding prayer, etc., of 23, 24, 26, 28, 30 (some part), 31, 32, 35 (in the main), 37, 38 (large part), 40–43; in Book II., §§ 5 (prayer of dismissal), 7 (prayer of exorcism), 9 (interpolations in Confirmation prayer), 12, 15, 18, 19, 22, 23 (large parts of it), 25 (last sentence), 26, 27.

Of the *general characteristics*, in addition to the theological, may be mentioned the enthusiastic praise of widows, and to a lesser extent of deacons, asceticism with regard to celibacy, especially as compared with A.C. (but the writer does not explicitly express all that he would wish, hinting rather than laying down hard and fast rules; see especially Notes to I. 20, 29, II. 1); but, on the other hand, less strict asceticism with regard to fasting, the rules as to this being less stringent and the fasts less numerous than in A.C. Among general characteristics we must name great diffuseness, especially in the interpolated passages of the prayers.

The *characteristics of phraseology* are very striking, and some of the principal ones are noted here. An asterisk is placed against the references when the Compiler's own work is probably in question.

(*a*) "He who sent me" (or the like), I. Preface*, 3, 8, 17*, 18*, 26*, 43* (cf. A.C. ii. 59, Lagarde, 90^{10}).

(*b*) "Children of light," light opposed to darkness (especially darkness of error), illumination, etc. (a very favourite idea), I. Preface*, 1*, 3, 12, 15*, 21* (interpolation in the Ordination prayer), 23* (deacon's admonition, Eucharistic thanksgiving interpolation, concluding prayer), 26* (passim), 28*, 30* (in interpolation), 31*, 32*, 37*, 38* (interpolation in Ordination prayer, twice), 43*, II. 5*, 7* (often), 9* (interpolations), 24 (so in Eg. C.O. and H.), 27*. Cf. A.C. ii. 46 (Lagarde, 74^{10}).

(*c*) Types. The fondness of the writer for finding a type in making ecclesiastical rules and in his teaching, is frequently shown. Thus we have the Eucharistic species as a type, I. 23* (omitted in the derived Anaphora of our Lord), II. 10 (where it is not peculiar to Test.; see Notes at both places); lights for a type (I. 19*; see Note there, and cf. II. 11); the number of loaves to be offered as a type (I. 23* *ad init.*); the double Amen of the communicant, typical of the Body and Blood (I. 23* s.f.); the dimensions of the baptistery are typical of prophets and apostles (I. 19*); the "place of commemoration" is a type of heaven (I. 19*); good women are figures of the kingdom of heaven (I. 16*); the triple song is a figure of the kingdom (I. 26*, third prayer), as also are the gospel-life (I. 28*) and Easter Even night (II. 19*), cf. also I. 32* (third prayer); our Lord in His Incarnation showed a type of incorruption (I. 28*); priests are to be types of archangels and of holiness (I. 31* s.f.); the "princes and priests" are types of heaven, and the three days' feast of the resurrection (I. 21*); the bishop's fasts are a type of our Lord's "entrances" to His passion (I. 22*); the oil is a type of spiritual fatness (I. 24*); late comers are types of the day of judgment (I. 36*); souls have "figures" before God (I. 40*); evening is a type of the resurrection (II. 24, also in the parallels).

(*d*) Personification of Power, Thought, Wisdom, etc., as names of our Lord, and fondness for the name "the Word"—*e.g.* I. 23* (Eucharistic prayer), 26* (often), 28* (so in Arabic Didascalia), 30* (interpolation), 31* (perhaps), 32*, 38* (the parallel phrase in Hauler personified), 43*, II. 7*, 16* (in interpolation), 24* (also in H., but more full in Test., "His Word and Wisdom").

(*e*) Christ in or with Christians, I. Preface, 1*, 8, 17*, 18*, 22*, 40*, II. 25* (in interpolation).

(*f*) Christians as holy vessels, I. 3, 30* (presbyters), 41* (widows), II. 9* (in interpolation). Cf. A.C. ii. 24 (Lagarde, 49^5) of St. Paul.

(*g*) "A work" (or the like), I. 13, 31* (often), 35* (thrice), 36*, 37* (see Note there), 40*, 42*, 46*, 47*, II. 3, 10, 24* (in interpolation).

(*h*) Antithesis, of corruption and incorruption, light and darkness, etc., I. 28* (often), II. 7*; and see (*b*), above.

(*i*) Eternal or heavenly habitations (or the like), I. 1*, 21* (in interpolation), 26*, 32*, 45*, II. 7*, 9* (in interpolation). Cf. I. 18 s.f.

(*j*) God "loving man" (φιλάνθρωπος), and "love of man" (φιλανθρωπία), I. 23* s.f., 31*, II. 9* (in interpolation).

(*k*) The "Testament," Title*, I. 17*, 18*, II. 26*.

(*l*) The bishop a "shepherd," I. 28* (twice), 39*, II. 5*, 10*, 13*. Only once in Ap. C.O. (§ 18). In Test. I. 39, II. 10 and 13 it represents "bishop" of the Eg. C.O. parallel. Perhaps Test. got the name from Ap. C.O. In the Prelude (I. 8) "shepherds" is used of the clergy generally.

(*m*) Among other phrases, etc., may be mentioned the angels visiting man (I. 22*, 23* deacon's admonition, 35); "incorruptibility" (I. 23* in interpolation, 28* passim, 26*, 32*, II. 7*); our Lord clothing Himself with man (I. 28*); the angel hierarchy (I. 23 [Eucharistic prayer— the reference much enlarged in Test.], 28*, 32*, II. 7*, 24); nature trembling (I. 23* oblation, 26* third prayer, II. 7*, 8 in interpolation); souls bound by death (I. 26*, 28*, II. 7*); the nails—fixing of our Lord on the Cross (II. 7*, 24 [so in Eg. C.O. parallel]); humiliation (I. 8, II. 7*); testing spirits (I. 8, 14, both in the perhaps independent Prelude; in I. 22*, 31*, II. 6*, the "testing" is repeated, but the word "spirits" is there absent); "rest" (I. 35*, 44*, II. 15*, and cf. Notes on I. 18, 37); "meekness" (passim, *e.g.* I. 21*, 23* in interpolation, 31*, 41*, 44*, II. 3*, 6, 9* in interpolation).

Other phrases have been already referred to in § iv. as bearing on the question of a Montanistic source. Turning to characteristics which are rather remarkably absent, we may note that the Compiler had little hold on the doctrine of justification by faith, and the Prologue writer had as little (cf. I. 12); and that we find nothing about being buried with Christ in baptism.

3. QUOTATIONS FROM THE BIBLE. The Compiler is not so fond of quoting Scripture as the A.C. writer is. This may, partly at least, be due to the "apocryphal pretence." A comparison

of the quotations shows that the Compiler drew very freely from the Pauline Epistles, especially 1 Tim., Rom., and 1 Cor., and that he clearly used disputed books like 2 Peter, Hebrews, and Revelation. In using N.T. quotations from O.T., he follows St. Paul and not the O.T. [a reservation must here be made, however, that James of Edessa might have altered these quotations to suit the form he knew best himself]. The Compiler seldom quotes O.T., seldom even the Psalms. Of the Gospels he shows the influence of St. John most. He usually uses no formula of citation ; when he does he makes an egregious blunder (I. 28 s.f.). In translating quotations into Syriac, James of Edessa seems to have rendered the Greek directly, without having his Bible open before him. In quoting 2 Peter he uses the text now commonly printed in Syriac Bibles (I. 31).

4. DELIBERATE OMISSIONS of what the Compiler had before him in his materials. The most striking instances are, " This do in remembrance of me," our Lord's words over the Cup, and the mention of the Holy Spirit in the Invocation (I. 23), the milk and honey for the newly baptized, and a formula in administering the Cup (II. 10). See Notes in those places. Perhaps we must add the clause about the Resurrection in the Baptismal Creed. See Note to II. 10.

5. DOES THE TESTAMENT EMANATE FROM A SECT? It has been thought from the alleged severity in the case of post-baptismal sin (but see Note to I. 37), from the prohibition of military service (but see Note to II. 2 ; the parallel Orders are nearly as unpractical), and the generally ascetic tone (but see p. 21, above), that the *Testament* is a sectarian work. The number of bishops in I. 21 points rather the other way. And with all his supposed Apollinarian leanings, the Compiler exhibits no actual heresy. We may compare the Apostolic Constitutions, which are the work of a not very orthodox individual, yet not, probably, of one who founded a sect or was in any way separated from the Church. Similarly it is unneces-

sary to suppose that the *Testament* was written for the use of a sect. Loose theological expressions were current in many widely different circles before the nomenclature of theology was fixed. An example from (perhaps) the same age as the *Testament* Compiler is seen in the extraordinary Invocation of the Word in Bishop Sarapion's Prayer Book (see Note to I. 23).

§ vi. DATE

The question of the date of the *Testament* is made extremely difficult by its almost entire dependence on internal evidence. We need not wonder, then, that different writers have ascribed it to different ages. Mgr. Rahmani considers that it belongs to the age of Irenaeus, the end of the second century. But no other scholar follows him here. Dr. Zahn attributes it to about 350 A.D. (see § vii., below); Dom Morin dates it not later than that year; Bishop Wordsworth ascribes it to the school of Apollinarius, and names about 400 A.D., with which date on other grounds Prof. Harnack in his "Preliminary Remarks" on the *Testament* agrees; M. Batiffol in the *Révue Biblique Internationale* of the Dominican Convent of St. Stephen at Jerusalem, thinks it is not earlier than the fifth century, and may be later; and Dr. Funk generally agrees with this.

Before discussing this question, it will be proper to remark that the argument from the absence of a custom or office in these Church Orders must be treated with some care. They are only indirectly books of canons. They are the works, probably, of individual authors, whereas canons are put out by synods. Hence the Church Orders need not be expected to be complete, and the argument from silence, always precarious, is unusually so in their case.

1. THE QUESTION HERE CONSIDERED. So great a diverg-

ence of view about the date as that mentioned above may be partly due to another question not having been first settled, namely: What do we mean by the *date* of the *Testament*? If by this word we mean the year in which the last touch was put to it, there is no reason why we should not date it from the time of James of Edessa himself, who may not improbably have added something to the work (see below). But the question we are now considering is not when the last touches were put to it, but when the apocryphal writer composed the book as a book. A late feature may conceivably be an addition by a later copyist. An early feature, on the other hand, may as conceivably have been put in by the apocryphal writer to give the work an antiquarian air. Therefore we must first ask, What was the aim of the writer? Was he a conscious forger, who wished his work actually to pass as the words of our Lord, or did he merely put his words into our Lord's mouth for dramatic effect? The Jewish and early Christian apocryphal or pseudepigraphic Old Testament literature was hardly what we should call forgery. There is no need to suppose that the writer or writers of the Book of Enoch actually intended the reader to think that it was written before the Flood. Similarly we can suppose that the writer of Ecclesiastes put his book into the mouth of Solomon as a mere dramatic fiction. Thus, although no doubt writers of the fourth or fifth century were capable of producing a deliberate forgery, it is not *a priori* necessary to suppose that an apocryphal work of those ages was meant actually to deceive its readers and to pass as an ancient book. It was the fashion to ascribe these Church Orders to the Apostles. Our writer has gone a step further, and has ascribed his to our Lord.

The question of a conscious forgery largely depends on the motive of the work. If a forgery, it must have been forged with some object. But, in this case, such an object is difficult to find. It could hardly be to propagate Apollinarianism, for if so that heresy would have been clearly stated, which is not the case (see p. 18, above). None of the "tendencies" mentioned in § v. (not, for instance, one of the most clearly marked, the advocacy of a ministry of "widows" for women) is strong enough to make it probable that we have here a conscious forgery, in which the author deliberately takes the obsolete customs of an earlier age and describes them as if they were going on in his day. The obvious and undisguised anachronisms in the *Testament* (*e.g.* I. 35*, the "foundation of the Apostles"; I. 43*, "God of the Apostles"; II. 8, "the ascension and session of our Lord"; II. 9*, "the holy Apostles"; II. 24*, "the Apostles singing psalms") make such a conscious forgery unlikely; as also do the profuse references to and direct quotations from the New Testament. These are not abstruse points which might well escape a forger's notice, like the word "its" in Chatterton's poems, but anachronisms which any one would see at the first glance. These considerations lead us rather to take up the idea of a "dramatic fiction."

The important result of such reasoning will be that the customs described and the Compiler are *in the main* contemporary. The writer would mean his work to be used; and we can hardly conceive that (if he is not a conscious forger) he introduced obsolete forms of worship and customs wholesale. It would indeed be permissible to suppose that he allowed some antiquarianisms to *remain,* provided that they did not pervade the whole work. It makes all the difference whether he retained what was in his sources, giving sometimes a slightly different turn to an obsolete phrase (as, for example, where it is possible to suppose that he retained references to persecutions, applying them not, as before, to the ill-treatment of Christians by the heathen, but to that inflicted by one Christian body upon another; see, however, below), or whether he invented an antiquated feature. There is no trace of the latter in the *Testament*; the former is what is done at this day by all Christians who use ancient liturgical formularies. Also it would be permissible to suppose that a later editor has added a few phrases, or even a complete section, provided again that these additions also did not pervade the whole book. Further, the above argument would not preclude the independence and priority, in whole or in part, of the Apocalyptic Prelude (see Note at the beginning of Book I.)

2. SUPERIOR LIMITS. We may with some confidence (but with the reservations mentioned below) say that the *Testament* is later than the Canons of Hippolytus, the Egyptian and Ethiopic Church Orders, and Hauler's Latin fragments.

(*a*) That Test. is later than the *Canons of Hippolytus* (allowing for some interpolations in the latter) appears from C.H. not having an apocryphal form, from their having only one Ordination prayer for bishops and presbyters (Test. has two), and from their being simpler in that prayer, in festivals, in not developing the ministry of women, and so forth. What then is the date of C.H.? It is impossible here to reproduce the arguments used for an early date by Achelis, or for a late one by Funk; and reference may be made to *Die Canones Hippolyti* of the former, and to *Apost. Konstitutionen* of the latter. Achelis considers that they date, if we omit interpolations, from the beginning of the third century, and that they are the work of Hippolytus. This date is agreed to by Duchesne and Bishop J. Wordsworth, though they dispute the Hippolytean authorship; Brightman also agrees with this date. Dom Morin thinks they were the book which Dionysius of Alexandria, probably early in the third century, sent to the Romans " by Hippolytus " (Eusebius, H.E. vi. 46). Funk, however, differs greatly from these views. He thinks that the eighth book of the Apostolic Constitutions is the original of the " Constitutions through Hippolytus " (§ iii. 1 θ), and that of the Egyptian Church Order, and that both of the Canons of Hippolytus and of our *Testament;* and thus he assigns C.H. to the sixth century or perhaps later. His arguments appear to be inconclusive, and Achelis' hypothesis of an early document with later interpolations is much more probable.

(β) That the *Egyptian Church Order* is earlier than Test. appears from its having, like C.H., only one Ordination prayer for bishops and presbyters; from the much less decided tone of its theology, as if the great Arian controversy had not then arisen; and from a careful comparison of passages in Test. (*e.g.* about confessors, I. 39; catechumens, II. 6; the agapé, II. 13; prayer at the sixth hour and evening, II. 24), which are almost impossible to understand by themselves, with the parallels in Eg. C.O. which explain them. It would be difficult to obtain the good sense of the latter out of the chaos of the former. It is generally agreed that Eg. C.O. precedes Test.[1] But what is its date? Probably the very beginning of the fourth century, before the rise of Arianism. This does not mean that the Egyptian Heptateuch dates from that time; the last part of that compilation is derived, probably, from A.C. viii.; and, as Harnack (on the Canons of the Apostles) has pointed out, St. Athanasius still held the Didaché in honour; therefore he probably did not know the Apostolic Church Order which replaces the Didaché (§ iii. 2 β), and which forms the first book of the Heptateuch. Also this need not mean that Eg. C.O. in its Coptic translation is as early as the date named. But the Greek original

---

[1] Test., however, derives some parts from C.H. independently of Eg. C.O.; *e.g.* the formula of submission to God in baptism, not in Eg. C.O. (H. wanting here); and in much of the baptismal section Test. is nearer to C.H. and H. than Eg. C.O.; in II. 11 s.f., Test. derives from C.H. 164 ff. without reference to Eg. C.O. or H.

may be assigned to that time; and with this conclusion Harnack agrees.

(γ) Is the *Ethiopic Church Order* earlier than Test. ? In the sections which follow, the various arguments are treated shortly, and references are given to the Notes where they are dealt with in detail. As only a portion of the Ethiopic Statutes has as yet been printed, it is not easy to assign a date to them; we can, however, arrive approximately at a date for Statutes 21–23, which Ludolf has published, or rather for the Greek which underlies them. These Statutes supplement the Eg. C.O. by giving us ordination prayers and a liturgy, and these forms must be pronounced certainly earlier than the corresponding parts of Test. The latter are greatly amplified; and amplification in *liturgical parts* is more likely than compression, as we see in later liturgies, which are all greatly amplified, not condensed. There can hardly be any question that the Test. Eucharistic Liturgy (see Note in I. 23) is derived from Eth. C.O. by interpolation, and so the prayer for the ordination of presbyters [1] (I. 30). Again, the Test. arrangement in which all the bishops say a formula in ordaining a bishop, and then one bishop says the ordination prayer itself, appears to be a combination of two practices which the Compiler had before him, namely, that of Eg. C.O., where one bishop says everything, and that of Eth. C.O., where all the bishops say everything (see Note on I. 21). Thus we must assign the priority to the Eth. C.O. forms. But this need only mean that their Greek original is earlier than Test., and that the Eth. C.O. Compiler was perhaps more conservative in retaining ancient material than the Test. Compiler. What then is the date of the Greek original of Eth. C.O. ? The absence of the Sanctus and the simplicity of the liturgy, for example, as compared with A.C. viii., would point to a date before the middle of the fourth century.

[1] This prayer in Eth. C.O. shows that that Order is later than Eg. C.O.

§ vi.]   DATE   31

(δ) *Hauler's Verona Latin fragments*, or rather their Greek originals, are probably a direct source of Test. Their Eucharistic Liturgy, down to the blessing of the oil, and their Ordination prayer for a presbyter, are almost the same as those of Eth. C.O., and the remarks made above apply to them. H., however, gives part of the Ordination prayer for a deacon, which is clearly the original of the Test. prayer (see Note on I. 38). Moreover, in the presbyter's Ordination prayer, where H. differs from Eth. C.O., Test. follows the former as against the latter (see Note on I. 30); and so in the phrase about the deacon being the counsellor of the clergy (I. 34), Test. follows the wording of H. rather than of Eth. C.O., though it flatly contradicts them both. In parts of H. and Test. which are not in Ludolf's Eth. C.O., we find them agreeing together against other authorities. In the Baptismal Creed (II. 8) both insert "living" or its equivalent before "from the dead," and have the past tense "He *sat* down." Both omit the formula of baptism given by C.H. (Eg. C.O. omits it also). The anointing and invocation after baptism in Test. (II. 8, 9) is an amplification of H., not of C. H. In the communion of the people, Test. (II. 10), while omitting the milk and honey of H., etc., agrees with H. in speaking of the water as the "sign of the laver" and of the "inner psychic man," phrases not in C.H. or Eg. C.O. In the agapé, Test. (II. 13) agrees nearly with the phrase of H. about that which remains over, as against the others. In the first fruits, H. and Eg. C.O. are almost the same; Test. (II. 16) amplifies the prayer, but omits details of the fruits. In the fast before Easter, Test. agrees with H. in mentioning women with child, while Eg. C.O. speaks of any sick man (masculine). In the hours of prayer, where H. and Eg. C.O. are almost one, Test. (II. 24) personifies "verbum suum" of H. into "His Word and Wisdom," just as in I. 38 the "desiderium" of H. is personified into "Thy Thought, Thy

Wisdom, Thine Energy, Thy beloved Son Jesus Christ," in the characteristic manner of Test. This last peculiarity would be sufficient in itself to show the priority of H.; the converse change is inconceivable. All these considerations, which are dealt with in detail in the Notes to the passages cited, make it probable that the Greek original of H. is a source of Test. What then is the date of these fragments? Dr. Hauler assigns the Greek original to the first part of the fourth century. We are not here concerned with the date of the *compilation*, that is to say, the date when the Didascalia, Ap. C.O., and the form of our Church Order were joined together in H., but merely with the date of the Greek original of the last part; and the same considerations which enabled us to put that of Eth. C.O. before 350 A.D., will lead us to agree with Dr. Hauler's opinion as to the Verona fragments.

3. INFERIOR LIMITS. The *Testament* seems to be earlier than the Apostolic Constitutions (as compiled in their present form), than the Arabic Didascalia, the Abyssinian Anaphora of our Lord, and the fifth century developed liturgies, such as the East Syrian (Nestorian) Liturgy of the Apostles Addai (Adai) and Mari.

(*a*) *The Apostolic Constitutions* in their present form must probably be pronounced later than Test. The eighth book gives us the best material for comparison, as containing in part a form of the "Lost Church Order." A.C. is more elaborate than Test., its prayers have more interpolations; it has the rule of three bishops ordaining a bishop, not found in any of its predecessors, but probably founded on the rule of Nicaea (which, however, has a somewhat different meaning; see Note on Test. I. 21); it has a much more elaborate system of festivals (Ascension, Pentecost, Easter, Christmas, Epiphany, Apostles' Days, St. Stephen and All Martyrs); subdeacons, readers, and deaconesses are appointed by laying on of hands (contrast Eg. C.O., Test., and, for readers, C.H. and Const. H.); catechumens, demoniacs and penitents are sent away before the Eucharist with elaborate dismissals; in the Liturgy the recital of the work of creation and redemption is very much more elaborate than in Test., and the Sanctus, wanting in Test., is given; in the Oblation ("Remembering therefore," etc.) A.C. is much more freely interpolated than Test., while the latter is more freely interpolated than Eth. C.O. and H.; the intercession in A.C. is elaborate, while that of Test. is rudimentary (see Note there, I. 23); and the A.C. intercession does not refer, as Test. does, to the charismata; the A.C. invocation is of the later style, specifying the transformation of the elements, unlike Test., H., Eth. C.O.; the deacon's litany after the Eucharistic Intercession and the bishop's accompanying prayer are in A.C. much more elaborate than in Test., where there is only one sentence; in the communion the charismata are not mentioned in A.C. as in Test. (but they are referred to in A.C. viii. 25 = Test. I. 47); and the post-communion thanksgiving and dismissal are more elaborate in A.C. The only part of the Liturgy where Test. develops a point not found in A.C. is the prayer said by the communicant. Again, the renunciation and submission at baptism in A.C. vii. 41 are more elaborate than in Test. II. 8. In A.C. viii. 31 the rule as to rejecting soldiers, found in Test. II. 2, Eg. C.O., etc., is softened down. These considerations make it extremely probable that Test. is older than A.C. as we now have it; and as it is generally agreed that A.C. is to be dated about 375 A.D., it follows that Test. must be put earlier than that year.

(β) *The Arabic Didascalia* borrows from Test., and is therefore a later document. Reasons for saying that Ar. D. 35–39 are derived from Test., and that the obligation is not the other way, are given in the Notes to Test. I. 21, 22, 28, and especially 23. Bishop J. Wordsworth's suggestion (*Revue Internat. de théol.* vol. xxxi. p. 461), that the Mystagogia in Ar. D. is of an older form than that in Test., appears to be unnecessary in itself (see Note to I. 28), the process having been probably that the Ar. D. writer suppressed phrases which by his time had acquired an Apollinarian meaning: it involves, moreover, an extremely complicated hypothesis, unless we further suppose that the other chapters (35–38) of Ar. D. are also earlier than the Test. parallels, which it is almost impossible to believe (see Notes to Test. I. 21, 22, 23). For, if not, the suggestion would mean that Test. had a predecessor very like itself, having an older form of the Mystagogia, and also using the name "Testament," which appears in the title to the Mystagogia in Ar. D. (see Appendix II.). Then, are we to suppose that the points in which Ar. D. differs from Test.—such as the dimensions of the oblong baptistery—are derived from this hypothetical predecessor of Test.? All this is complicated and unnecessary. It is far more probable that the Ar. D. writer, in quoting Test., altered what he did not approve of. As to the date of Ar. D., it is difficult to come to a determination, as we do not know its §§ 1–34 which have not been published. In § 38 it mentions incense in the preanaphoral service. Incense is mentioned in the Pilgrimage of Silvia, about 385 A.D. And from verbal coincidences and simplicity of the Liturgy described in Ar. D. (the text is not given), it seems probable that it and Test. are not very greatly removed from one another in time. We may probably date Ar. D., as far as the chapters we know are concerned, between 380 and 400 A.D.

(γ) *The Abyssinian Anaphora of our Lord* (see Appendix I.) is clearly derived from Test., but inserts an Invocation of the later form (retaining that of Test.), and adds a very rudimentary intercession in the middle of the Eucharistic Thanksgiving, like the modern Abyssinian and Coptic Liturgies. But, like

Test., it has no Sanctus, and does not give our Lord's words over the Cup; and from its form it is unlikely to be later than the beginning of the fifth century. This date is given on the supposition that the diptychs with "Genetrix Dei" are a later insertion. If they are an integral part of the Anaphora of our Lord, we must date that Anaphora a few years later.

(δ) *The East Syrian* (*Nestorian*) *Liturgy of the Apostles Adai* (*Addai*) *and Mari* has little in common with Test., but it may help us to decide the date of the latter; for some considerable interval is necessary for the development of such a Liturgy by a remote people, from a very much less formed type such as that of Test., Eth. C.O., etc. But it is difficult to believe that this East Syrian Liturgy can date from after 431 A.D. It has not the slightest reference to the Nestorian controversy; and its very rudimentary Invocation, greatly resembling that of Eth. C.O., and its omission of the Words of Institution, both point to a date not later than the first quarter of the fifth century (see Notes on I. 23).

4. VARIOUS MARKS OF DATE. Most of these are treated elsewhere in detail, and will only be shortly referred to in this place.

(*a*) *The theology* of the *Testament* (see § v. 1, above) points to a date before the actual outbreak of Apollinarianism, but when phrases which were afterwards used by Apollinarius were current in anti-Arian circles; it necessitates a date later than the rise of Arianism. This limits us to the half-century 325–375 A.D. The omission of the mention of the Holy Spirit in the Eucharistic Invocation (considering the devotion of the Compiler to the Holy Spirit) points to a date before the rise of the Macedonian controversy (see Note on I. 23, and below *o*).

(b) *References to persecution and the Empire* (cf. I. 8, 23,[1] 35, 39, II. 5, for persecutions; I. 26, third prayer, "the prince and his people," and I. 35 twice, for the Empire). Other considerations make it impossible to suppose that the Test. Compiler lived before Constantine, and the direct references to the Emperor and the Empire are such as we should expect of post-Constantinian times. The fact that regular church buildings are assumed as a matter of course to be universal, with other buildings attached, leads us to the same conclusion. But, on the other hand, the references to persecution tend the other way. Are we then to take these as deliberately inserted to produce an antiquarian effect? A more probable solution is that given above (p. 27). The Compiler seems to have adopted references to persecution which occurred in his predecessors' works, and which these (or their originals) applied to heathen persecutions, and to have applied them to the persecutions of the Catholics by the Arians, or (if a later date be the right one) of the Apollinarians by the Catholics. It is not unlikely, however, that the author, who possibly remembered the heathen persecutions in his childhood, thought that they might probably recur, especially if the alternative date given below be correct, namely, during the reign of Julian the Apostate. In connection with the references to the State, we must notice the prohibition of military service and the theatrical profession. The latter prohibition calls for no remark, as it was universal in the fourth century. For the former see Note to II. 2. The Test. Compiler is hardly more stringent than his predecessors, though much less so than A.C., and this makes for a comparatively early date.

(c) *The "chief deacon."* See Notes to I. 19, 34. The limited reference in Test., which implies that neither the

---

[1] This is a very slight reference interpolated into the Eucharistic Thanksgiving. It is very noteworthy that there is no reference to the persecuted in the Eucharistic Intercession in I. 23.

name nor the distinct office of an archdeacon was yet known, will suit any date in the fourth century, especially one somewhat early in the century. The "chief deacon" is merely one of the deacons chosen for a special duty because of his special qualifications, and is not of a distinct rank. There seems to be no reason for saying that the references necessitate a date about 400 A.D. On the contrary, the menial offices ascribed to the deacons imply an earlier date (I. 34, II. 23, etc.).

(*d*) The mention of a *stole* in I. 34 (see Note there) as a badge of office, not as used in service, is a mark of date a good deal earlier than the Council of Laodicea (*cir*. 380 ?).

(*e*) *Absence of metropolitans.* There are none in Test. nor yet in A.C. In Ar. D. there is just a trace of a primacy, and possibly in Eg. C.O. (see note to I. 21). Metropolitans are mentioned by name in 325 A.D. at Nicaea (can. 6), and towards the end of the fourth century at Laodicea. But the name was not used in Africa in the fourth century (Hefele, *Councils*, ii. 396, 410, Eng. trans.); and only some districts were then organised as provinces. Thus no deduction can be made from the absence of metropolitans in Test., except that it is not likely to have been compiled later than the fourth century. A sort of province is implied by the "neighbouring bishops" in I. 21.

(*f*) *Absence of chorepiscopi.* They are first mentioned in Asia Minor at the beginning of the fourth century (Councils of Ancyra, Neocaesarea, Nicaea); in the West, not till the Council of Riez in 439. They were afterwards numerous, especially among the East and West Syrians (Nestorians and Jacobites). Their absence from Test. is a mark of early date. The rise of this order was probably not universal even in the East, and we can well understand that by the middle of the fourth century they were unknown or little known in some countries.

(*g*) *Absence of penitential "stations."* They were common

in early times; the penitents were divided into classes called "stations." They are taken for granted in the councils of the fourth century (Ancyra, Nicaea, Neocaesarea, Laodicea), and we find traces of them (*e.g.*, the "hearers") in Tertullian and Cyprian, though some hold that those fathers apply that term to the catechumens, and not to penitents (but in Tertull. *de Poenitentia* 6, "auditor" applies to a "penitent" almost certainly). The "stations" are found in A.C., in the writings of St. Basil, St. Gregory of Nyssa, etc. At Elvira in Spain (*cir.* 305 A.D.) we do not find distinct traces of "stations"; the assembled fathers divided the penitents into natural classes, according to their offences, and as common sense dictated. The same remark applies to the Council of Arles in Gaul in 314 A.D.

All this would show us that there were different customs in different places. The Test. Compiler refers to penitents (I. 37, see Note there), but not to "stations." Probably in his time and in his country the latter were dying out, or had never been used. Public penitential stations were apparently abolished at Constantinople about 400 A.D. (see Brightman, L.E.W. 532[2]). On the whole, the bearing of the question on the date of the *Testament* is indecisive.

(*h*) *Absence of monasticism.* Neither monks nor ascetics are mentioned. In A.C., similarly, ascetics are only once mentioned (viii. 12, Lagarde, 259[21]). Monastic communities seem to have arisen in the fourth century for the first time in the Christian Church, and at the end of that century we find frequent references to them, and they were vigorously promoted by St. Basil, St. Jerome, St. Chrysostom, and St. Augustine. The absence of them, and also of any class of ascetics, in a writer given to strictness like the Test. Compiler, must be pronounced to be a distinct mark of a date earlier than the last quarter of the fourth century.

(*i*) *The Singers* do not form a class or order. See Note on

I. 26. This indicates a date before the Council of Laodicea and A.C.

(*j*) *The "widows who sit in front"* (προκαθήμεναι), also called "presbyteresses." See Note on I. 40. References to them pervade the work, and cannot be a mere antiquarianism. Test. represents them as not merely existing, but as in their fullest vigour; they are far from being a survival only. This is a decided mark of the priority of Test. to the Council of Laodicea (*cir.* 380 ?), for by its time they were dying out. In Epiphanius' writings, at the end of the fourth century, there are no presbyteresses as an official class (see Note to I. 40).

(*k*) *The doxologies to the prayers.* A decided mark of early date. See Note to I. 21.

(*l*) *The anomaly of the Son being addressed* in the Eucharistic prayers of Test., and the confusion which arises both there and elsewhere from the sudden transitions, the Father being addressed and then the Son in the same prayer, or *vice versâ* (see above, § v.), are examples of the sort of thing which led to the prohibition of the practice at Hippo in 393 (see Note to I. 23, Invocation).

(*m*) *The fasts* in Test. are rather remarkably few in a book which on some points (*e.g.*, celibacy) has an ascetic tone. The forty days of Lent are merely times for solemn prayer, and only the Friday and Saturday of Holy Week are ordered as fasts. This is an indication of early date, before A.C., bk. v. In an ascetic community the strictness of neighbours was likely to be imitated. Fasting for forty days grew up and spread rapidly in the fourth century (see Note on I. 22 and II. 8). And therefore it is unlikely that Test. is to be put late in the fourth century. From the first fasting increased out of emulation. In this connection we note that in Test. Good Friday is not mentioned as the day of commemorating the Passion, but as a preparation for Easter. The Passion and Resurrection seem to have been commemorated together on the Sunday.

(*n*) *The festivals* of Test. are Easter, Pentecost, and Epiphany only. Contrast the A.C. cycle of festivals as noted above (p. 32). The "Epiphany" was the commemoration of the Nativity; and throughout the fourth century, January 6 was observed in the East as this festival (τὰ ἐπιφάνια or τὰ θεοφάνια). In the West, December 25 was observed. The Western Christmas was introduced to Antioch *in addition* to the Epiphany about 375 (in A.C. they are two distinct festivals). In Silvia, however, the later date alone is observed at Jerusalem. Silvia, moreover, gives us another Jerusalem festival for the end of the fourth century, namely, Palm Sunday. For the Festival of the Cross, see below, § vii. Now in Test. there are indications that even the Epiphany is of recent introduction. It is only just mentioned, and no directions are given for it as for Pascha and Pentecost. This simplicity of the festal cycle points to a date in the first half of the fourth century.

(*o*) A possible mark of later date is the use of the phrases "the Lord," "Maker of Life," of the Holy Spirit, in I. 25, 41. These were added by the General Council of Constantinople (I.) to the Nicene Creed in 381 A.D. But that was only the culmination of a controversy which had been raging for a whole generation; and there is no reason to suppose that these phrases were novelties when they were added at Constantinople. The Test. Compiler being a strong anti-Arian, and holding firm to the Nicene faith as regards the Son, was not the least tempted towards the Arian or semi-Arian position which proceeded to attack the divinity of the Holy Ghost. He speaks of the Third Person as consubstantial with the Father (I. 41; see Note there); and it is therefore not unlikely that he would use the phrases "the Lord," "Maker of Life," of the Holy Ghost, before they were formally adopted at the General Council. Epiphanius used both, and A. C. the latter, before 381 (see Note to I. 41). It is a sound principle that the faith was in the Church, and had found expression, before a council put it in its creed. It is of course possible, if we adopt an early date for Test., that the words are interpolations by a later hand. But this is not a necessary supposition. As has already been said (p. 35), the Test. Compiler probably wrote before the Macedonian controversy, or at any rate before it became acute. But his predispositions were all in the direction of those who resisted the Macedonian heresy. We note that there is nothing in Test. about the procession of the Holy Ghost, which was much discussed at the end of the fourth century (see Dr. Swete's article, HOLY GHOST, *Dict. Chr. Biog.* iii. 113 ff.).

5. CONCLUSION. In reviewing the evidence, three possible hypotheses emerge—(*a*) That the author was an Apollinarian writer about 400, who inserted obsolete customs and an obsolete liturgy as a forgery. Want of motive makes this unlikely; (*b*) that he was an anti-Arian writer about the middle of the fourth century, who was a precursor in his doctrinal phraseology of Apollinarius; (*c*) that he was an anti-Arian writer about the middle of the fourth century, but that a later editor inserted the Mystagogia, and perhaps a few other interpolations. The second of these hypotheses appears to be the most probable; but in a case of this sort it is impossible to be dogmatic. It can only be said that a date about 350 A.D. seems to cover most fully all the facts.

An alternative, however, may be suggested. It is possible that the Compiler may have written in the reign of Julian the Apostate (361–363 A.D.), or at any rate after he became Caesar (356 A.D.). Julian was on his way to Antioch in 362, probably at Ancyra or Pessinus, when he issued the oppressive edict which forbade Christians to teach, and (indirectly) their children to learn. The *Testament* Compiler might well anticipate at his hands a repetition of the cruelties of Galerius. There was actual persecution at Antioch in 362. All this would account for the retention in the *Testament* of the references both to persecution and to military service. And further, the attempt to rebuild Jerusalem might possibly have suggested to the Compiler that Julian was Antichrist himself, and supplied the reason why he added the probably older Apocalyptic Prelude to his Church Order. It would not have been safe for him to speak very clearly of the reigning Emperor, but he might revive an old tract on the End, with a covert reference to a present or anticipated persecution. After Julian's death the anticipation of pagan persecution would have been much less strong.

This alternative suggestion would probably not greatly militate against the indications of early date mentioned in the foregoing pages, especially if we fix on a date shortly after 356, though in that case we must perhaps give up the Antichrist suggestion.

6. POSSIBLE ADDITIONS BY JAMES OF EDESSA. The general conclusion arrived at above will not be affected if it be found that the translator added something to the work. There are some instances of paronomasia in the Syriac of I. 18, 28, 30 (?), II. 7 (see Notes to those passages), which may be due to him. Also a clause in the Eucharistic Thanksgiving and the past tense in the *Benedictus qui venit* may be his work (see Notes to I. 23 and to Appendix I.).

§ vii. PLACE OF WRITING

This is even more difficult to ascertain than the date. That it was some place near the sea is determined by the direction to the deacon in I. 34 (not in Eg. C.O.) to search for those who have been drowned and thrown up by the sea. Travellers by sea are mentioned in I. 35. In the Copto-Arabic translation there is a reference to the sea in I. 19 (see Note there on the three Entrances). On the other hand, Test. omits the reference of Eg. C.O. to sailors (II. 20). From II. 8 we see that the writer's country was well watered, the reference of Eg. C.O. to scarcity of water in baptism being omitted.

Again, it was not a bilingual country. The absence of interpreters in Test. shows this. Sarapion (§ 25) has them. Syria (including Palestine) and Egypt are the only countries in which we have evidence for interpreters. Thus the absence of them in Test. argues to some extent against those countries.

Palestine is the country named in II. 27 (Jerusalem). But this is only part of the "apocryphal pretence." Palestine would seem to be precluded in a fourth century document by the absence of any festival of the Cross, especially when so much is made of the Cross as in Test. This festival was the anniversary of the dedication of Constantine's churches at Jerusalem in 335 A.D. Also the fact that the Jews are not mentioned makes Palestine unlikely.

We might get a clue from the countries where Test. exercised an influence. That influence has been chiefly felt in the Monophysite churches of Western Syria and Abyssinia, which appear to have greatly reverenced the *Testament*. It has left traces on the West Syrian ordinal (see I. 21), and on the Abyssinian liturgy (see I. 23 and Appendix I.) and litany (I. 35, 36). As far as is known, it only exists now in Syriac, Ethiopic, and Arabic translations. These considerations might point to Syria or Egypt as the country of origin.

Taking Syria first, we notice in its favour the mention of Syria in I. 10 before all other countries; and the connection between the language of Test. (see p. 17, above) and that of

Apollinarius, Bishop of the *Syrian* Laodicea. On the other hand, the chapter I. 10 is part of the Prelude, which is not improbably altogether independent of the Test. Compiler (see Appended Note at beginning of Book I.). And the second indication assumes—whatever date we fix upon for Test.— that the phraseology and influence which we may call " Apollinarian " were confined to the country of Apollinarius, a very unlikely assumption. Against the probability of Syria being the place of writing, we must set the absence of interpreters, the unlikeness of the Benediction before the Sursum Corda to Syrian usage (see Note to I. 23), the unlikeness of the ideas and theology to those of the Apostolic Constitutions, the fact that the forty days of Pascha include Holy Week, while in A.C. v. 13 (Lagarde, 141^{10} ff.) they do not do so, and the fact that in Test. there are no professed widows other than presbyteresses, while in A.C. there are (see Note on I. 40).

Next, taking Egypt, we have in its favour the fact that Eth. C.O. contains a source of the Test. Eucharistic Liturgy (but this consideration is discounted by the fact that the Verona fragments also have it [1]), and especially the likeness of the Benediction before the Sursum Corda to Egyptian (and Roman) usage as against all the rest of the East, and the position of the Benedictus qui venit (see I. 23 Notes); as also the fact that at any rate the Greek original of Eg. C.O. was probably before the Test. Compiler when he wrote. But the deliberate omission of the milk and honey at baptism (this edifying ceremony was preserved at Alexandria and in Abyssinia till modern times, cf. Dict. Chr. Ant. 164), the absence of the stated Wednesday and Friday fast, the absence as yet of the forty days' *fast* of Lent, the great difference of the Baptismal Creed from that of Eg. C.O., the plentifulness

---

[1] Bishop Wordsworth remarks that the mention of presbyteresses in H. 38^{25} makes it unlikely that the Verona fragments are either Roman or Alexandrian (*Ministry of Grace*, 29).

of the water (II. 8, see above), and the absence of interpreters, all tend to make Egypt unlikely.

A clue may be obtained if we consider attentively the material used by the Test. Compiler. Whether or no it be correct to conjecture a Montanist Church Order as such a source (see § iv., above), we may at least see distinct traces of Montanist influence in the Test. Church Order and in the Prelude; as also we see it in the Apostolic Church Order, which had so much influence on the Test. Compiler (§ iii. 2 β, above). This would lead us to think of Asia Minor as a probable place of writing for the fourth century Test. Compiler. Dr. Zahn has conjectured that Test. emanated from an Audian community in Asia Minor about 350 A.D. We must, however, remember that the Compiler was not a Quartodeciman (cf. Note to II. 8, and see also § v. 5, above). The absence of chorepiscopi may also make Asia Minor less probable (see p. 37, above). On the bearing of the phrase "day and night" on Asia Minor as the place of origin, see Note to I. 21.

On the whole, setting one probability against another, and disclaiming any wish to be any more dogmatic on this question than on that of the date of the work, we may conclude that while Syria is not an impossible country of origin, Asia Minor is the most probable country that has yet been suggested.

THE TESTAMENT OF OUR LORD JESUS CHRIST

THE[1] *TESTAMENT, OR WORDS WHICH OUR LORD, WHEN HE ROSE FROM THE DEAD, SPAKE TO THE HOLY APOSTLES, AND WHICH WERE WRITTEN IN EIGHT BOOKS BY CLEMENT OF ROME, THE DISCIPLE OF PETER*[2]

THE FIRST BOOK

IT came to pass, after our Lord rose from the dead, and appeared unto us, and was handled[3] by Thomas and Matthew and John, and we were persuaded that our Master[4] was truly risen from the dead, that falling on our faces we blessed the Father of the new world,[5] God, Who hath saved us by Jesus Christ our Lord; and being held[6] in very great fear, we waited prostrate as babes which speak not.[7] But Jesus our Lord, putting His hand on each one of us separately, lifted us up, saying, Why hath your heart thus fallen, and are ye stricken with great astonishment? Know ye not that He who-sent Me can do glorious things for the salvation of them that have from the heart believed on Him? Stand not then as [men] astonished, and staring,[8] neither [be] slothful,

[1] The number 77 is prefixed in M.

[2] Codex S.: The first book of Clement, which is called the Testament of our Lord Jesus Christ; the words which, after He rose from the dead, He spake to the holy Apostles. The Copto-Arabic version renders it with several variations. In Codex C. the preface is: And it came to pass after our Lord returned to life and rose from the grave on the third day and revealed Himself to His holy disciples and spake with them, they said unto Him afterwards: Tell us, O our Lord (as in chapter 2).

[3] Lit.: touched. 1 John i. 1.   [4] Lit.: Teacher.   [5] S.: worlds.

[6] S. has "we trembled" (root $\underline{H}RD$), as Lagarde renders it (see Payne-Smith's *Thesaurus Syriacus*, col. 1367).

[7] Lit.: without voice. Copto-arab.: we fell to the ground as dead.

[8] So S. B. understand it (Lagarde, ἐνεοὶ αἰδούμενοι). Or: as astonished ones, fashioned [like statues].

but as the children of light,[1] ask of My Father which is in heaven the Spirit of counsel and might,[2] and He will fill you with the Holy Ghost and grant you to be with Me for ever.

CHAPTER 1[3]

And we returned answer, saying, Lord,[4] what is the Holy Ghost, and what is His power, whom Thou badest[5] us to ask for? And our Lord said unto us, Verily I say unto you that ye shall not be the children of the light[1] except by the Holy Ghost. And we returned answer to Him, and said, O our Lord, give us this [Spirit]. And immediately Jesus[6] breathed on us.[7] And after we had received the Holy Ghost, He said unto us, Verily[8] I say unto you, that ye who have been made disciples unto the kingdom of heaven, and who have believed in Me with undoubting heart, and have cleaved unto Me, shall be with Me; and all those who through you know and do the will of My Father, who keep My words and know My sufferings,[9] shall be made holy, and shall dwell in the habitations[10] of My Father, and shall be delivered from the evil days that are about to come; and I will be with them, shewing them My ways in which they shall live.

CHAPTER 2[11]

And Peter and John answered and said unto Him:—Tell us, O our Lord, the signs of the end,[12] and all the deeds which shall then be [done][13] by them[14] who live in this world, so that we also may make [them] known to them who believe in

---

[1] Eph. v. 8; 1 Thess. v. 5; St. Luke xvi. 8; St. John xii. 36.
[2] Isa. xi. 2. Lagarde reads: "of glory and of perfection" ($\tau\hat{\eta}s$ $\delta \acute{o} \xi \eta s$ $\kappa a \grave{\iota}$ $\tau\hat{\eta}s$ $\tau \epsilon \lambda \epsilon \iota \acute{o} \tau \eta \tau o s$). This is due to a recent hand in S.
[3] C. omits this chapter.   [4] S.: O our Lord.
[5] Lit.: saidst.   [6] S. (recent hand): our Lord Jesus.
[7] St. John xx. 22.   [8] S.: Verily, verily.
[9] Cf. Phil. iii. 10.   [10] Cf. St. John xiv. 2.
[11] S. (in red ink) inserts: Questions of the Apostles (addressed) to our Lord about the end.
[12] St. Mark xiii. 3, 4.   [13] Lit.: are then [done].
[14] C.: all the troubles which shall then be from them . . .

Thy Name in all the nations, that those¹ generations may observe² [them] and live. But Jesus answered and said :— Did I not, before I suffered for those that dwell on the earth, tell you some things about the end³? We answered and said, [Yea,] O our Lord; but now we desire to know the deeds which [are] the signs of the end of this world, if our Lord hath judged that this is fitting for us to know⁴—for us, and for those who [shall] hear.

CHAPTER 3⁵

And Jesus answered and said:—In the time when I was in the world,⁶ I spoke unto you before I should be glorified, of signs that the end is near, thus:—that there shall be on earth famines and pestilences,⁷ tumults, and commotions, risings of nations against nations, and those other things whereof I have told you.⁸ But I commanded you to watch and pray.⁹ And now hear, ye children of the light; for My Father who hath sent Me to His inheritance hath predetermined¹⁰ in His foreknowledge,¹¹ that in the last days, out of the latest generation,¹² there should be vessels¹³ [of grace] holy, and honoured, and elect. Wherefore I make known unto you exactly [what are] the things which are about to be, and when he shall arise,¹⁴ that Son of Perdition,¹⁵ the Enemy, the¹⁶ Adversary,¹⁷ and what he is like.

¹ M. B.: all the.   ² Or: guard against. C. reads: may be preserved.
³ C.: before I suffered, tell you something concerning those that shall dwell on the earth in the latter time.
⁴ Cf. Acts i. 7.   ⁵ S. inserts: Of the signs of the end.
⁶ Lit.: in the time of my age (or world). S. reads: in my time; C.: at the time of my persecution.
⁷ St. Matt. xxiv. 7. The Syriac words for "tumults," "commotions," not as Pshiṭta.
⁸ C.: which are written in the Gospel (anachronism).
⁹ St. Matt. xxvi. 41.
¹⁰ Or (as C.): hath predetermined His inheritance. Copto-arab.: My Father, foreknowing the calamities which shall be in the last days, hath predetermined His inheritance and honoured vessels . . .
¹¹ Lit.: foreknowing.   ¹² So M. B. C.; S.: generations.
¹³ Cf. 2 Tim. ii. 20, 21; Acts ix. 15. C. reads: men.   ¹⁴ Lit.: ariseth.
¹⁵ Lit.: destruction. 2 Thess. ii. 3; St. John xvii. 12.
¹⁶ S.: and the.   ¹⁷ 2 Thess. ii. 4.

Chapter 4

There shall, then, be signs when the kingdom is approaching such as these. After the famines and pestilences and tumults among the nations,[1] then there shall rule, and rise to power,[2] princes who love money, who hate the truth, who kill their brethren, liars, haters of the faithful,[3] proud, lovers of gold,[4] allied by relationship but not allied in counsel,[5] for they wish each to destroy the life of his fellow. But there shall be in their hosts great affliction, and flight,[6] and bloodshed.

Chapter 5 [7]

But there shall arise also in the West a king of foreign race, a prince of great craft, godless,[8] a homicide, a deceiver, a lover of gold, great at devices,[9] a hater of the faithful,[10] a persecutor[11]; and he shall bear rule also over barbarous nations, and shall shed much blood. At that time silver shall be despised and gold be honoured; and in every city and every country there shall be spoiling and robbery, and there shall be [12] spilling of blood.

Chapter 6 [13]

Then there shall be signs in heaven. A bow[14] shall be seen, and a horn,[15] and lights; and noises out of season,[16] and

---

[1] So S. C.; M. B.: seas (by alteration of one letter).
[2] Lit.: the head.
[3] C. omits: who kill . . . faithful.
[4] See Appended Note for the remarkable addition of C. and Copto-arab.
[5] Lit.: thought.
[6] So S. M. C.; B. omits: and flight.
[7] S.: Of the king of foreign origin.
[8] C. inserts other epithets: valiant, a boaster.
[9] M. B.: reasoning.
[10] C.: of the faith.
[11] C. adds: of the Christians.
[12] Lit.: is. S. omits: there shall be.
[13] S.: Of the signs of heaven. The Trèves fragment begins this section (having prefixed our I. 11): But before this there shall be other signs in heaven.
[14] C. adds: in the heavens; Trèves fragm. similarly.
[15] M. B.: sounds; S. C. and Trèves fragm. as text.
[16] C.: lightnings and thunders. Trèves fragm. omits "out of season" and has "a sound and voice and raging of the sea," etc.

sounds,[1] and ragings of the sea [2] and a roaring [3] of the earth.

Chapter 7 [4]

But on the earth shall be signs; the birth [5] of dragons from mankind, and likewise also of wild beasts [6]; and young women newly wedded shall bring forth [7] babes who speak perfectly [8] and announce [9] the last times, and pray [10] to be put to death. And their looks shall be the looks of [men] far advanced in years; they shall be grey-headed when they are born.[11] Also women [12] shall bear babes with four feet: some [13] shall bear spirits only, and some [13] shall bear their progeny with [14] unclean spirits. Others [there] shall [be who] practise divination in [15] the womb, and shall speak with familiar spirits [16]; and there shall be many other horrible signs.[17]

Chapter 8 [18]

But in the assemblies,[19] and [20] nations, and churches, there shall be many tumults, for there shall arise evil

---

[1] C.: a sound of all sorts of storms. [2] St. Luke xxi. 25.
[3] Lit.: crying; S.: cryings. [4] S.: Of [signs] on earth.
[5] So C. M. B. Trèves fragm.; S.: births.
[6] Trèves fragm.: serpents.
[7] C.: others who being but boys take wives shall bring forth (*sic*); see Note. Cf. 2 Esdras vi. 21. Trèves fragm. has "a newly wed young woman shall bring forth" (mox nubserit femina pariet!).
[8] Lit.: perfect words. So also Trèves fragm.
[9] Or :- signify. [10] Lit.: persuade.
[11] Lit.: those who are born shall be white. (So Trèves fragm. also; C.: old men).
[12] Trèves fragm.: other women.
[13] Lit.: these. Trèves fragm.: but other women shall bring forth wind only (singular; the same Syriac word in plural is "spirits"); cf. Isa. xxvi. 18.
[14] Copto-arab.: possessed with. Trèves fragm., as S. M. B. C., has "with" only.
[15] Or: take omens by. Trèves fragm.: in utero divinabunt.
[16] C. omits: and shall . . . spirits.
[17] For monstrous births, cf. 2 Esdras v. 8.
[18] S.: Of disturbances and tumults of nations and shepherds (Lagarde: of disturbance and tumult, etc.).
[19] C. omits: the assemblies and; so also Trèves fragm.
[20] Lagarde: of.

shepherds,[1] unjust,[2] slothful,[3] avaricious, lovers of pleasures,[4] lovers of gains,[5] lovers of money,[6] talkative, boastful,[6] haughty, gluttonous,[7] perverse, rash, given to delights, vainglorious,[8] opposing the ways of [9] the Gospel and fleeing from the strait gate,[10] removing from themselves every humiliation and not sorrowing for My humiliation,[11] rejecting all the words of truth, and despising [12] all the ways of piety, and not mourning for their sins. Therefore [13] there shall be shed abroad among the nations unbelief,[14] hatred of the brotherhood,[15] wickedness, bitterness, slothfulness,[16] envy, hatred, strife, theft, oppression, drunkenness, debauchery,[17] lasciviousness,[18] licentiousness, fornication, and all such works as are contrary to the commandments of life. For from many mourning and gentleness shall flee away, and peace and meekness, and poverty and piety, and tears,[19] because the shepherds heard [20] these things, and did not do them, and moreover did not shew [21] My commandments, seeing that they [themselves] are examples of wickedness in the nation.[22] But the time shall come when some of them will deny Me, and will stir up [23] confusions in the earth,[24] and put their trust in a corruptible [25] king.[26] But they who in My Name endure [27] unto the end shall be saved.[28] Then they shall ordain commandments for men, [commandments] unlike the

[1] Cf. Zech. xi. 15–17.
[2] C. omits "unjust," and gives the adjectives in different order.
[3] Or: despisers. [4] S.: pleasure.
[5] S. margin: that is, unjust gains. [6] 2 Tim. iii. 2.
[7] So S. C.; M. B. omit: gluttonous. [8] κενόδοξος translated.
[9] So S. M. C.; B. omits: the ways of. [10] St. Matt. vii. 13.
[11] Lit.: wounding. Cf. II. 7. Lagarde: the humiliation (συντριβή) of my [people]. C. adds: for my sake.
[12] C.: slandering. [13] Lagarde: then.
[14] C. adds: recklessness. [15] C. S.: the brethren.
[16] Or: contempt (so Lagarde). [17] C.: avarice.
[18] C. omits: lasciviousness; S.: strifes, thefts, oppressions, drunkennesses, debaucheries, lasciviousnesses.
[19] Lit.: weeping. [20] So S. C. (cf. St. Jas. i. 22); M. B.: hated.
[21] I.e. teach. [22] C.: in their own persons. [23] Lit.: make.
[24] C. inserts: they shall become great. [25] I.e. mortal.
[26] S. C.: kings; Copto-arab.: mortal kings. Cf. Ps. cxlvi. 3, 4.
[27] St. Matt. x. 22, xxiv. 13; St. Mark xiii. 13.
[28] Lit.: live (so constantly in Syriac).

book of commandments[1] in which[2] the Father is well pleased[3]; and My elect[4] and My holy ones shall be rejected[5] by them, and called among them, as it were, the polluted. Yet these are the upright ones, pure, sad, merciful, quiet, kind, always knowing Him who is among them[6] at all times, and they shall be called mad for My sake, who have saved[7] them. It shall come to pass also in those days that My Father shall gather together[8] out of that generation the pure ones, even the pure and faithful souls, those to whom I will appear, and with whom I will make My habitation, and I will send to them the understanding[9] of knowledge and of truth, and the understanding[9] of holiness, and they shall not cease praising[10] and giving thanks to their God,[11] My Father who sent Me; and they shall speak the truth at all times, and they shall teach [others] whose spirit they have tried[12] [and have found] that they are upright[13] and worthy, as for the kingdom,[14] and shall instruct them in knowledge and strength and prudence. And those who suffer persecution because they live in piety shall receive the reward of their praise. And it shall be in those times that all the kingdoms shall be disturbed, and all the world[15] also [shall see] affliction[16] and want; and all this world shall be reputed as nothing; and all its possessions shall be destroyed

[1] S.: and the commandment.

[2] *I.e.* the commandments. Lagarde: in whom (but the text of S. is probably wrong).

[3] C.: precepts not according to my will, and traditions in which My Father is not well pleased.

[4] So C. S.; M. B.: my men (viri).   [5] Or: despised.

[6] Lagarde: knowing that he is among them (the text of S. is apparently corrupt).

[7] So C. M. B.; S.: commanded.   [8] St. Mark xiii. 27.

[9] Or: reasoning.   [10] Or: glorifying (so frequently).

[11] Misprint in Rahmani's Syriac here.

[12] Lit.: try; C.: whom My Father hath tried and chosen. Cf. 1 John iv. 1.

[13] Lagarde: they shall teach them that if they test their spirit they are upright.

[14] C.: rightly directed in their hearts towards the kingdom.

[15] Lagarde puts a full stop here.

[16] C.: all the kingdoms of the whole earth shall be swept together, and it shall be in want and affliction.

by many [destroyers], and there shall be great scarcity of crops, and the winter shall be very severe; and the princes[1] shall be few in number and small, who have rule over[2] gold and over silver, and are rich in all those things which are in this world; and the children of this world shall hold their storerooms and barns, and shall have rule over the markets of buying and selling.[3] Many shall be afflicted,[4] and on that account shall call upon their God that they may be delivered. Blessed are they who are not [alive] at that time; and [blessed] they [also] who shall be[5] [alive indeed], but[6] [shall] endure. For when these things shall come to pass, then soon she that travaileth is near to bring forth,[7] for the[8] time is fulfilled.

Chapter 9[9]

Then shall come the Son of Perdition, the Adversary, who boasteth and exalteth himself,[10] working many signs and miracles,[11] that he may deceive the whole earth,[12] and overcome the innocent,[13] My holy ones. Blessed are they who endure in those days. But woe to those who are deceived.

Chapter 10[14]

But Syria shall be plundered, and shall weep for her sons. Cilicia shall lift up her neck until He who judgeth her shall appear. The daughter of Babylon shall arise from the throne of her glory,[15] that she may drink that[16] wine[17] which is mixed for her. Cappadocia, Lycia,[18] Lycaonia shall bow down the

---

[1] C. omits: princes.   [2] *I.e.* possess.   [3] Cf. Rev. xiii. 17.
[4] C.: my faithful ones shall be afflicted, and so on (see Note).
[5] Lit.: are.   [6] Lit.: and.   [7] Cf. Mic. v. 3.
[8] So M. B.; C. S.: her.   [9] S.: Of the coming of the Devil.
[10] 2 Thess. ii. 4; lit.: is uplifted and upraised.   [11] 2 Thess. ii. 9.
[12] Cf. Rev. xii. 9; also St. Matt. xxiv. 24. C. reads: all that is under the heaven.
[13] C. omits: the innocent. The text of S. is corrupt here.
[14] S.: Of the destruction of the countries. C. omits this chapter and goes on to § 11 with "After a little."
[15] Cf. Isa. xlvii. 1.   [16] B. omits: that.
[17] Lit.: mixture. Cf. Rev. xvi. 19.   [18] Copto-arab.: Africa.

back, for many multitudes shall be depraved by the corruption of their wickednesses.[1] And then shall be opened the camps of the barbarians, for many chariots shall go forth so as to cover [the face of] the earth. In all Armenia, and in Pontus, and in Bithynia [2] the young men [3] shall fall by the sword, and the sons and the daughters shall be captives. [The sons and the daughters] of Lycaonia shall be mingled in [their] blood. Pisidia which boasteth, and trusteth in [her] riches, shall be overthrown [even] to the ground. The sword shall pass through Phoenicia, because [her inhabitants] are children of corruption. Judaea shall clothe herself with lamentation, and shall be made ready for the day of destruction, because of her uncleanness. Then shall she gather together the abomination of desolation.[4] The East shall be opened [5] by him [6]; also the ways shall be opened [7] by him. Sword and flame [are] in his hands: he burneth with anger and fiery indignation. This is the armour of the judgment of the corruption of them that are born in the earth; the extermination of the faithful, the way [8] of bloodshed [9]; for his way is in error and his power is to blaspheme,[10] and his hand for deception, his right hand in misery, and his left hand in darkness.

CHAPTER 11 [11]

And these are the signs of him [12]: his head [is] as a fiery flame [13]: his right eye shot with blood, his left [eye] blue-black, and he [14] hath two pupils. His eyelashes [15] are white;

[1] S.: wickedness.
[2] S.: to cover the land of all Armenia and of Pontus and of Bithynia.
[3] S.: islands; M. B. as text. [4] St. Matt. xxiv. 15.
[5] Perhaps, taken by assault.
[6] *I.e.* by Antichrist. S.: her (a manifest error).
[7] See note 5, above. [8] M.: ways.
[9] Lit.: effusion. [10] Lit.: for blasphemy.
[11] S.: Of the signs of the appearance and likeness of the Devil, what they are like. C. begins: Concerning the Son of Perdition he saith.
[12] *I.e.* of Antichrist. So explicitly the Trèves Latin fragm.
[13] Lit.: a flame of fire. So S. and Trèves fragm.: M. B.; a flame that burneth. Trèves fragm. adds: his eyes are those of a cat (fellini, for felini).
[14] *Sic*; see Note. C. has: the left one hath two pupils (Trèves fragm. similar).
[15] C.: eyebrows. So Trèves fragm.

and[1] his lower lip is large; but his right thigh slender;[2] his feet broad; his great toe[3] is bruised[4] and flat. This is the sickle of desolation.[5]

Chapter 12

Therefore I say unto you, [ye] children of the light, that the time is at hand, and the harvest is ripe[6] that sinners should be harvested in judgment. And to many the Judge shall arise as one who is kind,[7] and shall impute to them their own works.[8] But when He[9] shall be at hand, a sign shall be given to[10] the elect, who keep the law[11] of My Father.

Chapter 13 [12]

Then[13] those who fear My words, and do them in truth and with a faithful mind,[14] shall watch and pray[15] without ceasing,[16] reckoning continual supplication as a work, in nothing wandering or going about[17] in this world, and in nothing anxious, but[18] with an austere[19] soul and a mind that doubteth not,[20] daily taking on them the cross,[21] to do the will of My

---

[1] S. omits: and.

[2] Trèves fragm.: his right thigh lean, the shin bones slender. So in the Apocryphal Apocalypse of John, Antichrist has the legs of a cock (James, *Apoc. Anecd.* 156, 187).

[3] Or: finger.   [4] Trèves fragm.: broken.

[5] M. B. omit this clause. See Note for other MSS.

[6] Cf. Rev. xiv. 15 in the Greek. See Note for the reading of C.

[7] Lagarde vocalises the Syriac differently, and renders ὡς ἐν ἐπιθεσίᾳ. This is improbable.

[8] *I.e.* for merit; lit.: shall raise over them their works, *sc.* for a shield in the day of trial. In the day of judgment, they shall be justified by their works. Cf. II. 15, and p. 23. Possibly there is a reference to Rev. xiv. 13. See Notes for the Trèves fragm.

[9] C.: that Son of Perdition.   [10] Lit.: with.

[11] B.: laws; C.: laws and precepts.

[12] S.: Of the approach of the time of judgment.

[13] Copto-arab.: Then our Lord Jesus Christ commanded us, saying: Say to them who fear My words and fulfil them in truth that they pray . . .

[14] C. omits: with a faithful mind.   [15] St. Matt. xxvi. 41.

[16] 1 Thess. v. 17.   [17] Or: wrapped up.

[18] M. B.: also not.   [19] S. margin: contrite.

[20] B.: a doubting mind (error); C.: when also they take up with nothing but with a manly soul and unhesitating mind.

[21] Cf. St. Luke ix. 23.

Father which is in heaven, with a meek heart. For He who is anxious about them that trust in the truth, and careth for them,[1] is the Lord; and He sendeth to them those things which are right and fitting [2]—those things which He knoweth, and by the hands of them whom He knoweth.

CHAPTER 14

I have told you these things, therefore, that wherever ye go, ye may test the souls that are holy,[3] and tell them those things which are fitting and right, and those things which are about to be,[4] and all those things which, before I was [5] glorified,[6] I gave you in commandment,[7] so that believing [them] they may truly live.[8] From henceforth shall be [9] the beginning of travail,[10] and the mystery of destruction.[11] Turning therefore to the Church,[12] setting right,[13] duly ordering, and arranging, and doing all things in uprightness and holiness, speak to every man as is helpful to him,[14] so that your Father which is in heaven may be glorified.[15] Be ye wise, that ye may persuade those who are in captivity to error,[16] and those who are sunk in ignorance, that coming to the knowledge of [17] God, and living piously and purely, they may praise My Father and your God.[18]

CHAPTER 15

Now after Jesus had spoken these words, Peter and John

[1] Cf. 1 Pet. v. 7.
[2] C. omits the rest of this chapter, but adds: to their souls.
[3] Lit.: holy souls.   [4] C. omits: and those . . . about to be.
[5] Lit.: should be.   [6] C.: suffered.   [7] Lit.: commanded you.
[8] C.: while they believe in you they may live purely and holily.
[9] C.: worketh (2 Thess. ii. 7).   [10] St. Matt. xxiv. 8; St. Mark xiii. 8.
[11] C.: inquity (2 Thess. ii. 7). Here C. breaks off with: That of the Son of Perdition is ended without diminution.
[12] B.: Churches.   [13] S. here breaks off, and resumes in § 31.
[14] Copto-arab.: for "Turning . . . helpful to him," reads: Consolidate the Churches, and ordain for (impress upon) them the offices which suit each.
[15] St. Matt. v. 16.   [16] Or: who lead captive into error.
[17] Lit.: knowing.
[18] Cf. St. John xx. 17. Copto-arab.: My Father who is your Father, and my God who is your God.

and Thomas and Matthew and Andrew and Matthias (?) and the rest said: O our Lord, truly Thou hast spoken to us now also words of warning and of truth, and though we are not worthy Thou hast bestowed upon us many things, and hast granted also to those of future generations who are worthy, to know Thy words and to flee from the snares of the Evil One. But, O our Lord, we beseech Thee, make Thy perfect light to shine upon us, and upon those who are foreordained and separated to be Thine. Because[1] that we have many times asked Thee, we pray Thee teach us of what sort he ought to be who standeth at the head of the Church, or with what rule he should raise up and order the Church. For it is urgent that when we are sent to the nations to preach the salvation which is from Thee, it should not escape us as to how it is fitting to arrange the mysteries of the Church. Therefore from Thy mouth,[2] O our Saviour and Perfecter, we desire to learn without omission how the Chief of the holy things ought to please Thee, and [likewise] all those who minister in Thy Church.

Chapter 16 [3]

Then Martha and Mary, and Salome, who were with us,[4] answered and said:—Yea, O our Lord, teach us to know what we ought to do, that our souls may live unto Thee. Then Jesus answered and said unto them: I will that, persevering in supplication,[5] ye should always serve My Gospel, and be examples of[6] holiness, for the salvation of those who trust patiently[7] in Me; and in all things be figures of the kingdom of heaven.

Chapter 17

But to us also Jesus said:—Because that ye also have asked Me concerning the rule ecclesiastical, I deliver and make known to you how ye ought to order and command

---

[1] Copto-arab. abbreviates from here to the end of the chapter.
[2] Lit.: voice.   [3] Copto-arab. omits this chapter.
[4] Cf. Acts i. 14.   [5] 1 Tim. v. 5.
[6] Lit.: in.   [7] Or: endure.

him who standeth at the head of the Church, and to keep the perfect and just and most excellent rule, in which My Father who hath sent Me is well pleased. Verily I say unto you, that he who knoweth the power of this commandment and of this testament, and doeth according to those things which are written therein, shall be made like[1] unto the angels who praise My Father,[2] and shall be holy unto God.

But My Father is mediator,[3] and all His host, that if their sins are as the sand of the sea[shore] which cannot be numbered,[4] and any of them, understanding these words, shall do them, these sins shall be forgiven him, and he shall live in Me.

Chapter 18

But because in the midst of the assembly of the people [there are], more and more, many carnal desires, and the labourers are feeble[5] and few, only My perfect labourers shall know the multitude of My words, all also which at times[6] I spake to you in private before I should suffer, and which ye know; ye both have them and understand them. For My mysteries are given to those who are Mine, with whom I shall rejoice and be glad with My Father. When they shall be loosed from [this] life they shall come to Me.

But these remaining words, determining and appointing them, speak ye in the Churches.

But from the day that My faithful ones also have the desire to know, that they may do the things of My Father, what[soever is] in this My testament, I will be with them, and will be praised among them, and I will make My habitation with them, by power informing them of the will of My Father.

See that ye give not My holy things to the dogs, and cast not pearls before swine,[7] as I have often commanded you.

---

[1] Or: shall be like. There is a reminiscence of St. Luke xx. 36 (?).

[2] B.: the glorious angels of My Father.

[3] Or: arbiter.

[4] Jer. xxxiii. 22 (order altered and words applied to an altogether different object).

[5] Or: small.   [6] Or: many times.   [7] St. Matt. vii. 6.

Give not My holy things¹ to defiled and wicked men who do not bear My cross, and are not subject [to Me]; and My commandments shall be for derision among them. And it² shall be to him that is embittered³ and doeth them not, but giveth My words without profit, for the destruction of their souls.

But it⁴ shall be spoken and given to those who are firm and fixed, and do not fall away, who keep⁵ My commandments and this tradition, [to the end] that they, keeping these [things], may abide holy and upright and strong in Me, fleeing from the downfall of iniquity and the death of sin; the Holy Ghost [also] bestowing upon them His grace, that they may believe uprightly,⁶ that they may in the Spirit spiritually know the things of the Spirit,⁷ and in hope⁸ endure labour, and in joy serve My Gospel,⁸ and bear the reproach of My cross, not doubting but [rather] glorying⁹; for verily I say unto you, that such as these [men] and such as these [women] shall, after death, dwell¹⁰ in the third order of My Father who hath sent Me.

[CHAPTER 19¹¹]

I tell you therefore how the sanctuary¹² ought to be; then I will make known the holy rule of the priests of the Church.

Let the church then be thus: let it have three entrances as a type of the Trinity.

Let the diaconicum¹³ be on the right of the right hand entrance, that the eucharists,¹⁴ or offerings which are offered, may be seen. Let there be a fore-court, with a portico¹⁵ going round, to the diaconicum.

---

¹ M.: thing.   ² Masc.   ³ Or: provoketh [Me].
⁴ Fem.   ⁵ Lit.: do.   ⁶ *I.e.* rightly.   ⁷ Cf. 1 Cor. ii. 10-14.
⁸ Paronomasia in the Syriac between these two words.
⁹ Or: boasting. Cf. Gal. vi. 14.
¹⁰ Perhaps we should read: "after the rest (*or* quiet) of My Father who hath sent Me, shall dwell . . ." See Note.
¹¹ Number omitted in the Syriac.
¹² Lit.: house of holiness.   ¹³ Lit.: house of the deacons.
¹⁴ εὐχαριστίαι. The Greek is transliterated into Syriac from accus. pl.
¹⁵ στοά transliterated. See Note.

Then within the fore-court let there be a place [to serve] for a baptistery,[1] its length twenty-one cubits as a general[2] type of the prophets, and its width twelve cubits as a type of those who have been determined to preach the Gospel,[3] with one entrance and three exits.

Let the Church have a house of the catechumens, which shall be also the house of the exorcists. Let it not be detached from the Church; but so that those who enter and are in it may hear the lections[4] and spiritual hymns of praise and psalms.[5]

Let there be a throne by the altar[6]; on the right and on the left [let there be] the places of the presbyters, so that on the right may sit those who are more exalted and honoured, and those who labour in the word[7]; but those who are of middle age[8] on the left hand. But that place where the throne is, let it[9] be raised three steps, for there the altar ought to be.

Let that house have two porches, on the right and on the left, for men and for women.

Let all the places be lighted, both for a type, and also for reading.

Let the altar have a veil of pure linen, for it is without spot.

Also the baptistery likewise, let it be under a veil.

Let a place be built as for commemoration, so that the priest and chief deacon sitting with the readers may write the names of those who offer the oblations, or of those for whom they have offered [them], so that when the holy things are offered by the bishop, the reader or chief deacon may name them by way of commemoration, which the priests[10] and

---

[1] Lit.: Let a house be for the house of baptism. Cf. I. 34 *ad fin*.
[2] Or: complete; not same word as in I. 23, below.
[3] The Twelve Apostles.   [4] Of Holy Scripture.
[5] Cf. Eph. v. 19, and Col. iii. 16.
[6] So the MSS. (M.B.). See Note.
[7] Cf. 1 Tim. v. 17.   [8] Lit.: stature.
[9] In Syriac *masc.*; it refers to "throne" which is masc., and should refer to "place" which is fem.
[10] B.: priest.

people offer for them with supplication. For there is this type also in heaven.[1]

Let the place of the presbyters be within the veil, beside that place of commemoration.

Let the house of the offering and the treasury be quite [2] beside the diaconicum.

But let the place of the lection [3] be a little outside the altar.

Let the house of the bishop be beside that place which is called the fore-court.

Also that of those widows who are called "those that sit in front."

Also let that of the presbyters and deacons be behind the baptistery.[4]

Let the deaconesses abide beside the door of the Lord's house.

Let the Church have a house for entertaining near by, where the chief deacon shall entertain strangers.

CHAPTER 20

Now after the house is [built] as is fitting and right, let the bishop [5] be appointed, being chosen by all the people according to the will of the Holy Ghost,[6] being without fault,[7] chaste,[8] quiet, mild,[9] without anxiety, watchful,[10] not a money-lover,[11] blameless,[12] not quarrelsome,[13] ready to forgive, a teacher,[14] not given to much speaking, a lover of good things,[15] a lover of labour, a lover of widows, a lover of orphans, a lover of the

---

[1] There is a reference perhaps to St. Luke x. 20. Cf. Rev. xiii. 8, xvii. 8, xxi. 12.

[2] Lit.: all of it.   [3] Or: of reading.

[4] Lit.: behind that of the baptistery.

[5] The Pshitta in Tit. i., 1 Tim. iii., passages parallel to this, has qashîshâ (presbyter) for ἐπίσκοπος.

[6] Cf. Acts xiii. 2, xx. 28.   [7] 1 Tim. iii. 2 (but not as Pshitta).

[8] 1 Tim. iii. 2; Tit. i. 8.   [9] 1 Tim. iii. 3.   [10] 1 Tim. iii. 2.

[11] ἀφιλάργυρος, 1 Tim. iii. 3.   [12] Same root as Tit. i. 6.

[13] 1 Tim. iii. 3.   [14] 1 Tim. iii. 2.

[15] φιλάγαθος, Tit. i. 8., where R.V. renders "a lover of good," A.V. "a lover of good men," and A.V. margin, as has been done here by the Pshitta and by James of Edessa, "a lover of good things."

poor, experienced in the mysteries,[1] not lax[2] and distracted in company with this world, peaceful, and in all good things perfect, as one to whom the order and[3] place of God is entrusted. It is good indeed that[4] he be without a wife, but at any rate that he have been[5] the husband of one wife only,[6] so that he may sympathise with the weakness of widows. Let him be appointed when he is of middle age, not a youth.

CHAPTER 21

Being such as this, let him receive ordination[7] on the first day of the week, all consenting to his appointment, and bearing witness to him, with all the neighbouring presbyters and bishops. Let those bishops lay hands on him, having first washed their hands, but let the presbyters stand beside them, not speaking, in fear, lifting up their hearts in silence.

After [that], let the bishops lay hands on him, saying:

We lay hands on the servant of God, who hath been chosen in the Spirit, for the true and pious[8] disposing[9] of the Church, which alone hath the principality,[10] and which is not dissolved, of the invisible [and] living God, and for the delivering of true judgment and divine and holy revelations, and of divine gifts and faithful doctrines of the Trinity, by the cross, by the resurrection, by the incorruptibility, in the holy Church of God.

After this, one bishop, commanded by the other bishops, shall lay hands on him, saying his calling of appointment, thus:

PRAYER OF ORDINATION[11] OF A BISHOP

O God, who hast done[12] all things in power, and hast established them, and hast founded the inhabited world in reason, and hast adorned the crown of all these things which

[1] Or: sacraments. [2] M.B.: carried away. [3] M.: or.
[4] B. inserts: also. [5] Or: was.
[6] Not worded as 1 Tim. iii. 2 and Tit. i. 6; though the reference is clear. See Note.
[7] Lit.: laying on of the hand. [8] εὐσεβής translated. So always.
[9] κατάστασις transliterated. [10] Probably Greek μόναρχος (see p. 16).
[11] χειροτονία transliterated. [12] Or: made.

were made by Thee; who hast given to them to keep Thy commandments in fear; who hast bestowed upon us the understanding of the truth, and hast made known unto us that good Spirit of Thine; who didst send Thy beloved Son, the only Saviour, without spot, for our salvation; O God and Father of our Lord Jesus Christ, Father of mercies and God of all comfort,[1] who in the pure heights dost dwell eternally, who art high and adorable, dreadful[2] and great; who seest all things, who knowest all things before they are, with whom all things were before they were [made][3]; who gavest illumination to the Church by the grace[4] of Thy Only-begotten Son, having foreordained from the beginning those who delight in just things, and do those things that are holy, to dwell in Thy habitations; who didst choose Abraham, who pleased Thee by his faith,[5] and didst translate holy Enoch[6] to the treasure-house of life; who hast ordered princes and priests in Thine upper[7] sanctuary; O Lord, who didst call [them] to praise and glorify the Name of Thee and of Thy Only-begotten in the place of Thy glory; O Lord God, who before the foundation of the world didst not leave Thine upper[7] sanctuary without a ministry, and also, since the foundation of the world, hast adorned and glorified Thy sanctuaries [on earth] with faithful princes and priests, after the pattern[8] of Thine [own] heaven; Thou, Lord, even now also art[9] well pleased to be praised, and hast vouchsafed that there should be princes for Thy people: Cause to shine forth and pour out understanding, and the grace which cometh[10] from Thy princely Spirit, which[11] Thou didst deliver to Thy beloved Son Jesus Christ; give wisdom, O God, [give] reasoning,[12] strength, power, unity of spirit[13] to do all things by Thy

---

[1] 2 Cor. i. 3.   [2] Lit.: feared.
[3] Perhaps a paraphrase of Rev. iv. 11.
[4] Or: lovingkindness. So often.
[5] Cf. Heb. xi. 8.   [6] Heb. xi. 5.   [7] Lit.: high.
[8] Or: type.   [9] Lit.: wast.   [10] Lit.: is.
[11] *Sic.* In the parallels the relative refers to the Holy Spirit. See Note on this passage.
[12] M.: give glorious (*or* praised) wisdom, O God.
[13] There is, perhaps, a reference to Ps. lxxxvi. 11, and to Phil. ii. 13.

co-operation.[1] Give the Spirit which is Thine, O holy God; send to Thy holy and pure Church, and to every place which singeth to Thee "Holy," Him who was given to Thy Holy One; and grant, O Lord, that this Thy servant may please Thee[2] for doxology,[3] and for laud without ceasing, O God, for fitting hymns of praise, and for suitable times,[4] for acceptable prayers, for faithful asking, for an upright mind, for a meek heart, for the working of life and of meekness and of truth, for the knowledge of uprightness. O Father, who knowest the hearts,[5] [grant] to this Thy servant whom Thou hast chosen for the episcopate, to feed Thy holy flock, and to stand at the head of the priesthood without fault, ministering to Thee day and night; grant that Thy face[6] may be seen by him; vouchsafe, O Lord, that he may offer to Thee the offerings of Thy holy Church carefully [and] with all fear; bestow upon him that he may have Thy powerful[7] Spirit to loose all bands, as Thou didst bestow [Him] on Thy apostles, to please Thee in meekness; fill him full of love, knowledge, understanding, discipline, perfectness, strength, and a pure heart, when he prayeth for the people, and when he mourneth for those who commit folly and draweth them to [receive] help; when he offereth to Thee praises and thanksgivings and prayers for a sweet-smelling savour[8] through Thy beloved Son, our Lord Jesus Christ, by whom [are given] to Thee praise and honour and might, with the Holy Ghost, both before the worlds, and also now, and at all times, and for ever and ever without end. Amen.

And let the people say: Amen. *And then let them*[9] *cry out :* He is worthy, He is worthy, He is worthy.

After he is [ordained], let the people keep the feast three days, according to the mystery that in three days [our

[1] Lit.: work.
[2] Or: that this Thy servant who pleaseth Thee, may be for.
[3] δοξολογία translated. So always.
[4] Lit.: time; perhaps the Greek had "fitting and opportune hymns."
[5] Acts i. 24 (of our Lord).
[6] πρόσωπον transliterated.
[7] Or: free; not the same adjective as before. See Note.
[8] Eph. v. 2.   [9] Or: him.

Lord] rose from the dead. And let every one give him the Peace.

Chapter 22

Let him be constant at the altar; in prayers let him be persistent day and night, especially at the obligatory times of night; at the first hour, at midnight, and at early twilight when the star of the dawn riseth. Then also in the morning,[1] at the third, sixth, ninth [hours, and the] twelfth hour at the lamp [lighting]. If also at every hour he offer prayers without ceasing for the people and for himself, he doeth well. Let him abide in the house of the Church alone. If he have one or two likeminded[2] with himself, it is good that he should be with them for united supplication in unison.[3] For where two or three are gathered together in My Name, ye know that I have said unto you that I am in the midst of them.[4] But if he cannot abide all night long, yet let him remain these hours that I have said. For then the angels visit the Church.

Let him fast three days each [week][5] (?) all the year. But for three weeks after his appointment let him maintain the fast according to the number of the eighteen Exalted Entrances by which the Only-begotten passed when He came to the passion. But on the first day of the week only let him feed on bread with oil and honey and salt, and all fruits of trees; but let him in no wise taste wine, except only the cup of the Offering. This[6] let him use whether ill or well. For it is good that this be for the priests only.[7] And so after these weeks all the year, let him fast three days each[8] [week]; and for the rest of the time let him fast according to his strength. But in no wise let him eat meat,[9] not because if he taste or eat [meat] he is to be blamed, but because when he loveth infirmity these strong meats are not fitting,[10] and in order that he may watch.

---

[1] Copto-arab.: at the first hour of the day.
[2] So Phil. ii. 20 (in Harklean Version).   [3] ὁμόφωνος translated.
[4] St. Matt. xviii. 20, almost exactly.
[5] Lit.: three three days all the year. Cf. I. 31, and below.
[6] Perhaps: this [rule](?)   [7] St. Matt. xii. 4.   [8] Lit.: three three days.
[9] Lit.: flesh.   [10] B.: he doth not use these strong [meats].

Let the Offering[1] only be on Saturday, or on the first day of the week, and on a fast-day. On the eve[2] let him instruct and teach these things in the manner of a mystery to[3] those whom he hath tested[4] as having ears to hear.[5] But if he be sick in body, let him quickly take care to heal himself, feeding on fish, and constantly [taking] a little wine of the Holy thing, that the Church may not also come to an end because he is lying sick; but [that] those who learn may receive joy. But when teaching in the Church, let him speak thus carefully, as a man who knoweth that he is speaking for a testimony the doctrine of all the ministry of the Father of all, that [doctrine] which is accurately written. Let him say all these things—all those which he accurately knoweth and remembereth of old.[6] For if he knoweth what he saith, he may have hope that his hearers also [will] have known these things. And with all his labour, let him beseech the Lord, so that his word may bring forth the fruits[7] of the Holy Spirit in them that hear.

Let him do everything in order, and with knowledge. Let him dismiss the catechumens after he hath admonished them with meditations[8] and admonitions of the Prophets and Apostles,[9] with instructive words, so that they may know Him whom they confess. But let him teach the faithful after the manner of a mystery, having first dismissed the catechumens; and after the instruction in the mysteries let him offer, so that knowing in what mystery they are taking part, they may offer with fear.

Chapter 23

Let him offer on Saturday three loaves for a complete symbol[10] of the Trinity; but on the first day of the week let him offer four loaves for a complete symbol[10] of the Gospel.

---

[1] *I.e.* the Holy Eucharist.
[2] Lit.: in the evening.
[3] M. B.: and to.
[4] Lit.: testeth.
[5] Deut. xxix. 4 (not as in N.T. Pshiṭta).
[6] Or: beforehand.
[7] So pl. in Gal. v. 22, Pshiṭta.
[8] M.: meditation.
[9] Lit.: prophetical and apostolic admonitions.
[10] Not the same word as in I. 19, above; lit.: the filling up; so at end of this chapter, page 77. Or: according to the complete [number] of the Trinity . . . according to the complete [number] of the Gospel.

Because that the ancient people erred, when he offereth let the veil in front of the door be closed,[1] and within it let him offer with the presbyters and deacons and the canonical widows, and subdeacons and deaconesses and readers [and] those who have gifts. But let the bishop stand first in the middle, and the presbyters immediately behind him on either side, and the widows immediately behind the presbyters on the left side, and the deacons also behind the presbyters on the right hand side; the readers behind them, and the subdeacons behind the readers, and the deaconesses behind the subdeacons.

Let the bishop then place his hand on those loaves which have been set on the altar, and let the presbyters place their hands together with him, and let the rest stand only.[2]

Let not the loaf of catechumens[3] be received; not even if he have a believing son or wife and wish to offer on their behalf; let it not be offered[4] unless he is baptized.[5]

Before the bishop or presbyter offereth, let the people give the Peace[6] to one another.

Then, a great silence being made, let the deacon say thus:

ADMONITION OF THE DEACON ON THE EUCHARIST[7]

[Lift up] your hearts to[8] heaven.

If any man have wrath against his companion, let him be reconciled.[9]

If any man have[10] a conscience without faith, let him confess [it].

If any man have a thought foreign to the commandments, let him depart.

If any man have fallen into sin, let him not hide himself: he may[11] not hide himself.[12]

---

[1] Lit.: spread.
[2] *Sc.*, without speaking.
[3] So the MSS. (M. B.). Rahmani conjectures: a catechumen.
[4] Or: let him not approach.
[5] Cf. Lev. xxii. 25.
[6] The Kiss of Peace.
[7] εὐχαριστία transliterated.
[8] Lit.: in.
[9] St. Matt. v. 24.
[10] Lit.: be in.
[11] Or: can.
[12] Cf. Gen. iii. 8–10; Ps. lxix. 5; Jer. xvi. 17.

If any man have a disordered reason, let him not draw near.

If any man be defiled, if any man be not firm, let him give place.

If any man be a stranger to the commandments of Jesus, let him depart.

If any man despise the prophets,[1] let him separate himself: from the wrath of the Only-begotten let him deliver himself.

Let us not despise the cross.

Let us flee from threatening.

We have our Lord as onlooker, the Father of Lights [2] with the Son, [and] the angels [3] who visit [us].

See to yourselves that ye be not in [4] anger against your neighbours.

See that no man be in wrath: God seeth.

[Lift] up your hearts to offer for the salvation of life and of holiness.

In the wisdom of God let us receive the grace which hath been bestowed upon us.

Then let the bishop say, giving and rendering thanks with an awed voice:

Our Lord [be] with you.

And let the people say: And with thy spirit.
Let the bishop say: [Lift] up your hearts.
Let the people say: They are [lifted up] unto the Lord.
Let the bishop say: Let us give thanks to the Lord.
And let all the people say: It is meet and right.
And let the bishop cry: Holy things in holy [persons].
And let the people call out: In heaven and on earth without ceasing.

EUCHARIST [5] OR THANKSGIVING OVER THE OFFERING [6]

Let the bishop immediately say:

We render thanks to Thee, O God, the Holy One, Con-

---

[1] 1 Thess. v. 20.
[2] B.: Let us flee from the threatening of the Lord. We have an onlooker, the Father of lights. Cf. St. Jas. i. 17.
[3] 1 Cor. xi. 10.
[4] Lit.: keep not.
[5] εὐχαριστία transliterated.
[6] M.: offerings.

firmer of our souls, and Giver of our life, the Treasure of incorruptibility, and Father of the Only-begotten, our Saviour, whom in the latter times Thou didst send to us as a Saviour and Proclaimer of Thy purpose.[1] For it is Thy purpose [1] that we should be saved in Thee. Our heart giveth thanks unto Thee, O Lord, [our] mind, [our] soul, with all [its] thinking,[2] that Thy grace may come upon us, O Lord, so that we may continually praise Thee, and Thy Only-begotten Son, and Thy Holy Ghost, now and alway, and for ever and ever. Amen.

O Thou Power of the Father, the Grace of the nations, Knowledge, true Wisdom, the Exaltation of the meek, the Medicine of souls,[3] the Confidence of us who believe,[4] for Thou art the Strength of the righteous, the Hope of the persecuted, the Haven of those who are buffeted, the Illuminator of the perfect, the Son of the living God,[5] make to arise on us, out of Thy gift which cannot be searched into, courage, might, reliance, wisdom, strength, unlapsing faith, unshaken hope, the knowledge of Thy Spirit, meekness [and] uprightness, so that alway, O Lord, we Thy servants, and all the people, may praise Thee purely, may bless Thee, may give thanks unto Thee, Lord, at all times, and may beseech Thee.

And also let the bishop say:

Thou, Lord, the Founder of the heights, and King of the treasuries of light, Visitor of the heavenly Sion, King of the orders of archangels,[6] of Dominions, Praises, Thrones, Raiments, Lights, Joys, Delights, the Father of kings, who holdest all in Thy hand, and suppliest [7] [all] by Thy reason, through Thine Only-begotten Son who was crucified for our sins: Thou, Lord, didst send Thy Word, who is of Thy counsel and covenant,[8] by whom Thou madest all things, being well pleased with Him, into a virgin womb; who, when He was conceived,

---

[1] Or: thought. Cf. Jer. xxix. 11.   [2] Or: the intelligence.

[3] So Rahmani conjectures from the Ethiopic translation; M. B. read: Medicine of the meek, Exaltation of souls.

[4] Lit.: of us believers.   [5] St. Matt. xvi. 16.

[6] Lit.: of the archangelic orders of Dominions, etc.

[7] Or: managest.

[8] Lit.: Son of [Thy] counsel and Son of Thy promise.

[and] made flesh, was shown to be Thy Son, being born of the Holy Ghost and the Virgin[1]; who, fulfilling Thy will, and preparing a holy people,[2] stretched forth His hands[3] to suffering, that He might loose from sufferings and corruption and[4] death those who have hoped in thee; who when He was betrayed to voluntary suffering that He might raise up[5] those who had slipped, and find those who were lost, and give life to the dead, and loose [the pains of] death, and rend the bonds of the Devil, and fulfil the counsel of the Father, and tread down Sheol, and open the way of life, and guide the righteous to light, and fix the boundary, and lighten the darkness, and nurture the babes, and reveal the resurrection; taking bread, gave it to His disciples, saying, Take, eat, this is My Body which is broken for you for the forgiveness of sins.[6] When ye shall do[7] this, ye make[7] My resurrection. Also the cup of wine which He mixed He gave for a type of the Blood which he shed for us.

And also let him say:

Remembering[8] therefore Thy death and resurrection, we offer to Thee bread and the cup, giving thanks to Thee who alone art God for ever, and our Saviour, since[9] Thou hast promised[10] to us to stand before Thee and to serve Thee in priesthood. Therefore we render thanks to Thee, we Thy servants, O Lord.

And let the people say likewise.

And also let [the bishop] say:

We offer to Thee this thanksgiving, Eternal Trinity, O

[1] Or: a virgin. [2] 1 St. Pet. ii. 9; Ex. xix. 6.
[3] Cf. St. John xxi. 18. [4] So MSS. Rahmani conjectures: of.
[5] Lit.: set upright.
[6] The wording differs considerably from that in the N.T. It resembles most nearly St. Matt. xxvi. 27, 28, and 1 Cor. xi. 24, 25.
[7] The Syriac does equally well for "offer" in both cases. Cf. 1 Cor. xi. 26.
[8] Or: commemorating.
[9] ἐφ' ὅσα literally translated into Syriac.
[10] Rahmani conjectures: hast made us worthy, by omitting two letters in the Syriac.

Lord Jesus Christ, O Lord the Father before[1] whom all creation and every nature trembleth fleeing into itself, O Lord the Holy Ghost; we have brought[2] this drink and this food of Thy Holiness [to Thee]; Cause that it may be to us not for condemnation, not for reproach, not[3] for destruction, but for the medicine and support of our spirit. Yea, O God, grant us that by Thy Name every thought of things displeasing to Thee may flee away. Grant, O God, that every proud conception may be driven away from us by Thy Name which is written within the veils[4] of Thy sanctuaries, those high ones—a Name which, when Sheol heareth [it], it is amazed, the depth is rent, the spirits are driven away, the dragon is bruised,[5] unbelief is cast out, disobedience is subdued, anger is appeased, envy worketh not, pride is reproved, avarice rooted out, boasting taken away, arrogance humbled, [and] every root of bitterness[6] destroyed. Grant therefore, O Lord, to our innermost eyes to see Thee, praising Thee and glorifying Thee, commemorating[7] Thee [and] serving Thee, having a portion in Thee alone, O Son and Word of God, who subduest[8] all things. Sustain unto the end those who have[9] gifts of revelations.[10] Confirm those who have[9] a gift of healing.[11] Make those courageous who have[9] the power of tongues.[12] Keep those who have[9] the word of doctrine[13] upright. Care for those who do Thy will alway.[14] Visit the widows. Help the orphans. Remember those who have fallen asleep in the faith. And[15] grant us an inheritance with

---

[1] Lit.: from.   [2] See Note for the reading of M.
[3] M. omits: not.   [4] Lit.: faces of the doors.
[5] Cf. Rom. xvi. 20.

[6] Lit.: every nature that begetteth bitterness. The text has "master" here for "bitterness," but it seems to be either (1) a misprint of one letter—the correcting of which would yield "bitterness, or (2) "master" is taken for a masterful and overweening spirit, which would rather rule than be ruled, rather teach than be taught. Cf. St. Jas. iii. 1. See Appendix I for the parallels in the Abyssinian Anaphora of our Lord.

[7] Or: remembering.
[8] Or possibly: to whom all things are subdued.
[9] Lit.: are in.   [10] 1 Cor. xiv. 26, 30.   [11] 1 Cor. xii. 9.
[12] 1 Cor. xii. 10.   [13] 1 Cor. xii. 8.
[14] "Alway" may refer to either verb.   [15] B. omits: and.

Thy saints,[1] and bestow [upon us] the power to please Thee as they also pleased Thee. Feed the people in uprightness: sanctify us all, O God; but grant that all those who partake and receive of Thy Holy Things may be made one with Thee, so that they may be filled with the Holy Ghost, for the confirmation of the faith in truth, that they may lift up always a doxology to Thee, and to Thy beloved Son Jesus Christ, by whom praise and might [be] unto Thee, with Thy Holy Spirit for ever and ever.

Let the people say: Amen.[2]

The deacon: Earnestly let us beseech our Lord and our God that He may bestow upon us concord[3] of spirit.[4]

The bishop: Give us concord[3] in the Holy Spirit, and heal our souls by this offering, that we may live in Thee in all the ages of ages.

The people: Amen.

Let the people also pray in the same [*words*].

After these things the seal of thanksgiving thus: Let the Name of the Lord be blessed for ever.

The people: Amen.

The priest: Blessed is He that hath come[5] in the Name of the Lord.[6] Blessed [is] the Name of His praise.

And let all the people say: So be it, so be it.

Let the bishop say: Send the grace of the Spirit upon us.

---

[1] Eph. i. 18; Col. i. 12. [2] 1 Cor. xiv. 16. [3] ὁμόνοια translated.
[4] Or: of the Spirit. Not as Phil. ii. 1, Pshiṭta. [5] B.: cometh.
[6] St. Matt. xxi. 9.

If the bishop be polluted,[1] let him not offer, but let a [2] presbyter offer. Also let him not receive of the mystery,[3] not as though he were defiled, but because of the honour of the altar. But after he hath fasted and bathed in pure water, let him approach and minister. Similarly also a presbyter. And if also a widow be menstruous, let her not approach. Similarly if a woman or a layman or any of the company [of the clergy be polluted], let him not approach, for the honour [of the altar] except after fasting and bathing.[4]

Let the priests first receive, thus: the bishops, presbyters, deacons, widows, readers, subdeacons. After these those that have gifts, those newly baptized, babes.[5] The people thus: old men, virgins,[6] and the rest. The women [thus]: deaconesses, and after that the rest.

Let each one when he receiveth the thanksgiving [7] say before he partaketh: Amen. *After that let him pray thus; after that [8] he receiveth the Eucharist [9] let him say:* Holy, Holy, Holy, Trinity ineffable, grant me to receive unto life [10] this Body, [and] not unto condemnation. And grant me to bring forth the fruits that are pleasing to Thee, so that when I shall be shown to be pleasing to Thee I may live in Thee, doing Thy commandments; and [that] with boldness I may call Thee Father,[11] when I call for Thy kingdom and Thy will [to come] to me.[12] May Thy Name be hallowed [12] in me, O Lord; for Thou art mighty and [to be] praised, and to Thee be praise for ever and ever. Amen.

After the prayer let him receive.

---

[1] ἐν ὀνειρώξει translated.   [2] Or: the.
[3] Or: sacrament.   [4] Cf. Heb. x. 22.
[5] Cf. St. Matt. xviii. 1-4; St. Mark x. 15.
[6] *I.e.* male. Cf. 1 Cor. vii. 32, and Rev. xiv. 4.
[7] εὐχαριστία is here *translated* from the Greek, not transliterated as before.
[8] B. (recent hand): before that.
[9] εὐχαριστία transliterated.   [10] Or: salvation.
[11] Or: call on Thee, O Father. Cf. 1 St. Pet. i. 17 (?).
[12] Cf. St. Matt. vi. 9-13.

When he taketh of the Cup, let him say twice Amen,[1] *for a complete symbol*[2] *of the Body and Blood.*

After all receive, let them pray, giving and rendering thanks for the reception, the deacon saying:

Let us give thanks unto the Lord, receiving His Holy Things, so that the reception [of them] may be for the life and salvation of our souls. Let us beg and beseech [His grace], raising a doxology to the Lord our God.

After that let the bishop [*say*]:

O Lord, Giver of light eternal,[3] the Helmsman of souls, the Guide of saints; Give us understanding eyes which always look to Thee, and ears which hear Thee only, so that our soul may be filled with grace. Create[4] in us a clean heart,[5] O God; so that we may alway comprehend Thy greatness. O[6] God, Wonderful, who lovest man,[7] make our souls better, and, by this Eucharist[8] which we, Thy servants, who fail in much,[9] have [now] received, form our thoughts so that they shall not swerve: for Thy kingdom is blessed, O Lord God, [who art] glorified and praised in Father and in Son and in Holy Ghost, both before the worlds, and now, and alway, and for the ages and for ever and ever without end.

The people: Amen.

CHAPTER 24

If the priest consecrate oil for the healing[10] *of those who*

---

[1] There may be a reference, in the saying of the Amen *twice*, to the words of Gen. xli. 32.

[2] See at the beginning of this chapter, page 69.

[3] Or: Eternal Giver of light.   [4] Lit.: form.

[5] Ps. li. 10.   [6] M.: of (a manifest error).

[7] φιλάνθρωπος translated.   [8] εὐχαριστία transliterated.

[9] Lit.: thy deficient servants.   [10] See St. Jas. v. 14–16.

suffer, let him say thus, quietly,[1] *placing the vessel before the altar :*

O Lord God, who hast bestowed upon us the Spirit, the Paraclete,[2] the Lord,[3] the saving and unshaken Name, which is hidden from the foolish but revealed unto the wise [4]; O Christ, who didst sanctify us, and by Thy mercies dost make the servants whom Thou choosest wise with the wisdom that is Thine, who didst send the knowledge of Thy Spirit to us sinners by the holiness which is Thine, bestowing on us the power of the Spirit; who art the Healer of every sickness and of every suffering [5]; who didst give the gift of healing [6] to those who were counted worthy of this by Thee; send on this oil, which is the type of Thy fatness, the delivering [power] of Thy good compassion, that it may deliver those who labour and heal those who are sick, and sanctify those who return, when they approach to Thy faith; for Thou art mighty and [to be] praised for ever and ever.

The people : Amen.

CHAPTER 25

Likewise, the same also over water.

CHAPTER 26

At early dawn let the bishop assemble the people, so that the service may be finished before the rising of the sun.[7]

When he saith the First Hymn of Praise, of the Dawn, the presbyters and deacons and the rest, the faithful also, [standing] close by, let him say thus :

---

[1] *I.e.* in a low voice.   [2] Here only in Test.
[3] As in Constantinopolitan Creed. See Introduction, pp. 20, 40.
[4] Not as in St. Matt. xi. 25, or St. Luke x. 21. The reference would rather be to St. John xiv. 17.
[5] St Matt. iv. 23.   [6] St Mark xvi. 18 ; 1 Cor. xii. 9.
[7] Lit.: until the sun riseth.

Praise to the Lord.

And let the people say: It is meet and right.

HYMN OF PRAISE FOR THE DAWN

The bishop: It is meet and right that we should praise and laud and give thanks to Thee, who didst make all, ineffable God. Stretching forth[1] our souls upward, we raise to Thee, O Lord, a hymn of praise for the morning,—to Thee who art all-wise, powerful, great in mercies, O God, the Confirmer and Raiser-up of our souls; we praise Thee, the Word who before the worlds wast begotten of the Father, and restest alone with Thy saints,[2] who art praised with the hymns of the archangels,—Thee the Maker, who wast not made with hands, and who makest known holy things which are invisible, pure, and spotless,—Thee who hast made known to us the hidden mysteries[3] of wisdom, and didst promise to us immortal light; we lift up praise to Thee in pure holiness, we Thy servants, O Lord.

And let the people say: We praise Thee, we bless Thee, we give thanks to Thee, O Lord; and we beseech Thee, O our God.

Also [let] the bishop say: O God, the Begetter of light, the Principle[4] of life, the Giver of knowledge, the Gift of grace, the Maker of souls, who makest things [that are] beautiful, the Giver of the Holy Ghost, the Treasure of Wisdom, and the Maker of good things, the Lord, the Teacher of holiness, who rulest[5] the worlds by Thy will, the Receiver of pure prayers; we praise Thee, the Only-begotten Son, the First-born and Word of the Father, who didst bestow all Thy

---

[1] B.: having stretched forth.
[2] Or: delightest alone in. Cf. Ps. iv. 3 and xvi. 3; and, by contrast, the Morning Psalm, v. 4.
[3] Cf. 1 Cor. ii. 6, 7.
[4] Lit.: head, or beginning.
[5] Lit.: holdest.

grace on us who call upon Thee, the Helper, and upon the Father who begat Thee; who hast an essence that cannot be injured, where neither moth nor worm [1] doth corrupt [2]; who givest to all that with all their heart trust in Thee those things which the angels have desired to behold; [3] who art the Guardian of light eternal and [of] treasures incorruptible; who hast by the will of Thy Father shed light on the darkness which [is] in us; who from the depth hast raised us up to light; who hast given us life out of [4] death, and bestowed upon us freedom out of [4] slavery; who by the cross hast made us of the household of [5] Thy Father, and by Thy gospel hast guided us to the heights of heaven, and hast comforted us by Thy prophets; who in Thine own Person hast made us of the household of [5] God the Father of lights [6]; grant us, O Lord, that we may praise Thee, our God, so that always with unceasing thanksgiving [7] we may speak praises to Thee, we Thy servants, O Lord.

The people: We praise Thee, we bless Thee, we give thanks to Thee, we beseech Thee, O our God.

Let the bishop also say: We sing to Thee with our mouths this triple hymn of praise as a figure of Thy kingdom, O Son of God, who [art] by [8] eternity; who [art] above all, with the Father; whom all creation praiseth, trembling with fear of Thy Spirit; at whom all nature trembleth in fear and [whom] every soul of the righteous blesseth; with whom all we have taken refuge; who hast made confusion, storms, [and] wind to cease from us; who hast been to us an haven of rest,[9] and a place to flee unto from corruption; in whom we have hope of eternal salvation; who makest the peacefulness of fine weather [10] for those who are buffeted on the seas and with the tempests; who in sicknesses [11] art

---

[1] Not rust. See Thes. Syr. 180.   [2] St. Matt. vi. 19, almost exactly.
[3] 1 St. Pet. i. 12.   [4] Lit.: from.   [5] Or: brought us home to.
[6] St. Jas. i. 17.   [7] B.: thanksgivings.
[8] Or: through (the preposition is causal, not temporal).
[9] Lit.: rests.   [10] Cf. Ps. cvii. 29 sqq.   [11] B.: sickness.

entreated and healest without price; who art with those that are shut up in prison; who hast loosed us from the bonds of death; [who art] the Comforter of the poor, and of those who mourn, and of those who have laboured and wearied themselves with the cross; who turnest away from us every menace[1]; who for us hast reproved the craft of Satan; who drivest away his menaces,[2] and givest us courage; who thrustest away all error from those that trust in Thee; whom the prophets and apostles praised secretly: we praise Thee, O Lord, we lift up to Thee a doxology, so that, having known Thee, we may rest in the habitations of life, doing Thy will alway. And grant to us, O Lord, to walk according to Thy commandments, and in mercy visit us all, both small and great, the prince and his people, the shepherd and his flock; for Thou, O Lord, art our God, and blessed and praised [is] Thy kingdom—[the kingdom] of the Father, and of the Son, and of the Holy Ghost, both before the worlds, and now and always, and for the ages, and for ever and ever without end.

And let the people say: Amen.

Let them sing psalms and four hymns of praise; one[3] *by Moses, and of Solomon, and of the other prophets. Thus: little singing-boys*[4]; *two virgins*[5]; *three deacons; three presbyters. And so let the hymn of praise be said by the bishop, or by one of the presbyters.*

Let it be said thus: The grace of our Lord [be] with you all.

And let the people say: And with thy spirit.

And let the priest say: Also let us praise our Lord.

---

[1] Or: assault.   [2] Or: assaults.

[3] In M. this (rightly) refers to the hymns; in B., to the Psalms.

[4] Or: little psalm-singing boys; lit.: psalm-singers, little boys; or: singers, little boys.

[5] Masculine, as above, p. 76.

And let the people say: Meetly and rightly.

Let the priest say: Let your hearts be fixed.

And let the people say: We have [them fixed] with the Lord.

HYMN OF PRAISE OF THE SEAL [1]

O Lord, the Father, the Giver of light, the Author of all power and of all spirits, the Sealer of eternal light, and the Guide of life, the Maker of felicity and immortality, who hast made us to pass through material darkness, and hast bestowed upon us [2] immaterial light; who hast loosed the bonds of disobedience and crowned us with the faith which is Thine; who dost not keep far off from Thy servants, but art in them always; who dost not neglect those [souls] which with labour and in Thy fear beseech Thee; who knowest all things before they are thought,[3] and searchest out all things before they are considered,[4] and givest what Thou wilt give [5] before we ask Thee [6]; who art well pleased to hear [7] those who with heart undoubting serve Thee, O King of the highest lights and the soldiery [8] of heaven, who hearest the archangels when they praise Thee,[9] and art pleased in them; Answer us, O Lord, we beseech Thee. Grant us with boldness [with] unceasing voice to praise Thee, to laud Thee, to lift up to Thee a doxology; so that being guarded by Thee and guided in light, we Thy servants, O Lord, may constantly praise Thee.

The people: We praise Thee, we bless Thee, we give thanks to Thee, O Lord; and we beseech Thee, O our God.

The priest: O Lord Jesus, hear us, O Holy One, who

---

[1] *I.e.* Blessing.
[2] B. omits : upon us.
[3] Lit.: before reasoning.
[4] Lit.: before thoughts.
[5] Future (not "willest to give").
[6] This is the literal translation; the meaning, however, may be: "who givest before we ask Thee to give." Cf. Isa. lxv. 24.
[7] Lit.: Thou Good Will to hear.
[8] Lit.: heavenly soldiers; or: workmen; or: servants.
[9] Lit.: art the Hearer of the archangels who praise Thee.

wast the Voice of the dumb and the irrational, the Strength of the paralysed, the Giver of light to the blind, the Guide of the lame, the Cleanser of the lepers, the Curer of material fluxes, the Healer of the deaf and dumb, the Reprover of death, the Tormentor of darkness, the Ray of light, and the Lamp that is not quenched,[1] the Sun that is not darkened[2] [and] resteth [not]; but who always givest light unto[3] Thy saints; who hast established all things together for the good likeness[4] of comeliness; who art the well-tempered Reason;[5] who hast plainly given light to all; who art the Saviour of the sons of men,[6] and the Converter of souls; who art the Provider of all things as is right, the Maker of the angels, who adornest all; the Thought of the Father; who didst found the worlds in prudence and wisdom, and didst establish them together; and wast sent from Thy eternal Father unto us; the Intelligence of the Spirit who may not be apprehended or understood, the Maker-known of things invisible; Thou art glorious, and Thy Name is Wonderful.[7] Therefore we also, Thy servants, O Lord, give praise to Thee.

The people: We praise Thee, we bless Thee, we give thanks to Thee, O Lord; we beseech Thee, O our Lord.

The priest: We sing, O holy Lord, this threefold hymn of praise to Thee, who didst give us a faith in Thee which cannot be loosed, whereby Thou didst make us to conquer the bonds of death; who didst create upright minds in[8] them that trust in Thee, that they might be gods[9]; who by the Spirit didst give unto us to tread under foot all the power of the enemy[10] that we[11] may not profane those things which may not be

---

[1] Cf. 2 Sam. xiv. 7 and xxi. 17.
[2] Cf. Eccl. xii. 2 and Isa. lx. 20.   M.: quenched.   [3] Lit.: in.
[4] Perhaps εὐμορφία translated.
[5] Lit.: Reason of well-temperedness (εὐκρασία).
[6] Common Syriac expression for "mankind."   [7] Isa. ix. 6.
[8] Lit.: to; or: for.
[9] There is a reference perhaps to Ps. lxxxii. 6, with our Lord's commentary thereon, St. John x. 34; or to 2 St. Pet. i. 4.
[10] Cf. St. Luke x. 19.   [11] Or: he.

profaned; who by Thy mediation hast made friendship for us with Thy Father. Answer us Thy servants, O Lord, [Thou] whom without ceasing[1] we entreat,[2] who at our supplication givest[3] [us] power against the adversary; whom alway we ask, as [it were], for the overthrow of the Evil one; Hear us, O King Eternal; comfort the widows, help the orphans; pity and cleanse those who are possessed with unclean spirits, give wisdom to the unwise[4]; convert those who go astray; deliver those who are in prison; guard us all, for Thou, O Lord, art our God; blessed and glorious is Thy kingdom.

The people: Amen.

CHAPTER 27

After this let the prayer be completed, and let the reader then read the Prophets and the rest; let the presbyter or deacon read the Gospel; and then let the bishop or presbyter teach those things which are convenient and profitable. After that let there be a prayer, and let the catechumens receive a laying on of the hand.

CHAPTER 28

After that let the bishop teach the mysteries[5] to the people. But if he be not present,[6] let a[7] presbyter speak so that the faithful may know to whom they are approaching and who is their[8] God and Father. Then let the teaching[9] of the mysteries be said thus:

[MYSTAGOGIA OR] INITIATION[9] INTO THE MYSTERIES WHICH IS SAID BEFORE THE OFFERING TO THE FAITHFUL

[We confess] Him who is pre-existent,[10] and was present,

---

[1] Lit.: remission; or: neglect.   [2] Lit.: persuade.
[3] The text has "gavest"—a mistake occasioned by the misplacing of a point.
[4] B.: unwise [things]; or: unwise [women].
[5] Lit.: the things of the mysteries.   [6] Lit.: near.
[7] Or: the.   [8] Lit.: to them.
[9] These are different words in the Syriac; the latter is exactly μυσταγωγία translated into Syriac.
[10] Or: went before; or: was before.

and is, and cometh [1]; who suffered and was buried,[2] and rose, and was glorified by the Father; who loosed our cords from death, who rose from the dead; who is not only Man [3] but therewith also God; who by the Holy Ghost restored the flesh of Adam with [his] soul to immortality, because He preserved [4] Adam by the Spirit [5]; who clothed Himself with dead [6] Adam and made him to live; who ascended into heaven; under whom, after the cross,[7] Death fell, and [8] was conquered, when its bonds, whereby the Devil sometimes [9] waxed strong and prevailed against us, were dissolved; [and] through whose passion [Death] was manifested useless and weak when [Jesus] cut his cords and his power, when his snares were cut, and He struck him on his face,[10] [even Death] who was filled with darkness and was shaken, and feared, beholding the Only-begotten Son; who in His [human] soul [11] descended in the Godhead into Sheol [12]; who descended from the pure heights above the heavens; Him [we confess] the indivisible Thought who is from the Father, and [is] of one will with Him [13]; Him the Maker, with His Father, of heaven; who is the Angels' Crown, the Archangels' Strength, the Raiment of the Hosts and the Spirit of the Dominions; Him, the Ruler of the everlasting Kingdom, and Prince of the Saints, the unfathomable Intelligence of the Father; Him who is the Wisdom, the Power, the Lord, the Thought, Intelligence, Hand, Arm [14] of the Father.[15]

As we believe, we confess Him who is our Light, Salvation, Saviour, Protector, Helper, Teacher, Deliverer, Rewarder, Assister, Strength, Wall; our Shepherd, Entrance, Door, Way,

[1] Rev. i. 8.   [2] Cf. Constantinopolitan Creed (cf. p. 110).
[3] Lit.: Son of Man.   [4] Or: in order that He might preserve.
[5] This seems the best rendering, but other translations might be given, "in spirit" or "in the spirit."
[6] Rahmani renders: "qui Adam jam mortuum induit," but his "jam" is not in the Syriac.
[7] *I.e.* the crucifixion.   [8] M. omits: and.   [9] Or: once.
[10] $\pi\rho\acute{o}\sigma\omega\pi o\nu$ transliterated; not the usual word.   [11] See Note, p. 184.
[12] Gr. Hades: the "Hell" of the English version of the Apostles' Creed.
[13] Lit.: the Equality in His will.   [14] Cf. Isa. li. 9, liii. 1.
[15] In the Syriac all the above is one sentence, depending on the "we confess" of the next paragraph.

Life, Medicine, Provision, Drink, [and] Judge. We confess Him passible [yet] not passible, Son[1] [yet] not created,[1] dead [yet] alive, the Son of the Father, incomprehensible [yet] comprehensible; who, [Himself] sinless, hath borne[2] our sins when He left the Father's heaven; whose Body being broken becometh our salvation, and [His] Blood and Spirit [our] life and holiness, and the water[3] our cleansing; who giveth light[4] to the hearts of those who fear Him, being with them in all things; who hath made us strangers to the whole way of the Devil; the Renewer of souls, in whom we all have put our trust.

He, being God, and before the worlds with[5] the Father, eternal God,[6] when He saw the world perishing in the bonds of sin, and trodden down by the power of a crafty wild beast, and made subject to death through ignorance and error, determining to heal the race of mankind, came to a virgin womb, though hidden from all the camps of the heavenly ones, and cast into ignorance [the] opposing hosts. But when [He], the Incorruptible, clothed Himself with corruptible flesh, making flesh which was under death to be incorruptible, He thus showed in the flesh of dead Adam, wherewith He clothed Himself, an example[7] of incorruptibility, by which example[7] the things of corruption were abolished.

He delivered indeed holy commandments through the Gospel, which is the fore-proclaiming of the kingdom; by which Gospel as[8] a figure of the kingdom we learned to live[9]; through which Gospel the bonds of the Devil have been cut, so that we may attain[10] immortality instead of[11] death, and instead of[11] ignorance may receive [the grace] of watchfulness.

He, then, having become Man,[12] the Son of God, the Lord, who took [on Him] the dead race of Adam in all its kinds,[13] by emptying [Himself[14]], He who is the First, came to birth,

---

[1] Paronomasia.   [2] Or: taken away.   [3] *Sc.*, from His side.
[4] So Rahmani conjectures (see Note, p. 184).   [5] *Sic.*, not (as Rahmani) ex.
[6] These words seem to refer to our Lord.   [7] Or: type.
[8] B. omits: as.   [9] Or: to live as a figure, etc.
[10] ἐπιτυχῶμεν.   [11] Lit.: from.   [12] Or: Son of Man.
[13] Lit.: by kinds. See Note, p. 185.   [14] Phil. ii. 7 (same root).

as Man,[1] though He is God; He who was foreknown by the prophets,[2] and preached by the apostles, and lauded by angels, and glorified by the Father of all.[3] He was crucified for us; and His cross is our life, our strength, [our] salvation, for it is the hidden mystery,[4] the ineffable joy, and through it the whole nature of mankind,[5] always bearing it, is made inseparable from God, for it is the virtue[6] benign[7] and inseparable[8] from God, that cannot be spoken as is meet by these lips, [and] that was hidden from the beginning; but now the mystery which is revealed, which is for the faithful, shall be, not as it seemeth to be, but as it is.

This cross in which we boast, so that we may be glorified, [and] the bearers whereof, the faithful and perfect, separate their souls from everything that can be felt, from everything that is seen, as from a thing which is not true,[9] —by this ask for yourselves, O ye who quit you like men[10]; make deaf your visible ears[11]; make blind your bodily[12] eyes; so that ye may know the will of Christ and all the mystery of your salvation. Holy men[13] and women, whose property it is to make your boast in the Lord, listen to the inward man.[14]

Our Lord, when He taught us and appointed to us a covenant, and made us of [His] household, and came, after His passion,[15] into Sheol, made captive all the earth—He who made the nature of death captive to life, and Death when it saw Him descending in His soul[16] to Sheol, was deceived, and hoped that He was food for him, as was his custom. But when he saw in Him the beauty of the Godhead, he cried out with [his] voice, saying: Who is this that hath clothed Himself with Man[14] who [was] under me, and hath conquered

---

[1] Or: Son of Man.　　　　　　　　[2] Cf. Rom. xvi. 25, 26.
[3] The allusion is clear to 1 Tim. iii. 16.　　[4] Cf. 1 Cor. ii. 7.
[5] Lit.: sons of men.　　　　　　　[6] Or: excellence.
[7] Or: pitiful.　　　　　　　　　[8] Lit.: cannot be separated.
[9] The paragraph here in Rahmani's text seems wrong.
[10] 1 Cor. xvi. 13. (1 Sam. iv. 9 is different.)
[11] Lit.: hearings.　　　　　　　　[12] Lit.: open; or: revealed.
[13] Viri.　　[14] Homo; lit.: Son of Man.　　[15] Lit.: after He suffered.
[16] Lit.: endowed with a (human) soul; as above.

me? Who is this that snatcheth from destruction flesh which was bound by me? Who is this¹ that hath clothed Himself with earth but [Himself] is heaven? Who is this that was born in corruptibility, but suffereth no corruption²? Who is this [that is] a stranger to my laws? Who is this that maketh captive those that are mine? Who is this that striveth with the power of burning Death,³ and conquereth darkness? What is this new glory which [is] in this vision that preventeth me from doing the things which I would? Who is this new dead One without sin? Who is this that by the abundance of light extinguisheth darkness, and doth not allow⁴ me to have rule over those that are mine, but draweth to heaven the souls which were given unto me? What is this glory which preventeth the body from being corruptible? Who is this whom I cannot touch⁵? What is this glory unsearchable⁶ to its surroundings? Woe⁷ is me! I am put to flight⁸ by Him and by those things which are His, for I cannot⁹ injure them.

He, being the Christ, who was crucified, by whom the [things] that were on the left hand were¹⁰ [placed] on the right hand, and those which were beneath [were] as those which [were] above, and those which [were] behind as those which [were] before, when He rose from the dead, and trod down Sheol, and by death slew Death¹¹; after¹² He rose on the third day He gave thanks to the Father, saying: I give thanks to Thee, O My Father, not with these lips which are fixed together, nor yet with a corporeal tongue through which truth and lying¹³ go out, nor with this created and material word¹⁴; but I give thanks to Thee, the King, with that Voice which through Thee understandeth all [things], which cometh not by a bodily organ, which falleth not on carnal ears, which

---

¹ B. omits: this.   ² Cf. Acts xiii. 37.   ³ Lit.: the flame of Death.
⁴ Lit.: give.   ⁵ Lit.: handle.   ⁶ ἀνεξιχνίαστος translated.
⁷ Rahmani's paragraph seems to be wrong.
⁸ Or: I have fled from Him.   ⁹ Lit.: I have nothing whereby to.
¹⁰ Lit.: became.   ¹¹ Heb. ii. 14.
¹² B.: He who *before*. M. and Arab. Didascalia as text.
¹³ Cf. St. Jas. iii. 10.
¹⁴ Lit.: word (*or* speech) which goeth out of workmanship, thus material.

is not in the world and is not left on earth, but with this Voice, the Spirit who¹ is in Us, only speaking to Thee, O Father, loving Thee, praising Thee, through whom¹ also the whole choir of perfect saints calleth Thee beloved, [calleth] Thee Father,² [calleth] Thee Sustainer, [calleth] Thee Helper; for Thou art all, and all [are] in Thee; for whatever is, is Thine and not another's, but is Thine alone, who art for ever and ever. Amen.

Let the shepherd know the mysteries³ of all⁴ nature.

After I have prayed to the Father, as ye know and see, I am taken up, saith Jesus.

Therefore it is right that the shepherd should speak the teaching of the Initiation into the mysteries,⁵ so that they may know of whom in the holy things they are partaking, and what⁶ memorial they are making⁷ through the Eucharist.⁸

And at the end, after this, let him say thus: As then we also have taken refuge in Him, and have learnt that it is in Him alone to give, let us beg from Him those things which He said that He would give⁹ us, which eye hath not seen and ear hath not heard, and [which] have not entered¹⁰ into the heart of man,¹¹ the things which God hath prepared for them that love Him,¹² as Moses¹³ and some of the saints have said. As then we have hoped in Him, let us give to Him praise; and to Him be glory and might for ever and ever. Amen.

Let the people say: Amen.

---

¹ Masculine; therefore it means the Holy Ghost.
² There is a reference to Rom. viii. 15; Gal. iv. 6.
³ B.: mystery.   ⁴ Or: every.
⁵ See p. 84, footnote.   ⁶ Or: whose; or: of what.
⁷ Or: offering.   ⁸ εὐχαριστία transliterated.
⁹ Lit.: giveth.   ¹⁰ Lit.: gone up.   ¹¹ Lit.: a son of man.
¹² 1 Cor. ii. 9 (almost exactly); not as in Isa. lxiv. 4.
¹³ The reference is perhaps to Deut. xxix. 4; but it is more probably a blunder.

After the people are taught the Initiation[1] into the mysteries, let the Eucharist be offered; but let not the Initiation into the mysteries be said each time, but only at Pascha,[2] on Saturday, and on the first day of the week, and on the days of the Epiphany and of Pentecost.

Chapter 29

OF WHAT SORT A PRESBYTER OUGHT TO BE

Let a presbyter be ordained,[3] being testified to by all the people, according to what has been said before[4]; skilled in reading, meek, poor,[5] not money-loving,[6] having laboured much in ministrations among the weak, proved to be pure, without blame; if he have been as a father to the orphans, if he have ministered to the poor; if he have not grown cold [in his love] for the Church[7]; if[8] in all things he be pious, quiet, so that being [thus] he may in all respects be worthy to have those things that are fitting and suitable revealed to him by God, and also may be counted worthy of the gift of healing.

Chapter 30

Then let the appointment[9] of the presbyter be thus. All the priestly company conducting him, the bishop laying his hand on his head, the presbyters touching him and holding him, let the bishop begin, and say thus:

---

[1] See at the beginning of this chapter, p. 84, footnote.

[2] πάσχα transliterated. So always.

[3] χειροτονηθείς transliterated from accusative singular (?), but the termination is misprinted in Rahmani's Syriac text.

[4] Copto-arab. adds: in the chapter about the appointment of the bishop.

[5] Copto-arab.: a lover of the poor.

[6] ἀφιλάργυρος. See I. 20.

[7] B.: if he have not neglected (*or* left uncultivated) the Church; Copto-arab.: diligently frequenting the church.

[8] Lit.: that.

[9] The Greek word underlying this would be κατάστασις. So often. See Note on I. 20, p. 153.

PRAYER OF ORDINATION[1] OF A PRESBYTER

O God, the Father of our Lord Jesus Christ, the Ineffable One, the Light,[2] who hast neither beginning nor ending,[3] the Lord, who hast ordered[4] all things, and set bounds to [them[5]], and by reason hast defined the order of all things by Thee created; Hear us, and look upon this Thy servant, and make him partaker of, and grant unto him, the Spirit[6] of grace and of reason and of strength, the Spirit[6] of the presbyterate[7] who doth not grow old,[7] and is indissoluble, homogeneous,[8] loving the faithful, rebuking, that he may help and govern Thy people by labour, by fear, by a pure heart, by holiness, by excellency, by wisdom, and by the working of the Holy Spirit, through Thy care, O Lord. In like manner as when Thou didst look upon Thy People, the Chosen, Thou didst command Moses[9] to ask for the elders,[10] and filling [them] with Thy Spirit didst bestow Him on Thy minister,[11] so now, O Lord, bestow[12] on [this man] abundantly[13] Thy Spirit, whom Thou didst give to those who by Thyself were made disciples, and to all those who through them truly believed in Thee.[14] And make him worthy, being filled with Thy wisdom and Thy hidden mysteries, to feed[15] Thy people in holiness of heart; pure, and true; praising, blessing, lauding, giving thanks, offering a doxology alway, day and night, to Thy holy and glorious Name; labouring with cheerfulness and patience to be a vessel of Thy Holy Spirit; having and bearing alway the cross of Thy Only-begotten Son, our Lord Jesus Christ, through whom [be] praise and might to Thee with the Holy Ghost for ever and ever.

---

[1] χειροτονία transliterated.
[2] Or: the Shining One.
[3] Heb. vii. 3; Rev. xxi. 6, xxii. 13.
[4] *I.e.* set in order.
[5] Lit.: placed [them] in a boundary.
[6] Masculine, and therefore the Holy Spirit ("Spirit" is otherwise feminine in Syriac).
[7] Paronomasia. See Note, p. 188.
[8] ὁμογενής translated.
[9] Num. xi. 17–29.
[10] Or: presbyters.
[11] Moses. See Note, p. 187.
[12] M.: Thou hast bestowed.
[13] Lit.: without lack.
[14] St. John xvii. 20. For the confusion of Persons, see p. 20.
[15] Lit.: to shepherd.

Let the people say: Amen.

Let both the priests and people give him the Peace, with an holy kiss.[1]

CHAPTER 31

After he is [ordained] let him be constant at the altar, making prayers laboriously without ceasing. But sometimes alone in some house let him take a rest from the things which belong to[2] the house of the Lord; but not ceasing, or diminishing [one] hour, from prayers.

Let him fast three days each [week?] all the year, [on the] one [hand] that he may be perfected in intelligence; and moreover [let him fast] according to his strength, not wandering about and going hither and thither with every spirit, but doing everything with energy.

If it be revealed to a presbyter or bishop to speak, let him speak; but if not, let him not neglect and despise his work.

If it be revealed to a presbyter to visit his parishes,[3] and speak the word, let him go; but if not, let him entreat God[4] with supplication; and if it be revealed to him to speak to them, let him speak to them, always taking the burden and load of Him who was crucified for him, and praying for all the people.

Let not a presbyter or bishop be anxious about food or raiment.[5] God taketh thought and careth for His own in the [things[6]] which He knoweth. But if, when he receiveth from any one food or clothing,[7] it be said to him that he should receive also from another, let it suffice him to receive from [the first] alone, and that [only] in so far as is fitting, and as he needeth, and not to excess.

In respect of firmness of faith, let a presbyter always be unchangeable; for it is such as these that God desireth;

---

[1] Rom. xvi. 16, etc..
[2] Are in.
[3] παροικίαι translated.
[4] B. omits: God.
[5] Allusion to St. Matt. vi. 25 ff.
[6] Or: [ways].
[7] Lit.: a covering.

and let him prove the heart of each one; lest evil,[1] kept and buried within, make him a stranger to the grace of God.

Let him not allow tares to grow in the good wheat, but let him take them away from it, and cut off, those who bring [them] into it. Let not darkness cover his light. Let him teach all the faithful at all times that they accomplish their course, as it were, in the day [2]; because the children of light walk not in darkness.[3] Let the teaching of the presbyter be fitting, and quiet and moderate, coupled [4] with fear and trembling; and that of the bishop also in like manner. And in teaching let them not speak vain things; but let him say such things as the hearers when they hear may keep [in memory]. Let the presbyter be mindful of all the things that he teacheth. For in the day of the Lord the Word, it will be [5] demanded [of him] that he should testify to the people the things which he spake, so that those who did not hear [6] may be reproved. For he must [7] stand before the glory of God,[8] speaking those things which he hath taught. Thus, then, let him teach,[9] that he perish not. Let him pray for those who hear, that the Lord may give them understanding of the Spirit, of knowledge, of truth; and let him not vainly cast pearls before swine [10]; but let him search out [those] who are worthy, those who have heard and have performed [11]; lest if the Word have not brought forth fruit in them, but have perished, he himself should prove the cause [12] of its perishing. Let him not give the holy things to dogs.[10] Let him discern the signs of those who hear the word and bring forth good fruits. But in all things let him, without anxiety, keep [the matter] for the bishop.

Let him not neglect nor despise those who do good works [13]

---

[1] So Rahmani conjectures; M.B.: "in evil."
[2] Rom. xiii. 13.   [3] St. John viii. 12.
[4] Lit.: mingled.   [5] Lit.: is.
[6] Or: paid no attention.   [7] Lit.: is about to.
[8] Rom. xiv. 10; 2 Cor. v. 10.   [9] B. omits these five words.
[10] St. Matt. vii. 6.   [11] Lit.: done.
[12] Lit.: he give the reason (or word) of its perishing.
[13] B. omits: those . . . works.

through teaching.¹ But let him watch for signs in them; [and] of those [signs appearing] in them let him judge spiritually ² by [their] sighs, weeping, earnest conversations, silence, sadness, patience, humble bowing of the head.³ But that which best traineth and causeth suffering is weeping and groaning.

But the work [these do] is watching, continence, fasting, quietness, unceasing prayer, meditation, faith, meekness, philanthropy,⁴ labour, weariness, love, subjection, goodness, gravity, and every [work of] light.⁵

[On the other hand], the signs of those who do not bring forth the fruits of life are [these]:—sloth, love of pleasure, eyes wandering in all directions, disobedience, complaining, restlessness,⁶ a laziness⁷ that will not move,⁸ wandering about.

But the work [these do] is gluttony, debauchery, anger, unbelief, idle and unseasonable laughter, confusion, neglect, error, disturbance, wantonness, love of gains, love of money, envy, contention, drunkenness, high-mindedness,⁹ vain talking, love of praise, and every [work of] darkness.¹⁰

Let him recognise products such as these, and let him speak to those who are worthy. But let him not waste time ¹¹ upon those who do not receive [his teaching]. For those who sow on earth without fruits shall reap miseries.

Let ¹² the presbyter, as is right and fitting, go about to the houses of those who are sick with the deacon, and visit them; let him consider and say to them those things that are fitting and proper, especially to the faithful. Let him exhort that the sick who are poor be helped by the Church, so that they also who do [deeds] of kindness may enter into the joy

---

¹ As the Syriac is punctuated, "through teaching" qualifies "neglect or despise."
² M.: [being] spiritual,—a reference perhaps to 1 Cor. ii. 15.
³ Lit.: asceticism (*or* voluntary poverty) of the head.
⁴ φιλανθρωπία translated. ⁵ Lit.: all light.
⁶ Or: fidgeting (literally, spasms). ⁷ So Rahmani's text; M.B.: slothful.
⁸ Lit.: without moving. ⁹ Lit.: exaltation of thought (*or* mind).
¹⁰ Lit.: all darkness. ¹¹ Lit.: delay.
¹² S. resumes here with a title:—35 (*sic*) That the presbyter should visit the sick, and especially the faithful.

of their Lord.¹ Let² him confirm those who have newly become catechumens³ with prophetical and evangelical utterances, with the word of teaching. Let him not neglect his prayers, for he is the figure of the archangels: but let him know that God did not spare the angels who sinned.⁴

Let him fast; and if it is proper, let him receive of the cup. Let wine suffice him, as much as, in his judgment, profiteth and helpeth him, lest that drink which was for [his] healing he receive to [his] loss. In sickness, let him eat herbs and fish,⁵ and also that he may have care for his work. In everything let the priest be an example⁶ to the faithful of the work of holiness.⁷

Let the presbyter praise and give thanks in the same way as the bishop.

CHAPTER 32

Let them say the daily hymn of praise in the Church, each of them at his own time, thus:

DAILY HYMN OF PRAISE

The grace of our Lord [be] with you all.
The people: And with thy spirit.
The priest: Praise ye the Lord.
The people: It is meet and right.
The priest: Thee, O Father of incorruptibility, Deliverer of our souls, Confirmer of the thoughts, and Guardian of our hearts, who hast illumined our hearts and hast brought to an end the darkness of our intelligence, by the knowledge which is in Thee; who hast by the cross of Thy Only-begotten brought back anew⁸ to incorruptibility the old man⁹ which was given over to corruption¹⁰; who hast brought error to an

---

¹ St. Matt. xxv. 21.
² S.: 36. Also how a presbyter ought to conduct himself, and how he should teach and not neglect his prayers.
³ M. B.: become disciplined.
⁴ 2 St. Pet. ii. 4 (usual printed version) almost exactly.
⁵ Plural; S.: a fish.   ⁶ Lit.: type.   ⁷ Here S. breaks off.
⁸ Lit.: renewed again.   ⁹ Lit.: son of man.   ¹⁰ Eph. iv. 22.

end, and by Thy commandments hast made man [1] to pass to immortality; who didst seek that which was lost, we [Thy] servants [and] also [Thy] people praise.

The people: We praise Thee, *and the rest.*

The priest: We praise Thee, O Lord, whom continually the unceasing doxologies of the Archangels singing praise, and the hymns of praise [2] of Glories,[2] and chants of Dominions praise. We praise Thee, O Lord, who didst send Thy Thought, Thy Word, Thy Wisdom, Thy Energy,[3] [namely] Him who [is] of old, and was with Thee before the worlds, the uncreated Word of the Uncreated one, but appeared, incarnate, in the end of times, for the salvation of created [4] man,[5] Thy beloved Son Jesus Christ, who made us free from the yoke of slavery. Therefore we also, as we are accustomed, [we] Thy servants, O Lord [and] also [thy] people, praise Thee.

The people: We praise Thee, *and the rest.*

The priest: We sing to Thee a triple hymn of praise from our hearts, O Lord who givest life, to Thee who dost visit the souls of the poor, and neglectest not the spirits of those who are afflicted, the Assister of those who are persecuted, the Helper of those who are tossed on the sea, the Deliverer of those who are buffeted, the Provider for those who are hungry, who takest vengeance for those who are wronged, the Lover of the faithful, the Companion of the saints, the Habitation of the pure, the Dwelling-place of those who call on Thee in truth, the Protector of widows, the Liberator of orphans, who givest to Thy Church a right government, and hast founded [6] in it love-feasts, ministrations, receptions [7] of the faithful, the partaking of the Spirit, gifts of grace and powers. We praise Thee; we cease not alway in our hearts picturing the image of [8] Thy kingdom in ourselves, for Thy sake [and] also [for the sake] of Thy beloved Son Jesus Christ, by whom [be] praise and might to Thee with the Holy Ghost, for ever and ever, Amen.

And let the people say: Amen.

---

[1] Lit.: son of man.   [2] Same root.   [3] Or: Action.
[4] Lit.: made.   [5] Lit.: sons of men.   [6] Lit.: planted.
[7] *I.e.* feasts.   [8] *I.e.* prefiguring.

But if also any one saith prophetical words, let him say [them]; he hath a reward.

But at midnight let the sons of priestly service, and those of the people who are more perfect, give praise by themselves. For also in that hour our Lord, rising, praised His Father.

See, O Children [1] of the light; he who believeth the words of the Lord, walketh as He walked in this world, that where He is, there he may be also.

CHAPTER 33 [2]

OF DEACONS

The deacon is appointed,[3] chosen like the things which have before been spoken of. If he be of good conduct,[4] if he be [5] pure, if he have been chosen for purity and for abstinence from distractions [6]; if not, yet [if he] be the husband of one wife,[7] borne [8] witness to by all the faithful, not entangled [9] in the businesses of the world, not knowing a handicraft, without riches, without children.[1] But if he be married [10] or [11] have children,[1] let his children [1] be taught to work piety [12] and to be pure, so that they may be approved by the Church,[13] according to the rule of the ministry. But let the Church take care for them, so that they may persevere in the law and in the work of the ministry.

CHAPTER 34 [14]

But let him accomplish in the Church those things which are right. Let [his] ministry be thus. First, let him do

[1] Or: Sons.
[2] S. resumes here with the words: 37. Of the deacon.
[3] S.: let the deacon be appointed. For the word, see p. 90.
[4] εὐβίοτος or (Lagarde) εὔτροπος translated.
[5] M. omits: he be.   [6] Or: enticements.
[7] Lit.: of (or from) the marriage of one wife. Cf. 1 Tim. iii. 12.
[8] S.: and borne.   [9] S. [Lagarde]: disturbed by.
[10] Lit.: if he be from (of) a wife.   [11] S.: and if he.
[12] So S.; M.B.: work fear well (error).
[13] M.B.: as they are who are approved, etc.
[14] S. carries this on as a part of the preceding chapter.

only those things which are commanded by the bishop as for proclamation[1]; and let him be the counsellor of the whole clergy,[2] and the mystery[3] of the Church; who ministereth to the sick, who ministereth to the strangers, who helpeth the widows, who is the father of the orphans, who goeth about all the houses of those that are in need, lest any be in affliction or sickness or misery. Let him go about in the houses of the catechumens, so that he may confirm those who are doubting and teach those who are unlearned.[4]

Let him clothe those men[5] who have departed,[6] adorning [them]; burying[7] the strangers; guiding those who pass from their dwelling, or go into captivity. For the help[8] of those who are in need let him notify the Church; let him not trouble the bishop; but only on the first day of the week let him make mention about everything, so that he may know.

Let him be watchful at the hour of the assembly, going about in the church, and let him see that no one be [there who is] proud, or[9] a buffoon, or a spy,[10] or one who speaketh idle [words]. Let him rebuke [such], every one seeing and hearing, and let him thrust out him whom he hath condemned[11] to receive punishment, so that the others also may fear.[12] And if [the offender] persuade him to permit him to partake, let him give[13] him comfort. But if the man persist in his transgression[14] or disorderliness, let him take [word] about him up to the bishop, and let him be separated seven days, and then called; so that he be not taken captive.[15] But if when he cometh he still continue and persist in his folly, let him be cut off until he, repenting truly, come to himself, beseeching [to be received back].

If he be in a city on the seashore, let him go quickly[16]

---

[1] S.: patience (error). See Note, p. 190.   [2] κλῆρος transliterated.
[3] Or: sacrament.   [4] ἰδιῶται, transliterated.   [5] Viros.
[6] Lit.: finished; S. (margin, first hand): dead.
[7] Lagarde reads QRR (when it is cold) for QBR (burying).
[8] So S.; M.B. have: memorial (or, remembrance).
[9] S.: and.   [10] S.: a disturber.   [11] S.: who is guilty.
[12] Lit.: obtain fear.   [13] Lit.: make.   [14] Lit.: fall.
[15] Sc. by the Devil?   [16] S. omits: quickly.

about the places on the seashore, lest[1] there be any one dead in the sea[2]; let him clothe him and bury him. Similarly also let him search out the guest house,[3] lest there be any one who is staying in the place sick or in need or dead; and let him make [it] known to the Church, so that it may provide what is right for each one. Let him cause the palsied and infirm to bathe[4] as is right, so that they may have a breathing space from their pains.[5] Let him give through the Church to each one what is right.[6]

In the Church let twelve presbyters, seven deacons, fourteen subdeacons, thirteen widows who sit in front,[7] be known.[8]

But of the deacons let him who is considered among them to be most earnest, and best in governing, be chosen to be the receiver of strangers. Let him alway be in the place[9] of the guest house which is in the church, clothed in white garments, a stole[10] only on his shoulder.

Chapter 35

Let him be in everything as the eye of the Church, with fear admonishing,[11] so that he may be an example to[12] the people of piety Let him admonish thus:

ADMONITION OF THE DEACON

Let us arise.
Let every one know his place.
Let the catechumens depart.
See [that] no one polluted, no one slothful [remain].
[Lift] up the eyes of your hearts.
The angels are looking on.
See [that] he who trusteth not, withdraw.

---

[1] *I.e.* to see if. [2] See p. 42. [3] S.: guest houses.
[4] Or: wash the palsied and infirm. [5] Or: diseases.
[6] S. here breaks off and goes on to the middle of I. 36.
[7] Same words as in I. 19, p. 64. [8] *I.e.* recognised.
[9] Lit.: house; cf. I. 19, p. 63, a place for a baptistery?
[10] Gr. Orarium transliterated. [11] Lit.: making known; see p. 70.
[12] Lit.: a type of.

Let us beseech in concord.[1]

Let no fornicator, no wrathful man[2] [remain]; if one who is a servant of evil be [here], let him withdraw.

See, as children[3] of the light, let us beg [and] beseech our Lord and our God and our Saviour Jesus Christ.

When the presbyter or bishop beginneth the prayer, let the people pray and kneel.[4]

Then let the deacon say thus:

For[5] the peace which is from heaven let us beseech, that the Lord in His mercy may give us peace.

For our faith[6] let us beseech, that the Lord may grant unto us to keep truly unto the end the faith which is in Him.

For harmony and concord let us beseech, that the Lord may keep us together in concord of the Spirit.

For patience let us beseech, that the Lord may bestow [upon us] patience unto the end in all afflictions.

For the Apostles let us beseech, that the Lord may grant to us to please Him, as they also pleased Him, and may make us worthy of their inheritance.

For the holy prophets let us beseech, that the Lord may number us with them.

For the holy confessors let us beseech, that the Lord God may grant us to fulfil [our course] with the same mind [as they].

For the bishop let us beseech, that our Lord may grant him to us for length of days[7] in faith, rightly dividing[8] the word of truth, and standing at the head of the Church purely and without blame.

For the presbyterate let us beseech, that the Lord may not take away from them the spirit of the presbyterate, but bestow on them earnestness and piety until the end.

For the deacons let us beseech, that the Lord may grant

---

[1] ὁμόνοια translated.
[2] Homo.
[3] Or: sons.
[4] Or: genuflect.
[5] Or: With reference to (so throughout).
[6] Misprinted.
[7] Lit.: long in days.
[8] Lit.: cutting. 2 Tim. ii. 15.

unto them to run a perfect course, and to perfect holiness, and that He may remember their work and their love.

For the presbyteresses let us beseech, that the Lord may hear their supplications and keep their hearts perfectly in the grace of the Spirit and help their work.

For the subdeacons, readers, deaconesses let us beseech, that the Lord may grant to them to receive a reward in patience.

For the faithful laymen let us beseech, that the Lord may grant unto them to keep the faith perfectly.[1]

For the catechumens let us beseech, that the Lord may grant unto them to be counted worthy of the laver of forgiveness, and may sanctify them with the seal of holiness.

For the kingdom let us beseech, that the Lord may bestow upon it tranquillity.

For the exalted powers let us beseech, that the Lord may grant to them prudence and the fear of Him.

For all the world let us beseech, that the Lord may provide for each one such things as are meet.

For those who travel by sea,[2] and those who go on journeys let us beseech, that the Lord may guide them [3] with the right hand of mercy.

For those who are persecuted let us beseech, that the Lord may grant to them patience and knowledge, and may bestow on them also a completed [4] labour.

For those who have fallen asleep from the Church let us beseech, that the Lord may bestow upon them a place of rest.

For those who have fallen [5] let us beseech, that the Lord may not remember their follies unto them, but moderate [His] threats unto them.

And let us all also, who need prayer, beseech that the Lord may protect and keep us with the [6] peaceful Spirit.

Let us persuade and beseech the Lord, that He may receive our prayers.

After the deacon commemorateth, let the bishop make a sign with his hand.

[1] B.: perfect faith.   [2] Lit.: who sail.   [3] B. omits: them.
[4] Or: perfect.   [5] Lit.: are in a fall.   [6] Or: in a.

Let the deacon say: Let us arise in the Holy Ghost, that, being made wise, we may grow in His grace, boasting in His Name; being built on the foundation of the Apostles,[1] let us beg [and] beseech the Lord that, being persuaded, He may receive our prayers.

Then let the bishop complete [*the prayer*]. *And let the people say:* Amen.

Chapter 36

Let the deacon be such as this, so that he may appear with fear and modesty and reverence. With regard to fervour of spirit,[2] let him have a perfect manner of life. Let him observe and look at those who come into the house of the sanctuary. Let him investigate who they are, so that he may know if they are lambs or wolves. And when he asketh, let him bring in him that is worthy, lest, if a spy enter, the liberty of the Church be searched out,[3] and his sin be on his head.

If[4] any one come late to the [service of] praise,[5] either when that of the dawn[6] is being said or when the Offering is being offered, whoever he be, let him remain outside, and let not the deacon bring him in,—for it[7] is a type of the day of judgment[8] which is to come,—lest by the noise of the entrance there be distraction to those who are praying. But when he cometh and findeth that the door is shut,[8] let him not knock, because of what hath been said already.

But after the hymn of praise which is placed first is finished, let the faithful man or faithful woman enter. Let the deacon say, either, Over the offering[9]: or, For[10] the

---

[1] Eph. ii. 20. See p. 15.

[2] B.: because he is the shewing forth (*or* example) of the Spirit. Rom. xii. 11.

[3] *I.e.* attacked.

[4] Here S. resumes with the title: 49. Of those who come late to the church, that they enter not when the service is going on, but be outside till it endeth.

[5] S.: service.   [6] S.: the beautiful one (transposition of a letter).

[7] Or: he.   [8] St. Matt. xxv. 12.

[9] S.: offerings.   [10] Or: with regard to, as in Chap. 35.

hymn of praise, let us beseech that the Lord may write our supplication [1] in the book of life, and [that] God who [is] for ever may remember us in His holy habitations of light. For [2] [this] brother who is late, let us beseech that the Lord may give him earnestness and labour, and turn away from him every bond [3] of this world, and give him the will of affection and love and [4] hope.

Similarly also [5] for [6] a sister or for [6] a deaconess, for [6] those who are [7] late or remain [8] outside, let him admonish [9] that all the people may beseech for them. For thus when a deacon mentioneth and admonisheth about them,[10] earnestness is strengthened and the bond of love [11] is fulfilled, and the despiser and the slothful is disciplined.

CHAPTER 37

If [12] any woman whatsoever suffer violence from a man, let the deacon accurately investigate if she be faithful [13] and have truly suffered violence; if [14] he who treated her with violence was [15] not her lover. And if she be accurately thus, and if she that suffered mourn about the violence that happened to her, let him take it up to the hearing of the bishop, that she may be shewn to be in all things in communion with [16] the Church. If he who treated her with violence be faithful, let not the deacon bring him into the church for partaking,[17] even if he repent. But if he be a catechumen and repent, let him be baptized and partake. Let the deacon catechise [18] those who repent and bring them to the presbyters or to the bishop that they may be catechised and taught knowledge. But if [his] power suffice [19] to accom-

[1] S.: supplications. [2] Or: with regard to. [3] S.: all the bonds.
[4] So S.; M.B.: in. [5] S.: either. [6] Or: with regard to.
[7] Lit.: were. [8] Lit.: remained. [9] Lit.: make known.
[10] Masculine (*i.e.* both sexes). [11] Cf. Col. iii. 14.
[12] S. inserts title : 43. Of a woman who is treated by a man with violence.
[13] S. omits : if she be faithful.
[14] S. inserts: also. [15] B.: is.
[16] Lit.: daughter of the partaking of.
[17] So S.; M.B. omit : for partaking. [18] Or : instruct.
[19] Rahmani conjectures : doth not suffice.

plish perfectly the office of the diaconate, let him abide only in prayer; and let him consider supplication and meditation, love, the [1] way, mourning, and [to have] fear before his eyes, as a work; and he shall be called a son of the light.

Chapter 38

Let the appointment of a deacon be thus. Let the bishop alone lay a hand [2] on him, because he is not appointed to the priesthood, but for the service of attendance on the bishop and the Church.[3] Over the deacon then, let the bishop say thus:

PRAYER OF ORDINATION [4] OF A DEACON

O God, who didst create all things, and didst adorn [them] by the Word; who dost rest [5] in the pure ages; [6] who didst minister to us eternal life by Thy prophets; who didst enlighten us with the light of knowledge; O God, who doest great things,[7] and [art] the Maker of all glory,[8] Father of our Lord Jesus Christ,[9] whom Thou didst send to minister to Thy will,[10] that all the race of mankind might be saved, and didst make known to us and didst reveal Thy Thought, Thy Wisdom, Thine Energy, Thy beloved Son, Jesus Christ, the Lord of light, the Prince of princes, and God of gods; give the spirit of grace and earnestness to [11] this Thy servant, that there may be given to him earnestness, quiet, strength, power to please Thee; give him, O Lord, as a worker in the law without shame, kind, a lover of orphans, a lover of the pious, a lover of widows, fervent in spirit,[12] a lover of good things [13]; and

---

[1] S.: and the way. Lagarde conjectures: the duty of the way.
[2] S.: hands.
[3] Here S. breaks off and goes to Chap. 46.
[4] χειροτονία transliterated.
[5] Or: delightest.
[6] Or: worlds.
[7] Job v. 9 (as printed in the Pshiṭta, *didst*).
[8] Or: praise.
[9] Rom. xv. 6.
[10] Or: to minister Thy will (as Hauler's Verona fragments, p. 110[11]).
[11] Lit.: in (cf. Hauler *ubi sup.*, "in hunc servum tuum").
[12] Rom. xii. 11? (not as Pshiṭta).
[13] φιλάγαθος, Tit. i. 8.

enlighten,[1] O Lord, him whom Thou hast loved and chosen to minister to Thy Church, offering in holiness to Thy holy place [2] those things which are offered to Thee from the inheritance of Thy high priesthood; so that ministering without blame and purely and holily and with a pure conscience, he may be counted worthy of this high and exalted office, by Thy good will, praising Thee continually through Thy Only-begotten Son Jesus Christ,[3] our Lord, by whom [be] praise and might to Thee for ever and ever.

The people: Amen.

CHAPTER 39

[OF CONFESSORS]

If [one] be borne witness to and confess that he was in bonds and in imprisonment and in afflictions [4] for the Name of God, a hand is not therefore laid on him for the diaconate. Similarly not for the presbyterate. For he hath the honour of the clergy,[5] having been protected by the hand of God, by [his] confessorship. But if he be appointed bishop, he is also counted worthy of laying on of the hand. And [even] if he be a confessor who hath not been judged before the power, and hath not been buffeted in bonds, but only hath confessed, he is counted worthy of laying on of the hand. For he receiveth the prayer of the clergy. But let him [6] not pray over him repeating [7] all these words; but when the shepherd advanceth,[8] he will receive the effect.

CHAPTER 40

OF WIDOWS

Let a widow be appointed,[9] being chosen, if for a long time past she have abided without a husband; if though often

---

[1] M.: Thou hast enlightened.   [2] Or: to Thy sanctity.
[3] B. omits: Christ.   [4] B.: affliction.   [5] κλῆρος transliterated.
[6] *I.e.* the bishop?   [7] B.: again.   [8] See p. 116 below.
[9] Same word as above, pp. 90, 97, etc.

pressed by men¹ to be married,² because of the faith she have not been married.² But if not, it is not yet right that she should be chosen; but let her be proved for a time, if she be pious, if having³ children she have brought them up⁴ in holiness, if she have not taught them worldly wisdom, if she have made them examples of the holy law and of the Church, if she have loved and honoured strangers,⁵ if she have been constant in prayers,⁶ if she have lived meekly, if she have cheerfully aided those who are afflicted,⁵ if it have been revealed to the saints about her, if she have not neglected the saints,⁵ if she have ministered⁷ with all her power, if she be fit to bear and endure the burden, being one who prayeth without ceasing,⁸ being perfect in all things, being fervent in spirit,⁹ having the eyes of her heart¹⁰ opened in everything, being alway kind, loving innocency, not possessing anything in this world, but alway taking and bearing about the cross, crucifying¹¹ all evil, by night and by day¹² abiding by the altar, working cheerfully and secretly. If she have one or two or three likeminded¹³ in my Name, I am among them.¹⁴ But let her be perfect in the Lord, as one who is visited by the Spirit. Let her do the things which are made known to her with fear and earnestness. Let her instruct those women who do not obey; let her teach those¹⁵ [women] who have not learnt; let her convert those who are foolish; let her instruct them to be grave¹⁶; let her prove the deaconesses; let her make those who enter¹⁷ to know of what sort and who they are; also let her instruct them that they abide. To those who hear¹⁸ let her patiently counsel those things which are proper. To those who are disobedient after three instructions let her not speak. Let her love¹⁹ those who desire to be in virginity

---

¹ homines; lit.: sons of men. ² Lit.: for a husband.
³ Lit.: having gained, *or* possessed. ⁴ Same word as in 1 Tim. v. 10.
⁵ Cf. 1 Tim. v. 10. ⁶ B.: prayer. ⁷ M.: heard.
⁸ 1 Thess. v. 17. ⁹ Rom. xii. 11. ¹⁰ Eph. i. 18.
¹¹ Or: torturing. ¹² See Note, p. 159. ¹³ See pp. 68, 109.
¹⁴ St. Matt. xviii. 20. The var. lect. of M. (which is not grammatical) is the Pshiṭta unaltered. ¹⁵ Feminine pronouns throughout.
¹⁶ *Not* 1 Tim. iii. 8, 11, or Tit. ii. 2, Pshiṭta.
¹⁷ Heathen enquirers. ¹⁸ Catechumens. ¹⁹ Or: cherish.

or in purity; those who oppose themselves let her correct modestly and quietly. With every one let her be peaceful. Let her privately shut the mouth of [1] those who talk much and idly; but if they do not hear, let her take with her an aged woman, or let her take [it] up to the hearing of the bishop. But in the church let her be silent.[2] In prayer let her be persistent. Let her visit those [women] who are sick; on each first day of the week let her take with her one deacon or two and help them.[3] If she have any possession [4] let her give [5] it for the poor [6] and the faithful.[7] But if she have nothing, let her be helped by the Church. Let her do no secular work, as it were for a trial. But let her have these works of the Spirit; let her continue in prayers and fasts; let her ask for nothing deep; let her receive those things which the Lord giveth; let her not be anxious for [her] children [8]; let her deliver them to the Church, so that they living in the house of God may be fit for the service of the priesthood Her requests to God will be acceptable; they are the sacrifice and altar of God. For those [9] who have ministered well shall be praised [10] by the archangels. But as for them who are dissolute and raging and drunken, and babblers and curious and evil, that is, those who love pleasures much, the figures of their souls, which stand before the Father of light, perish and are carried to darkness to dwell. For their deeds which are visible, going up before the most High, drag them easily [11] to the pit, so that after this world is changed and passeth away the figures of their souls may stand against them as witnesses, not allowing them to look up. For the figure and type of every soul standeth before God from the foundation of the world.[12] Therefore let her be chosen who can go to meet the holy phials. Of them [13] are the twelve presbyters who praise My Father who is in heaven. These who receive the prayers of every holy soul, offer [them] to the most High [as] a sweet savour.

---

[1] Lit.: muzzle. Cf. St. Matt. xviii. 16.   [2] Cf. 1 Tim. ii. 12.
[3] Fem. (*i.e.* the sick women).   [4] Lit.: anything of her possession.
[5] Or: offer; lit.: make.   [6] Text: a poor man (points om. by error).
[7] Plural.   [8] Lit.: sons.   [9] Feminine.   [10] Or: glorified.
[11] Or: plainly; or: openly.   [12] Does this illustrate St. Matt. xviii. 10?
[13] Masc. (phials is fem.). Cf. Rev. v. 8.

Chapter 41

Let the appointment[1] be thus. As she prayeth at the entrance of the altar,[2] and looketh down, let the bishop say quietly, so that the priests may hear, thus:

PRAYER OF THE INSTITUTION[3] OF WIDOWS WHO SIT IN FRONT

O God, the Holy One, the Most High, who seest the [things][4] that are humble,[5] who hast chosen the weak[6] and the mighty;[6] the Honoured One who hast created[7] also[8] those [things] which are despised; give, O Lord, the spirit of power to[9] this Thine handmaid, and strengthen her with Thy truth, so that doing Thy commandment and serving[10] in the house of Thy sanctuary, she may be an honoured vessel[11] unto Thee, and may glorify[12] [Thee] in the day[13] when Thou wilt glorify[12] Thy poor, O Lord. And[14] grant to her power cheerfully to accomplish Thy teachings which Thou hast determined for a rule for Thine handmaid. Grant to her, O Lord, the spirit of meekness and of power and of patience and of kindness, so that, bearing with ineffable joy Thy burden, she may endure labours. Yea, O Lord God, who knowest our weakness, perfect Thine handmaid for the praise[15] of Thine house; strengthen her for edification and a good example,[16] sanctify [her], make [her] wise; comfort [her] O God; for blessed and glorious[17] is Thy kingdom, O God the Father. And to Thee [be] praise, and to Thine Only-begotten Son, our Lord Jesus Christ, and to the[18] Holy Ghost [who is] good and adorable and the Maker of life,[19] and of equal essence with Thee,[20] now

---

[1] Same word as before, pp. 90, 97, 105.
[2] See above, I. 19 (p. 63) and Note, p. 149. B. has: east (one letter different; cf. conjecture on p. 149 f.).
[3] M. has a letter wrong in this word.
[4] Or: women (fem. pronoun).
[5] Or: meek.
[6] Masculine. Cf. 1 Cor. i. 27.
[7] B.: called.
[8] B. omits: also.
[9] Lit.: on.
[10] Or: working.
[11] Rom. ix. 21; 2 Tim. ii. 21.
[12] Or: praise.
[13] M.: Name.
[14] B. omits: and.
[15] Or: glory.
[16] Lit.: type.
[17] Or: praised.
[18] B.: Thy.
[19] ζωοποιός translated (p. 40).
[20] ὁμοούσιος translated.

and before all the worlds and for the ages and for ever and ever.¹

The people: Amen.

CHAPTER 42

After she is [appointed] thus,² let her not be anxious about anything, but let her remain solitary and having leisure for supplications of piety. For the foundation of holiness and life for a widow such as this is solitude.³ For she hath loved none other but the God of gods, the Father which is in heaven. But at fixed⁴ times let her give praise by herself, in the night [and] at dawn. If she be menstruous let her abide⁵ in the temple and not approach the altar,⁶ not that she is as it were polluted, but that the altar⁶ may have honour. Afterwards, when she fasteth and batheth, let her be assiduous [at the altar]. In the days of Pentecost, let her not fast. In the feast of Pascha, let her give of those things which she hath to the poor, and let her bathe, and so let her pray. But when she giveth thanks or praise, if she have friends⁷ like-minded,⁸ virgins, it is well that they pray with her for the sake of the Amen. But if not, [let her pray] alone by herself, both in the church and in the house, especially at midnight. The times in which she should give praise are: Saturday,⁹ the first day of the week, either Pascha or Epiphany or Pentecost.¹⁰ At other time[s] let her give thanks meekly with psalms, with hymns of praise, with meditations; and thus let her labour. For the Most High will sanctify them¹¹ and will forgive all [their] sins, those which were before written¹² against¹³ them, and their error; My Father, the Heavenly One, shall strengthen them and enlighten their faces¹⁴ as the faces¹⁴ of

¹ M. adds: Amen.
² B. adds: as has been said.
³ M.: solitary (error).
⁴ Or: the appointed.
⁵ B. omits: let her abide.
⁶ *I.e.* the sanctuary, as I. 19.
⁷ Female.
⁸ So pp. 68, 106, above.
⁹ Lit.: Sabbath.
¹⁰ See Note to I. 28, p. 184.
¹¹ Fem.
¹² Fem. verb, "sins" being masculine, probably by forgetfulness of translator (as another form of the word "sin" is fem.).
¹³ Lit.: to.
¹⁴ πρόσωπον transliterated, not the usual Syriac word.

My sanctuaries;[1] they shall shine[2] in My glory in the day of recompense.

Chapter 43

Let her hymns of praise be said thus quietly:

NIGHT HYMN OF PRAISE OF WIDOWS

Holy, holy, without spot, who hast Thy dwelling in the light, God of Abraham, and of Isaac, and of Jacob, God of Enoch and David, of Elijah, of Elisha, of Moses, of Joshua, and of the prophets and of the others who in truth preached Thy Name, God of the Apostles, the God who hast guided all things by Thy reason[3] and hast blest them who lovingly trust in Thee; my soul praiseth Thee[4] with the power of the spirit of my power, my heart praiseth Thee, O Lord, and Thy might, alway. Let all my power praise Thee, O Lord, for if Thou wilt, I am Thine, O God, the God of the poor; for Thou art the Helper of them that lack, and Thou art He that looketh on the meek, and the Assister of the weak; assist me, O Lord, because by Thy grace[5] Thou wast well pleased in me that I should be Thine handmaid, for Thou hast bestowed upon me a great name, that I should be called a Christian. Thou who hast freed me from servitude that I may serve a servitude to God, the Mighty One who [art] for ever, who seest all, that I may praise Thee uncondemned. Yea, O Lord God, confirm my heart in Thee until it is perfected in the Holy Ghost. Rejuvenate us for the edification of Thy holy Church, Son and Word and Thought of the Father, the Christ who camest for the salvation of the race of man,[6] who didst suffer and wast buried, and didst rise, [and] also wast glorified by Him who sent Thee, turn, help, O Lord, set upright our thoughts[7] by the strong faith of the Spirit. Glorify Thy Name in us.

---

[1] Or: holy things.   [2] Or: appear.   [3] B.: reasonings.
[4] B. omits this clause (blank space left).
[5] Or: in thy lovingkindness (so throughout).
[6] Not in B. (space left); lit.: of sons of men.   [7] Lit.: reasonings.

For in Thy Father and in Thee and in the Holy Ghost is our hope for ever and ever.

With those who are with her let her say: Amen.

But let her say the hymn of praise at dawn thus:

HYMNS OF PRAISE AT DAWN OF WIDOWS WHO SIT IN FRONT

O Eternal God, Guide of our souls, Maker of light, Treasure of life, who restest[1] in the praises and prayers of the holy ones, Lover of compassion,[2] merciful, kind, King of all, and God, our Lord, my spirit praiseth [Thee], sending [up] to Thee the unceasing voices of Thine handmaid, O Lord, who beseecheth Thee that Thou mayest perfect in Thine handmaid the spirit of reason and of piety and of right knowledge. I praise Thee, O Lord, who didst take away from our poverty all disturbance and confusion (?), wrath and all contention and evil habit, who didst prepare [and] change the feelings of my understanding that I might serve Thee only, O God; who hast adorned Thy holy Church with various ministries, who drivest away from Thine handmaid all doubtfulness, fear, weakness; and holdest the thoughts of those who rightly serve Thee; I praise Thee, O God, who hast enlightened me with the light of Thy knowledge, through Thine Only-begotten Son, our Lord Jesus Christ, by whom [be] praise and might to Thee for ever and ever. Amen.[3]

And with those who are with her let her say: Amen.

CHAPTER 44

OF SUBDEACONS [4]

Similarly let a subdeacon be appointed[5] who is chaste,[6] the bishop praying over him. Let the bishop say over him on the first day of the week, in the hearing of all the people, thus:

[1] *I.e.* delightest.
[2] φιλέλεος translated.
[3] B. omits: Amen.
[4] ὑποδιάκονος transliterated.
[5] Same word as before.
[6] Or: modest.

Thou, O N., minister and hear the Gospel in the fear of God. Cultivate[1] holily the knowledge of thy soul; keep pureness; discipline thyself; observe and obey and hear meekly; neglect not prayers and[2] fasts, so that the Lord may give thee rest and make thee worthy of a higher degree.[3]

And let all the priests say: So be it, so be it, so be it.

CHAPTER 45

OF THE READER

A reader is instituted[4] [who is] pure, quiet, meek,[5] wise, with much experience, learned and of much learning, with a good memory,[6] vigilant, so that he may deserve a higher degree.[3] First let the book be given him in the sight of the people, on the first day of the week. But a hand is not laid on him. But he heareth from the bishop [the following]:

Thou, O N., whom Christ hath called to be a minister[7] of His words, be careful, and strive that thou mayest appear approved[8] both in this rule and in a higher degree,[3] even by our Lord Jesus Christ; so that He in His everlasting habitations may pay thee a good reward for these things.

And let the priests say: So be it, so be it, so be it.

CHAPTER 46 [9]

OF MALE AND FEMALE VIRGINS [10]

A male or female virgin is not instituted[11] or appointed[12] by man,[13] but is voluntarily separated and[14] named [a virgin].

---

[1] Or: work out; or: serve (M.: serving, etc.).
[2] B. omits: and.
[3] Or: office. Same word as in 1 Tim. iii. 13.
[4] Cf. I. 41, p.108, above.
[5] M. omits: meek.
[6] Or: well remembered.
[7] Same word as "deacon."
[8] 2 Tim. ii. 15 (not as Pshiṭta).
[9] Here S. resumes, and numbers the chapter 52.
[10] S.B.: Of virginity; but S. margin (later hand) has: Of monks.
[11] Same word as above.
[12] Same word as before.
[13] Homo.
[14] M. omits: and.

But a hand is not laid on him, as for virginity. For this division[1] is of [their] own free will. But it is right for virgins[2] that they be fixed and bound in the suffering of a sound body, that they be constant in fasts and in prayers, in weeping and in mourning daily; but[3] that they alway expect a departure from the flesh, and strive as at[4] the departure. Let them not serve[5] raging or debauchery or drunkenness or vain talking, or [be engaged] in worldly work or in distraction,[6] but they are as one who is on[7] the cross; let their hearts be [lifted] up, with all meekness of thought and comeliness, with meditation on the Holy Scriptures, with faithful thoughts,[8] with kind consolations, so that when they pray they may be answered[9] concerning those things which they ask for the faithful who wish to provide for them. Let them not despise[10] [these things (?)],[11] so that through them also[12] a portion of life may be divided to those.[13] Let them be confirmed in love and kindness and in true and perfect grace.[14] Let them be constant in consolation,[15] consoling their neighbours, catechising[16] and teaching those who have lately been made faithful, in[17] understanding and in knowledge and in kindness, inciting[18] those who are very young, being examples[19] of holiness among them in all good things. Similarly also let the females do. But in order and in grace[14] and in knowledge let them speak and work,[20] that they may truly be the salt of the earth[21] as it is called. But[22] let females[23] who are virgins have their heads covered in the church, and let them hide only their hair; but let them be counted worthy

[1] Or: class. [2] Masc. [3] B. omits: but.
[4] B.: expect as it were. [5] Or: cultivate. [6] Or: enticement.
[7] Lit.: in.
[8] S.: thoughts, faithfulnesses (error of one letter).
[9] Lagarde conjectures (unnecessarily?) σχολάζωσι.
[10] Or: reject.
[11] Lagarde puts a stop after "ask" and goes on: Let them not despise the faithful who . . ., perhaps rightly.
[12] M.B. omit: also. [13] The faithful. [14] Or: lovingkindness.
[15] M.B.: consolations. [16] Or: instructing. [17] S. omits: in.
[18] S.: let them incite. [19] Lit.: types. [20] Or: visit.
[21] St. Matt. v. 13. [22] S. omits: but.
[23] So S.; M.: old women; S. marg. adds: The name of male and female virgins in Greek are (sic) not distinguished from one another in diction.

of honour from every one, in order that the rest [of the women] who desire, may emulate them.

Chapter 47 [1]

OF A GIFT

If any one appear in the people to have a gift of healing or of knowledge or of tongues,[2] a hand is not laid on him, for the work is manifest. But let them have honour.

The First Book of Clement is ended.

[1] S. omits this chapter. [2] 1 Cor. xii. 1–10.

THE SECOND BOOK OF CLEMENT

COMMANDMENTS AND RULES AND A DEFINITION[1] *WHICH OUR LORD JESUS CHRIST LAID DOWN FOR THE ORDER*[2] *OF THOSE WHO ARE BAPTIZED*[3]

CHAPTER 1

OF LAYMEN THUS:

LET those who first come[4] to hear the Word, before they enter among[5] all the people, first come[4] to teachers[6] at home,[7] and let them be examined as to all the cause[8] [of their coming] with all accuracy, so that their teachers may know for what they have come, or with what will. And if they have come with a good will and love, let them be diligently taught. But let those who bring them be such as are well on in years, faithful who are known by the Church; and let them bear witness about them, if they are able to hear [the word]. Also let their life and conversation be asked about: if they be not contentious, if quiet, if meek, not speaking vain things[9] or despisers or foul speakers,[10] or buffoons or leaders astray,[11] or ridicule mongers. Also if

---

[1] *Sic*, singular. Perhaps error (plural points omitted).
[2] τάξις transliterated (so constantly).
[3] Title in B.: A commandment which has in it the definition which our Lord Jesus Christ laid down. S. has only extracts from this book, headed: From the Second Book of Clement.
[4] Lit.: approach.
[5] Lit.: to.
[6] B.: doctrines.
[7] Or: to the house.
[8] Or: reason; B.: causes.
[9] ματαιολόγοι translated.
[10] αἰσχρολόγοι translated.
[11] B. omits: or leaders astray.

any of them have a wife or not; and if of his own free will[1] he have not [a wife], let him[2] be instructed[3] carefully and diligently and persuaded with all kindness to amend his failings. And let the bishop provide for him in the Lord with prophetical instructions which lead him to purity; and if he maketh progress,[4] also with apostolic doctrines[5] and then with Gospel [doctrines] and with the perfect word of doctrine; and if he be worthy, let him be baptized. And if thus he be worthy of the hidden things, let him hear [them] by himself, and also make progress in that which is hidden.

Let[6] there be no obstacle at all to him who desireth to marry, so that he be not caught by the Evil One with fornication. But let him marry a Christian, a faithful [woman] of the race of the Christians, who is able to keep her husband in the faith; at the bidding of the bishop, he thus providing for him.

And also let him who cometh[7] be asked if he be a slave or free[8]; and if the slave of one who is faithful, and if also his master permit him, let him hear. But if his master be not faithful and do not permit him, let him be persuaded to permit him. And if [his master] say[9] truly about him that he[10] wisheth[11] to become a Christian because he hateth his masters, let him be cast out. But if no cause be shewn of hatred of servitude, but [if] he [really] wish to be a Christian, let him hear. But if his master be faithful and do not bear witness to him, let him be cast out. Similarly if [a woman] be the wife of a man,[12] let the woman be taught to please her husband in the fear of God. But if both of them desire to serve[13] purity in piety, they have[14] a reward.

[1] As the text is punctuated, these go with "instructed"; S. has "with the word of instruction" in margin (first hand).
[2] Lit.: this one. [3] Or: made a catechumen (so often).
[4] Or: advanceth (same word as at p. 105).
[5] M.: doctrine. [6] S. here resumes and has all the rest of §§ 1, 2.
[7] Lit.: approacheth. [8] Lit.: son of the free.
[9] S. inserts: accusations; or: causes. [10] M.B.: and he.
[11] S.: and sheweth that he wisheth. [There is a misprint in Rahmani's note.]
[12] Homo. [13] Or: cultivate. [14] S.: shall have.

Let him who is unmarried [1] not commit fornication, but let him marry in the law. But if he desire to persevere thus, let him abide [2] in the Lord.

If any one be tormented with a devil, let him not hear the Word from a teacher until he be cleansed. For the intelligence, when consumed [3] with a material spirit, doth not receive the immaterial [4] and holy Word. But if he be cleansed, let him be instructed in the Word.

Chapter 2

If a fornicatress,[5] or brothel keeper,[6] or a drunkard, or a maker of idols,[7] or a painter, or one engaged in shows,[8] or a charioteer,[9] or a wrestler,[10] or one who goeth to the contest,[11] or a combatant [in the games],[12] or one who teacheth wrestling,[13] or a public huntsman,[14] or a priest of idols, or a keeper of them, be [among those that come], let him not be received.

If any such desire to become faithful, let him cease [15] from these [things]; and being in deed faithful, and being baptized,[16] let him be received and let him partake. And if he do not cease,[15] let him be rejected.

If any one be a teacher of boys in worldly wisdom, it is well if he cease.[15] But if he have no other craft [17] by which to live, let him be excused.[18]

---

[1] Lit.: without marriage.
[2] 1 Cor. vii. 40.
[3] Lit.: burnt; S.: weighed down by.
[4] M.: material (error).
[5] M.: any fornicator.
[6] πορνοβοσκός (translated), as in the parallels. The Syriac phrase might be translated, "one (masc.) delighting in fornication." It occurs again in the Pshiṭta of Prov. xxix. 3, where the LXX has ὅς ποιμαίνει πόρνας.
[7] εἰδωλοποιός translated.
[8] = A.C.: τῶν ἐπὶ σκηνῆς τις ἀνὴρ ἢ γυνή.
[9] ἡνίοχος transliterated.
[10] μονομάχος as A.C.?
[11] σταδιοδρόμος as A.C.?
[12] ὀλυμπικός as A.C.?
[13] S. omits this phrase.
[14] Lit.: a huntsman of the public treasury (or of the State; δημόσιον transliterated).
[15] Lit.: remain.
[16] Or: when he in very deed believeth and is baptized; or: when he is by labour faithful, etc. (Lagarde, μόγις). For "being baptized" B. reads "doing" (error of one letter).
[17] Or: profession.
[18] Lit.: have forgiveness.

If any one be a soldier or in authority, let him be taught not to oppress or to kill or to rob, or to be angry or to rage and afflict any one. But let those rations¹ suffice him which are given to him. But if they wish to be baptized in the Lord, let them cease² from military service³ or from the [post of] authority, and if not let them not be received.

Let a catechumen or a believer of the people, if he desire to be a soldier, either cease from his intention,⁴ or if not let him be rejected. For he hath despised God by his thought, and leaving the things of the Spirit, he hath perfected himself in the flesh,⁵ and hath treated the faith with contempt.

If a fornicatress or a dissolute man or a drunkard do not⁶ [these things], and desire, believing, to become catechumens,⁷ they may [be admitted]. And if they make progress, let them be baptized; but if not let them be rejected.

If a concubine of a man⁸ be a servant, and desire to be faithful,⁹ if she educate those who are born [of her] and she separate from her master, or be joined¹⁰ to him alone in marriage, let her hear; and being baptized let her partake in the Offering,¹¹ but if not let her be rejected.

He who doeth things which may not be spoken of,¹² or a diviner or a magician¹³ or a necromancer,¹⁴ these are defiled and do not come to judgment. Let a charmer,¹⁵ or an astrologer,¹⁶ or an interpreter of dreams, or a sorcerer, or one who gathereth together the people, or a star-gazer, or a diviner by idols, either cease,² and when he ceaseth let him be exorcised and baptized; or if not let him be rejected.

If a man⁸ have a concubine, let him divorce her and marry in the law and hear the word of instruction.¹⁷

---

¹ Allusion to St. Luke iii. 14; but the word is not the same as in the Pshiṭta.
² Lit.: remain.   ³ M.: the work.   ⁴ Lit.: reasoning.
⁵ Syriac *BSRA*; S. reads: he hath despised (Syr. *BSR*), *sc.* the faith.
⁶ *I.e.* have ceased to do.   ⁷ Or: to be instructed.   ⁸ Homo.
⁹ Lit.: to believe.   ¹⁰ Lit.: partake with.   ¹¹ B.: offerings.
¹² ἀρρητοποιός translated, as in the parallels.
¹³ Or: magian.   ¹⁴ νεκρόμαντις translated.
¹⁵ Or: snake-charmer.
¹⁶ Lit.: a speaker by the stars (ἀστρολόγος translated).
¹⁷ S. goes on from this point to § 8.

Chapter 3

Let him who is instructed[1] with all care and heareth the perfectness[2] of the Gospel, be instructed not less than three years, and if he, loving, strive to be baptized, let him [then] be baptized.

But if he be quiet and meek and earnest, and persevering and abiding with him who teacheth him, with labour, with watching,[3] with confession,[4] with subjection, and with prayers, and [if] he desire to be baptized sooner,[5] let him be baptized. For it is not the time that is considered,[6] but the will of faith.[7]

Chapter 4

Let those who are instructed, after the teacher ceaseth, pray apart from the faithful and go out, so that the faithful may learn,[8] when the presbyter or deacon readeth the New [Testament] or Gospels.[9]

Let the faithful women stand in the church by themselves and the female catechumens by themselves apart from the faithful [women]. But all the [women] apart from the men; the girls also apart, each according to her order.

The men on the right and the women on the left; the faithful virgins[10] first, and the [women] who are being instructed to virginity behind them.

After the prayer let the female catechumens give the Peace to one another; also men[11] to men; also women to women.

Let every woman[12] cover her head with her hair also. Let the women becomingly and decorously show their modesty in their adornment,[13] and let them not be adorned with plaited hair[13] or with [precious] stones, lest the young men who are in the church be caught, but with modesty and knowledge. But

---

[1] Same word as for "catechumen." [2] Or: concord.
[3] B.: dawn (error). [4] Or: giving of thanks.
[5] Lit.: quickly. [6] Lit.: judged.
[7] Letter omitted in Syriac text.
[8] B. omits: and go . . . learn (homoiotel.).
[9] *Sc.* plural, unlike usual Syriac usage. [10] Fem.
[11] Viri. [12] Married women? [13] 1 Tim. ii. 9.

if not, let them be instructed by the widows who sit in front. But if they rebelliously resist, let the bishop reprove them.

Chapter 5

After the catechumens pray, let the bishop or presbyter, laying on them a hand, say the prayer of the laying on of the hand of catechumens:

PRAYER OF CATECHUMENS

O God, who dost send thunderings and preparest lightnings; who hast founded the heaven and established [1] the earth, and enlightenest the faithful and convertest them that err; who hast quickened those who were dead and hast given hope to those who [were] without hope, and hast freed the universe from error by the coming down of Thy Only-begotten Son Jesus Christ; hear us, O Lord,[2] and give to these souls intelligence, perfectness, undoubting faith, knowledge of the truth, that they may be in a degree higher than this, through the holy Name of Thee and of Thy beloved Son Jesus, our Lord, through whom [be] praise and might to Thee with the Holy Ghost, both now and alway and for ever and ever. Amen.

After this let them be dismissed. If any one, being a catechumen, be apprehended for My Name and be judged with tortures, and hasten and press forward to receive the laver, let not the shepherd hesitate, but let him give [it] to him. But if he suffer violence and be killed, not having received the laver, let him not be anxious. For, having been baptized in his own blood, [he is] justified.[3]

Chapter 6

But if they are severally chosen to receive [4] the laver, let them be proved and investigated first,[5] how they have lived

[1] Or: spread.
[2] B. omits: O Lord.
[3] Or: [God] justifieth [him].
[4] Lit.: who received.
[5] B. transposes these verbs.

while catechumens,[1] if they have honoured widows, if they have visited the sick, if they have walked [2] in all meekness and love,[2] if they were earnest in good works.[3] But let them be borne witness to by those who bring them.

And when they hear the Gospel, let a hand be laid on them daily.

Let them be exorcised from that day when they are chosen. And let them be baptized in the days of Pascha. And when the days approach, let the bishop exorcise each one of them separately by himself, so that he may be persuaded that he is pure. For if there be one that is not pure, or in whom is an unclean spirit, let him be reproved [4] by that unclean [5] spirit.

If then any one is found under any such imagination,[6] let him be removed from the midst [of them], and let him be reproved and reproached that he hath not heard the word of the commandments and of instruction faithfully, because the evil and strange spirit abided in him.

Let those who are about to receive the laver be taught on the fifth day of the last week only, to wash and bathe [7] their heads. But if any woman then [8] be in the customary flux, let her also take in addition another day, washing and bathing beforehand.[9]

Let them fast both [on] the Friday and [on] the Saturday.

Chapter 7

On the Saturday let the bishop assemble them who receive the laver, and let him bid them to kneel while the deacon proclaimeth.[10] And when there is silence let him exorcise [them], laying a hand on them, and saying:

EXORCISM BEFORE THE LAVER

O God of heaven, God of the lights,[11] God of the arch-

---

[1] Or: being instructed.   [2] Eph. v. 2.   [3] Tit. ii. 14.
[4] Or: he will be convicted.   [5] B. omits: unclean.
[6] Or: suspicion.   [7] Or: cleanse.   [8] M. omits: then.
[9] "Washing" and "laver" have the same root.
[10] Not same word as "admonish" on pp. 70, 99.   [11] Cf. St. Jas. i. 17.

angels who are under Thy power, God of the angels who are under Thy might, King of glories and of dominions,[1] God of saints,[2] Father of our Lord Jesus Christ;[3] who hast loosed the souls that were bound by[4] death; who hast enlightened him that was bound in darkness and fixed firm, by the firm-fixing[5] of the suffering of Thy Only-begotten; who hast loosed our cords and hast loosed every weight from [off] us; who hast repelled from us every attack[6] of the Evil One; O Son and Word of God, who hast made us immortal by Thy death; who hast glorified us with Thy glory; who hast loosed all the bands of our sins by Thy passion; who hast borne the curse of our sins by Thy cross, and by Thy resurrection hast taught [mankind] to pass from [being] sons of men to become gods; who hast taken on Thee our humiliation[7]; who hast trodden the way to heaven for us; who hast changed us from corruption to incorruptibility[8]; hear me, O Lord, who cry to Thee in pain and fear, O Lord God, and Father of our Lord Jesus Christ,[9] before Him before whom stand the holy hosts of archangels and of cherubim and armies[10] without number, of princes and of seraphim; whose veil [is] the light, and before whose face[11] [is] fire; the throne of whose glory is ineffable; the habitations of whose delights, which Thou hast prepared for Thy saints, are ineffable, the raiments and treasures of which are visible to Thee alone and to Thy holy angels; before whom all things tremble, giving praise[12]; whose glance measureth the mountains, and whose Name, when uttered, cleaveth the depths; whom the heavens which are shut up by Thy hand, hide from view; before whom the earth and the depths together tremble; before whom the sea and

---

[1] Col. i. 16.   [2] Not Rev. xv. 3 (Syr. as R.V.).
[3] Rom. xv. 6.   [4] Or: unto.
[5] Simply inserted for paronomasia. Perhaps with reference to the nails; same root as in II. 24, below.
[6] Lit.: war.
[7] Same word as p. 54; lit.: breaking; or: wounding.
[8] Cf. 1 Cor. xv. 50–54, where the Pshiṭta apparently makes a difference between "that which is not in a state of corruption," and "incorruptibility."
[9] Rom. xv. 6.   [10] Or: ministries.
[11] πρόσωπον transliterated; not the usual Syriac word.
[12] Or: glorifying [Thee].

the dragons that [are] in it quake; of whom the wild beasts,[1] trembling, stand in awe; through whom the mountains and the firmament[2] of the earth melt with fear; at whose power the tempest of the winter quaketh and trembleth, and the raging whirlwind keepeth its limits; because of whom the fire of vengeance doth not overpass that which hath been prescribed to it, but abideth when reproved by Thy commandment; because of whom the whole creation travaileth, groaning[3] with groans, being bidden to tarry till its time; from whom all nature and creation that opposeth itself fleeth; because of whom the whole army of the adversary is subdued, and the Devil is fallen, and the serpent is trodden down, and the dragon is killed; because of whom the nations which have confessed Thee are enlightened[4] and strengthened in Thee, O Lord; because of whom life is revealed and hope confirmed, and faith strengthened and the Gospel[5] preached; because of whom corruption is brought to naught and incorruptibility waxeth strong; through whom man[6] was fashioned from the earth, but having believed in Thee he is no longer[7] earth; O Lord God Almighty, I exorcise these in the Name of Thee and of Thy beloved Son Jesus Christ.

Drive away from the souls of these Thy servants every disease and illness, and every stumbling block and all unbelief, all doubt and all contempt,[8] every unclean spirit that worketh,[9] that is a witch,[10] that killeth, that is under the earth, that is fiery, dark, evil-smelling, given to witchcraft, lascivious, loving gold, uplifted,[11] money loving, wrathful.

Yea, O Lord God,[12] overthrow from these Thy servants who have been named in Thee the weapons of the Devil, all magic, witchcraft, fear of idols, divination, astrology,[13] necromancy,[14] observation of the stars, astronomy,[15] pleasure of the

[1] Lit. singular.   [2] Lit. plural.   [3] Rom. viii. 22.
[4] Lit.: shine; or: burn.   [5] Lit.: annunciation.
[6] Lit.: the son of man.   [7] Lit.: not also.   [8] Or: negligence.
[9] Or: visiteth.   [10] "spirit" is feminine in Syriac.
[11] *I.e.* proud.   [12] B.: my God.
[13] Lit.: speaking of the stars (ἀστρολογία translated).
[14] Lit.: divination by the dead (νεκρομαντεία translated).
[15] Lit.: legality of the stars (ἀστρονομία translated).

passions, love of disgraceful things, sadness, love of money, drunkenness, fornication, adultery, lasciviousness, contumacy, contentiousness, wrath, confusion, wickedness, evil suspicion.[1] Yea, O Lord God, hear me, and breathe on these Thy servants the spirit of tranquillity, that, being guarded by Thee, they may bring forth in Thee fruits of faith, of virtue, of wisdom, of purity, of self-discipline,[2] of patience, of hope, of concord,[3] of modesty,[4] of praise. For by [5] Thee they have been called as servants, in the Name of Jesus Christ, being baptized in the Trinity, in the Name of the Father and of the Son and of the Holy Ghost, the angels, glories, dominions, all the heavenly army being witnesses. O Lord, the real-essence [6] of our life and theirs, guard their hearts, O God, for Thou art mighty and glorious [7] for ever and ever.

And let all the people, also the priests, say: Amen, So be it, so be it, so be it.

If any one be in the endurance of any thing, rise suddenly while the bishop is saying [these words], and weep or cry out, or foam [at the mouth] or gnash with his teeth, or stare [8] or be much uplifted or altogether run away, being quickly carried off, let such an one be put aside [9] by the deacons, so that there be no disturbance while the bishop is speaking, and let such an one be exorcised by the priests until he be cleansed, and so let him be baptized.

After the priest exorciseth those who have drawn near, or him who is found unclean, let the priest breathe on them and seal them between their eyes,[10] on the nose, on the heart, on the ears ; and so let him raise them up.

Chapter 8

In the forty days of Pascha, let the people abide in the

---

[1] Or: expectation.   [2] Or: asceticism.   [3] ὁμόνοια translated.
[4] Or: chastity.   [5] Or: to.
[6] Quûmâ. See Note to I. 26, p. 180.   [7] Or: praised.
[8] Lit.: looketh hard.   [9] Lit.: hidden.
[10] Or: on their foreheads.

temple, keeping vigil and praying, hearing the Scriptures and hymns of praise and the books [1] of doctrine.[2]

But [3] on the last Saturday let them rise early [4] in the night, and [5] when the catechumens are being exorcised till the Saturday midnight.[6] Let those who are about to be baptized not bring anything else with them except one loaf for the Eucharist.[7]

But let them be baptized thus. When they come to the water, let the water be pure and flowing. First the babes, then the men, then the women.

But if any one desire to approach as it were to virginity, let him [8] first be baptized by the hand of the bishop.

Let the women, when they are baptized, loose their hair. Let all the boys who can answer in baptism make the responses [9] and answer after the priest. But if they cannot, let their parents make the responses for them, or some one of their households.[10]

But when they who are being baptized go down [to the water], after they make the responses and say [the answers], let the bishop see if [11] there be any of them—either a man having a ring of gold, or a woman having on her gold; for no one should have with him any strange thing in the water, but let him deliver it to those who are near him.[12]

But when they are about to receive the oil for anointing, let the bishop pray over it and give thanks, and let him exorcise another [oil] with an exorcism, the same as in the case of catechumens. And let the deacon bear that which is exorcised, and let the presbyter stand by him. Let him then who standeth by that [oil] on which a giving of thanks over [13] the oil [is said] be on the right hand; but him who standeth by that which is exorcised, on the left.

---

[1] Or: treatises.   [2] B.: doctrines.
[3] S. resumes here, prefixing the words "And after a little."
[4] Or: come early; or: hasten.   [5] B. omits: and.
[6] Lagarde conjectures a lacuna here.   [7] εὐχαριστία transliterated.
[8] Lit.: this one.   [9] S.: enter (error of a letter).
[10] Lit.: from their houses.   [11] S.: lest.
[12] S. here breaks off, and with "After a little" goes on to § 13 (s.f.).
[13] Lit.: of.

And when he taketh hold of each one, let him ask—*he that is being baptized turning to the West*—*and let him say:* Say, I renounce thee, Satan, and all thy service,[1] and thy shows,[2] and thy pleasures,[3] and all thy works. *And when he hath said these things and confessed, let him be anointed with that oil which was exorcised, he who anointeth him saying thus:* I anoint [thee] with this oil of exorcism for a deliverance from every evil and unclean spirit, and for a deliverance from every evil. *And also, turning him*[4] *to the East, let him*[5] *say:* [Say,[6]] I submit[7] to Thee, Father and[8] Son and[8] Holy Ghost, before whom all nature trembleth and is moved. Grant me to do all Thy will[5] without blame.

Then after these things let him give him over to the presbyter who baptizeth. And let them stand in the water naked. But let the deacon descend with him similarly. But when he who is being baptized goeth down into the water, let him that baptizeth him say, putting his hand on him, thus: Dost thou believe in God the Father Almighty? *Let him that is being baptized say:* I believe. *Let him immediately baptize him once. Let the priest also say:* Dost thou believe also in Christ Jesus the Son of God, who came from the Father, who is of old with the Father, who was born of Mary the Virgin by the Holy Ghost, who was crucified in the days of Pontius Pilate, and died and rose the third day,[10] [who] came to life from the dead, and ascended into heaven and sat down on the right hand of the Father, and cometh to judge the quick and the dead? *But when he saith:* I believe, *let him baptize him the second time. And also let him say:* Dost thou believe also in the Holy Ghost, in the holy Church? *And let him who is being baptized say:* I believe; *and thus let him baptize him the third time.*

Then when he cometh up let him be anointed by the presbyter with oil over which the giving of thanks has been said,

---

[1] Lit.: military service.
[2] Lit.: theatres.
[3] Misprinted in Rahmani's Syriac text.
[4] The baptized.
[5] The baptizer.
[6] So Rahmani conjectures.
[7] Lit.: consent.
[8] B. omits: and (twice).
[9] Lit.: wills.
[10] Lit.: to three days.

[*the presbyter*] *saying over him:* I anoint thee with oil in the Name of Jesus Christ. *But let women be anointed by widows who sit in front, the presbyter saying over them* [*the words*]. *And let those widows in baptism also beneath a veil receive them by a veil, the bishop saying those Confessions, and so those* [1] *whom they* [1] *cause them to renounce.* [2]

CHAPTER 9

Then let them be together in the Church, and let the bishop lay a hand on them after baptism, saying and invoking over them thus:

INVOCATION OF THE HOLY GHOST

O Lord God, who by Thy beloved Son Jesus Christ didst fill Thy holy apostles with the Holy Ghost, and by the Spirit didst permit Thy blessed prophets to speak; who didst count these Thy servants worthy to be counted worthy in Thy Christ [3] of forgiveness of sins through the laver of the second birth,[4] and hast cleansed them of all the mist of error and darkness of unbelief; make them worthy to be filled with Thy Holy Spirit, by Thy love of man,[5] bestowing upon them Thy grace, so that they may serve Thee according to Thy will, truly, O God, and may do Thy commandments in holiness, and cultivating alway those things which are of Thy will, may enter into Thine eternal tabernacles, through Thee and through Thy beloved Son Jesus Christ, by whom [be] to Thee praise and might ·with the Holy Ghost for ever and ever.

Similarly, pouring the oil, placing a hand on his head, let him say: Anointing I anoint [thee] in God Almighty, and in Jesus Christ and in the Holy Ghost, that thou mayest be His [6] soldier,[7] having a perfect faith, and a vessel pleasing to Him.

[1] Masc.
[2] *I.e.* the renunciations. The genders are confused in the text.
[3] So Rahmani conjectures. The MSS. (M. B.) have: by Thy oil. It is not certain that the MSS. are wrong.
[4] Lit.: birth again. Tit. iii. 5.   [5] $\phi\iota\lambda\alpha\nu\theta\rho\omega\pi\iota\alpha$ translated.
[6] Lit.: to Him.   [7] Or: workman.

And sealing him on his forehead, let him give him the Peace, and say: The Lord God of the meek be with thee. *And let him who has been sealed answer and say:* And with thy spirit. *And so each one severally.*

Chapter 10

Thenceforward let them pray together with all the people. Let the oblation be offered by the deacon. And so let the shepherd give thanks. But the bread is offered for a type of My body. Let the cup be mixed with wine,—mixed with wine and water, for it is a sign[1] of blood and of the laver[2]; so that also the inner man, that is to say, that which is of the soul,[3] may be counted worthy of those things which are like [them],[4] that is to say,[5] those things of the body also. And[6] let all the people, according to what hath been said before, receive with Amen of the Eucharist[7] which is offered. Let the deacons hover over [them],[8] as hath before been said.[9]

Let him who giveth [the sacrament] say: The Body of Jesus Christ, the Holy Ghost, for the healing of soul and body. *And let him who receiveth say:* Amen.

He who spilleth[10] of the cup gathereth up judgment to himself. Similarly also he who seeth and is silent and doth not reprove him, whoever he may be. Let those who take the Offering be exhorted by the priests to be careful to do good works, to love strangers,[11] to labour in fasting, and in every good work to engage[12] in servitude. And let them be taught also about the resurrection of the body[13]; before any one receiveth baptism let no one know the[14] word about the

---

[1] Or: shewing forth.
[2] So B.; M.: a sign (shewing forth) of blood and water of the laver.
[3] The Greek seems to have been ψυχικός, not πνευματικός.
[4] *I.e.* the antitypes.   [5] M.S. omit: that is to say.
[6] S.: of (error).   [7] εὐχαριστία transliterated.
[8] Or: wave [fans?].
[9] So text is punctuated, but the punctuation is loose throughout.
[10] Lit.: poureth forth.   [11] Heb. xiii. 2.
[12] Lit.: serve; or: cultivate; not same root as "servitude."
[13] Lit.: bodies.   [14] Or: a. Cf. Rev. ii. 17.

resurrection, for this is the new decree, which hath a new name that none knoweth but he who receiveth [it].

The deacon doth not give the Offering to a presbyter. Let him open the disc¹ or paten,² and let the presbyter receive.

Let the deacon give [the Eucharist] to the people in their hands.³ Let⁴ the deacon, when the presbyter is not present, of necessity baptize.

CHAPTER 11

If any one receive any service⁵ to carry to a widow or poor woman or any one constantly engaged in a Church work, let him give it⁶ the same day; and if not, on the morrow, let him add something to it⁶ from his own [property] and so give it.⁶ For the bread of the poor hath been kept back in his possession.

But in the last week of Pascha, on the fifth day of the week, let the bread and the cup be offered. And he who suffered for that which he hath offered, he [it is] who draweth near.

Let the lamp be offered⁷ in the temple by the deacon, saying⁸: The grace of our⁹ Lord [be] with you all. And let all the people say: And with Thy spirit. And let the little boys say spiritual psalms and hymns of praise by the light of the lamp.¹⁰ Let all the people respond Hallelujah to the psalm and to the chant sung together, with one accord, with voices in harmony; and let no one kneel until he who speaketh cease. Similarly also when a lection is read or the word of doctrine is spoken. If then the Name of the Lord

¹ πίναξ transliterated.
² *KPPTA*, an unusual word.
³ Lit.: in his hand ("people" being masculine and singular). Or: with his [the deacon's] hand. But this hardly makes sense.
⁴ B. omits from here to "possession" in II. 11.
⁵ Or: administration (fem.).   ⁶ Masc. (error).
⁷ Or: brought near.   ⁸ B.: and let him say.
⁹ B.: the.
¹⁰ *Sic.* Lit.: by (*or* close to) the burning of the lamp; or: the flame of the lamp.

be spoken, and the rest, as hath sufficiently been made known, let no one bow, having come creeping in.[1]

Chapter 12

Let the end[2] of Pascha be after the Saturday, at midnight.

[At] Pentecost let no one fast or kneel. For these are days of rest and joy.

Let those who bear the burdens of labour refresh[3] themselves a little in the days of Pentecost, and on every first day of the week.

Let the bishop, before he offereth the Offering,[4] say what is fitting for the Offering, while those who are clothed in white receive from one another and say [to one another] Hallelujah.

Chapter 13

[THE AGAPÉ]

In the supper or feast, let those who have come together[5] receive [a portion?] thus from the shepherd, as for a blessing. But let not a catechumen receive.

If any one be of the household of, or related to,[6] one who is a teacher of heathenism,[7] let him not accord with[8] him and give praise with him, also let him not eat with him because of relationship or for concord, lest he deliver ineffable things to a wolf[9] and he receive judgment.

Let those who are called with the bishop to the house of one who is faithful, eat with gravity and knowledge, not with drunkenness or to debauchery,[10] and not so that he who is present may laugh, or so as to annoy the household[11] of him

---

[1] Meaning? Perhaps *private* devotions forbidden during *public* service.
[2] Lit.: dissolution; or: loosing. [3] Lit.: assist.
[4] Lit.: before the oblation of the Offering.
[5] Lit.: come near together; or: are present together.
[6] M. omits: to (error). [7] Lit.: other things.
[8] Or: consent to; or: deliver [himself] to. [9] Cf. Acts xx. 29.
[10] Allusion perhaps to 1 Cor. xi. 21. [11] Lit.: house.

that called him; but so let them enter that he who called [them] may pray that the saints may enter into his house. For ye are the salt of the earth,[1] [as] ye have heard.

Because[2] when they eat, let them eat abundantly, [but] so that there may be left over both for you [and] also for those to whom he that called you wisheth [to] send, so that he may have them[3] as foods[4] left over[5] by the saints, and that he may rejoice at that which remaineth over.

Let[6] those who come to a feast, being called, not stretch out[7] a hand before them that are elder. But let the last eat[8] when[9] the first shall have done.

Let not those who eat strive[10] in speech, but let them eat in silence; but if any one desire, or the bishop or presbyter ask [a question], let him return answer.

But when the bishop saith a word,[11] let every one quietly, praising [him],[12] choose silence for himself, until he also[13] be asked [a question].

CHAPTER 14 [14]

[FIRST FRUITS]

If any one bring forward[15] fruits or the first produce of crops as first fruits, let him offer [them] to the bishop.[16]

CHAPTER 15 [17]

[PROPERTY]

If any one depart from the world, either a faithful man or a faithful woman, having children, let them give their

[1] St. Matt. v. 13.
[2] *Sic*, text.
[3] Masc. The text is ungrammatical.
[4] Fem.
[5] Masc.
[6] Here S. resumes.
[7] Lit.: throw.
[8] Or: let them eat last.
[9] Lit.: and.
[10] S.: be offended.
[11] Or: speaketh the word.
[12] Or: giving praise.
[13] M. omits: also.
[14] This chapter is also in S.
[15] Or: present; lit.: make.
[16] So punctuated. Perhaps "let him offer [them] as first fruits to the bishop." Lagarde thus punctuates, perhaps rightly: εἴ τις καρποὺς . . . ποιεῖ, τὰς ἀπαρχὰς προσφερέτω τῷ ἐπισκόπῳ.
[17] This chapter is also in S.

possessions to the Church, so that the Church may provide for their children, and [that] from the things which they have the poor may be given rest, that God may give mercy to their children and rest to those who have left [them] behind.[1] But if a man [2] have no children, let him have not much possessions, but let him give much of his possessions to the poor and to the prisoners,[3] and only keep[4] what is right and sufficient for him[self]. If a man [2] have children,[5] and he desire to discipline himself in virginity, let him give all his possessions to the poor, and discipline himself [6] and abide in the church, being constant in prayers and thanksgivings.[7]

Chapter 16

[First Fruits]

The fruits which are offered [8] to the bishop let him bless thus :

O God, we give thanks to Thee alway, and also in this day when we offer to Thee the first fruits of the fruits which Thou hast given us for food, having ripened [9] them by Thy power and by Thy Word, having commanded from the beginning of the creation [10] of the worlds that the earth should bring forth different fruits for the joy and delight of man [11] and of all beasts.[12] We praise Thee, O Lord, for all these things with which Thou hast benefited [13] us, adorning for us all the earth with various fruits. Bless also this Thy servant N., and receive his earnestness and his love, through Thine Only-begotten Son Jesus Christ, through whom [be] praise and honour and might to Thee with the Holy Ghost for ever and ever. Amen.

---

[1] S.: fallen asleep.
[2] Homo.
[3] Lit.: prisons.
[4] Lit.: possess.
[5] S.: possessions. Qy.: *no* children.
[6] S.: be constant.
[7] Here S. breaks off, and with "After a little" goes on to § 20.
[8] Or : brought near.
[9] Lit.: perfected.
[10] Lit.: making.
[11] Lit.: sons of men.
[12] Or : living creatures.
[13] εὐεργετέω translated.

Vegetables are not blessed, but fruits of trees, flowers,[1] and the rose and the lily.

CHAPTER 17

OF ALL THE FAITHFUL WHO RECEIVE AND EAT

Let them give and return thanks and not eat with offence or scandal. Let no one taste that which is strangled or sacrificed to idols.[2]

CHAPTER 18

[PASCHAL SOLEMNITIES]

On the days of Pascha, especially in the last days, on Friday and on Saturday, by night and by day, let the prayers be according to the number of the hymns of praise. But let the word be interpreted at length,[3] and let the lections [be] various and continuous.[4] And let the vigils and anticipations of the night be in good order.[5]

CHAPTER 19

OF THE DEACONS WHO GO AND PASS AMONG WOMEN, LEST THERE BE DISORDERLY YOUNG CHILDREN [6]

Let the readers assist them. Similarly also the sub-deacons. Let them not allow them to sleep.[7] For that night is a figure of the kingdom, and especially that of the Saturday.

Those who labour and work, let them work [8] till midnight.

Let the catechumens first be dismissed, having received blessings [9] from the bread which is broken.

---

[1] B.: flower.   [2] Cf. Acts xv. 29.   [3] Lit.: thick ; or : well filled.
[4] Lit.: dense.   [5] εὐσταθής translated.   [6] Lit.: babes (see p. 178).
[7] Lit.: nod.   [8] M.: weep.
[9] εὐλογίαι translated ; B.: a blessing.

When the faithful are dismissed, let them go in order[1] and knowledge to their houses. In their feasts[2] let them not forget the prayers.

Let the priests not abbreviate their ministrations.

Let the women go, each one cleaving to her husband.

Let the widows stay till dawn in the temple, having food there.

Let the virgins[3] abide together in the temple, and let the bishop help and provide for them, and let the deacons minister to them.[4]

Let the presbyteresses stay with the bishop till dawn, praying and resting.

Similarly also those who were lately baptized.

Let virgins[3] who are ready for marriage go, cleaving to their mothers. This is thus fitting.

Chapter 20[5]

Let the bishop command that they proclaim[6] that no one taste anything until the Offering is completed. And the whole body of the Church shall receive a new food. Then in the evening[7] let those who are to be[8] baptized be baptized, after one lection.

But if any one before he approacheth and receiveth of the Eucharist[9] eat something else, he sinneth and his fast is not reckoned to him.

When the catechumens are dismissed, let a hand be laid on them.

If a faithful because of sickness remain [away], let the deacon carry the Offering to him.

If any one be a presbyter who cannot come, let a presbyter carry [it] to him.

Similarly if a woman be pregnant [and] sick, and cannot fast these two days, let her fast that[10] one day,[11] taking on the

---

[1] B.: in their orders. [2] The Agapé?—B.: in a feast. [3] Fem.
[4] B. masc. (error). [5] Here S. resumes. [6] Or: preach.
[7] Lit.: from the evening. [8] Lit.: being.
[9] εὐχαριστία transliterated. [10] S. omits: that. [11] S. omits: day.

first [day] bread and water. And if she cannot come, let a deaconess carry [the Offering] to her.

CHAPTER 21 [1]

OF THOSE WHO ARE SICK

Let them take [it] up to the hearing of the bishop, so that if it seem good [2] to the bishop he may visit them; for the sick [man] is much comforted when the high priest remembereth him, and [3] especially when he is faithful.[4]

CHAPTER 22

[THE PSALMS]

In answer to him who singeth the psalms in the church, let the virgins [5] and boys respond and sing. But if they sing the psalms in a house privately, if they be two or three, let them respond to one another, singing the psalms. Similarly the men.

CHAPTER 23

[BURIALS]

If a poor man die, let those who provide for each one, provide for his clothing. If any one who is a stranger die and he have no place to be buried, let those who have a place give [it]. But if the Church hath [a place] let it give [it]. And if he have no covering, let the Church similarly give it. But if he have not grave clothes, let him be shrouded.

But if a man be found to have possessions, and do not leave them to the Church, let them be kept for a time; and after a year let not the Church appropriate them, but let them be given to the poor for his soul.

But if he desire [6] to be embalmed, let the deacons provide for this, a presbyter standing by.

---

[1] This chapter is also in S.
[2] M.B.: satisfy (letter omitted).
[3] S. omits: and.
[4] Here S. ends.
[5] Fem.
[6] Lit.: persuade.

If the Church have a graveyard, and there be one who abideth there and keepeth it, let the bishop provide for him from the Church, so that he be no burden to those who come there.

Chapter 24

[HOURS OF PRAYER]

Let the people alway take care about the early dawn, that arising and washing their hands they immediately pray. And so let each one go to the work which he willeth.

Let all take care to pray at the third hour with mourning and labour, either in the church, or in the house because they cannot go (to the church). For this is the hour of the fixing[1] of the Only-begotten on the cross.

But at the sixth hour similarly let there be prayer with sorrow. For then the daylight was divided by the darkness. Let there be then that voice which is like to the prophets, and to creation mourning.

At the ninth hour also let prayer be protracted, as with a hymn of praise that is like to the souls of those who give praise to God that lieth not, as one who hath remembered His saints, and hath sent His Word and Wisdom to enlighten them. For in that hour life was opened to the faithful, and blood and water were shed from the side of our Lord.

But at evening, when it is the beginning of another day, shewing an image of the resurrection, He hath caused us to give praise.

But at midnight let them arise praising[2] and lauding[3] because of the resurrection.

But at dawn [let them arise] praising[2] with psalms, because after He rose He glorified the Father while they[4] were singing psalms. But if any have a consort[5] or wife [not[6]] faithful,

---

[1] See p. 122, above.
[2] Lit.: in a praising manner.
[3] Lit.: in a lauding manner.
[4] The apostles.
[5] Lit.: daughter of the partaking of marriage.
[6] So Rahmani conjectures from Copto-arab. translation.

let the husband who is faithful go and pray at these times without fail.¹

Let those who are chaste not lessen [them]. For the adornments of heaven give praise, the lights, the sun, the moon, the stars, the lightnings, the thunders, the clouds, the angels, the archangels, the glories, the dominions, the whole [heavenly] army, the depths, the sea, the rivers, the wells, fire, dew, and all nature that produceth rain.

All the saints also give praise and all the souls of the righteous.² These, then,³ who pray are numbered together in the remembrance of God.

CHAPTER 25

[CONCLUSION]

When ye the faithful accomplish these things, teach and instruct one another, causing the catechumens to make progress, as loving all men⁴; ye do not⁵ perish, but will be in Me and I will be among you.⁶

But alway let the faithful take care that before he eat he partake of the Eucharist,⁷ that he may be incapable of receiving injury.

When ye teach these things and keep [them], ye shall be saved, and evil heresy⁸ shall not prevail against you.

Lo, then, I have taught you now all [things] that ye desire; and those things⁹ which I have spoken with you [of] from the beginning, and have taught and commanded you before I should suffer, ye know.

CHAPTER 26

And thou¹⁰ especially John, and Andrew and Peter, even now ye know all [the things] which I have spoken to you

---

¹ Lit.: of necessity.
² Cf. Song of the Three Children, verses 35–65.
³ Rahmani's text is misprinted. ⁴ Lit.: every man.
⁵ *I.e.* will not. ⁶ St. John xiv. 20.
⁷ εὐχαριστία transliterated. ⁸ αἵρεσις transliterated.
⁹ M.: and so. ¹⁰ *Sic.*

while I am with you, as also that which [is] in this Testament, in order that when ye deliver [them] to the nations the will of My Father may alway be accomplished, abiding¹ firm in carefulness, so that there may be good fruits in them that hear.

Ye know that I have spoken with you that a good tree cannot bring forth evil fruit.² All [things], then, that I have commanded you openly and secretly, do. And the God of tranquillity be with you.³

Chapter 27

And falling down we worshipped Him, saying, Glory to Thee, O Jesus, Name of light, who didst give us the teaching of Thy commandments, so that we may be like unto Thee,⁴ we and all those who hear Thee. And when He spoke to us and taught and commanded us, and showed many loosings⁵ and miracles, He was taken up from us, giving us tranquillity.⁶

John and Peter and Matthew wrote this Testament, and sent [it] in copies from Jerusalem by Dositheus⁷ and Silas and Magnus and Aquila, whom they chose to send [them] to all dioceses.⁸ Amen.

The Second Book of Clement is ended, translated from the Greek to the Syrian language by James the poor,⁹ in the year 998 of the Greeks.¹⁰

---

¹ *I.e.* the will. ² St. Matt. vii. 18.
³ Rom. xv. 33; 2 Cor. xiii. 11; Phil. iv. 9, but not as Pshiṭta.
⁴ Perhaps suggested by 1 John iii. 2 (cf. Rom. viii. 3; Phil. ii. 7, etc.), but quite different wording. ⁵ *I.e.* healings?
⁶ Or peace. But it is a different word from the [kiss of] peace. Cf. St. John xiv. 27 (but different word); cf also St. Luke xxiv. 51.
⁷ M.: Dositha. ⁸ παροικίαι translated.
⁹ Thus a scribe usually describes himself; so also the scribes of the ancient Irish and Scottish churches:—"The wretchock (misellus) who wrote it." Book of Daer, lx. ¹⁰ A.D. 687.

NOTES

NOTES

BOOK I

THROUGHOUT these Notes the "Testament Compiler" means the person who put the book, exactly or approximately, into its present form, probably in the fourth century, but possibly in the fifth. The phrase leaves the question of a later editor untouched. See Introduction, pp. 16, 25-42.

TITLE. The ascription to Clement of Rome is found also in the title of the Egyptian Church Order (Tattam, p. 32, etc.), and in the Apostolic Constitutions and in the heretical Clementine books.

THE APOCALYPTIC PRELUDE consists strictly of I. 2-14a inclusive, but has passages prefixed and added to weld it into the framework of the *Testament*. It appears in a perhaps earlier form than we have it here, in an eighth century uncial Latin manuscript in the Stadtbibliothek at Trèves (Trier), known as Codex Treverensis 36. The fragment found there was published by Dr. M. R. James in his *Apocrypha Anecdota*, i. 153, 154 (Cambridge *Texts and Studies*, 1893). It has our I. 11, with a sentence from I. 12, and then goes on to our I. 6 and I. 7, and ends with the beginning of I. 8 : " And in the peoples and Churches shall be many disturbances. But all these things shall be before the coming of Antichrist. Dexius shall be the name of Antichrist. The End." Harnack, in his *Preliminary Remarks* on the *Testament*, suggests that "Dexius" is Decius disguised, and that therefore we may date the Latin fragment about A.D. 250. When the Decian persecution was long past, the name Dexius would be omitted. Possibly the Latin fragment gives the original order and contents of the Prelude.

It is proper, however, to mention some considerations which rather point to the Trèves fragment being a curtailment of the longer form than the original of it. The fragment adds a sentence to I. 11 ("and many as it were Christ shall stand by") which, we can hardly doubt, is taken from our I. 12; it is scarcely possible that our I. 12 could have been enlarged out of this Trèves sentence. And the addition before our I. 6 of "But before this" in the Trèves fragment looks as if, having taken two previous chapters from its original, the writer inserted these words in order to tack those chapters on to I. 11; in Test. the connexion of I. 5 and I. 6 is very natural. But a more forcible consideration is that in four instances the text of the Trèves fragment points to a Syriac, not a Greek original. This certainly is not conclusive. For the original Greek might have been in the form of the fragment, then translated into Syriac, and thence into the Latin we have, before (*ex hypothesi*) it was enlarged into our I. 2–14*a*. But a more simple supposition is that the longer form was translated into Syriac (possibly in the shape given in Codex C., see below), and that the writer of the Trèves fragment took excerpts from that Syriac form. The four instances are: (*a*) In I. 7 Trèves has "serpents" (= Syr. *ḤWWTA*) where C. has "beasts" (= Syr. *ḤIWTA*), S.M.B. also having a similar word for "wild beasts." We can well understand the Trèves writer mistaking a Syriac *I* for *W*, but "beasts" could hardly have been got out of "serpentium." (*b*) Trèves reproduces the error in its sentence added to I. 11 (from I. 12, see Note, p. 147), ἐπὶ πολλοῖς, *to many*, for ἐπὶ πύλαις, *at the gates*, as if it had already been made in the Syriac, as in fact James of Edessa, at least, read it, and so passed into the Latin fragment. (*c*) Trèves reads in I. 11 "sinister [*i.e.* oculus] gaudens." This may, of course, be a mistake of the copyist for "*glaucus*"; "blue black" is the reading of C.S.M.B. (*ZMRTA*). But it looks as if the writer of the fragment had the Syriac before him, and read *ZMRTA* (as he might do) as if it meant "singing," and so rendered it "*gaudens.*" (*d*) At the end of I. 11 the Trèves fragment has "fallax dilectionis," which may be a mistake of the copyist for "falx desolationis," *the sickle of desolation*. But he may have had the Syriac given in Codex S. before him, namely, *MGDLA·DḤURBA*, *the tower of desolation*, and misread it *MDGLA ḌḤUBA*, which would be "fallax dilectionis." The last two suggestions are due to Mr. Norman M'Lean, Fellow of Christ's College, Cambridge; see James, *Apoc. Anecd.* 187. These considerations, then, make it at least possible that the Trèves fragment is an abbreviation, and that our longer form is the original.

But taking the other supposition as a working hypothesis, that the Trèves fragment is the original, we may conjecture that the next form which it took was that which we now have in Test. I. 2–14a; and if so the question arises, who thus enlarged it? Was it the Testament Compiler, or some earlier writer? It may be the former, and certainly some of his favourite expressions, such as "He who sent me" (I. 8), "children of light" (I. 3, 12), "vessels" (I. 3), "a work" (I. 13), appear in these chapters, so that if he were not the author of them he at least borrowed some phrases from them. On the other hand (see Introduction, p. 23), some phrases, such as "testing spirits," "shepherds," are used in one way in the Prelude and in another in the rest of the work. Also the preface and I. 1, as also I. 15–18, read as if they were added rather clumsily by another hand, in order to join them on to the Church Order which follows. The style of these portions is quite different from that of the Apocalyptic part; they introduce the idea of a "Testament." Probably also the latter portion of I. 14, "Turning therefore to the Church," was added by the later hand in order to pave the way for the change from the apocalyptic prophecy to the ecclesiastical organisation. It seems probable, therefore, that the chapters I. 2–14a are older than the Testament Compiler.

The evidence of Codex C., which Dr. Arendzen has only just brought to light, points in the same direction. It is a translation independent of James of Edessa, and looks as if it represented a Greek text altogether independent of Test. Compiler. Both it and S. break off in the middle of I. 14, and C. expressly says that the passage about the End is finished there. With regard to S., which certainly reproduces James's translation of the *Testament* in part, its breaking off only seven words lower down than C. and in the middle of a sentence, and its frequent following of C. as against M.B. (see the footnotes), raise the conjecture that the S. scribe knew the Prelude in an independent form, and that he was much influenced by it. (A somewhat similar phenomenon in the MSS. of the Apostolic Church Order, where S. is also concerned, is called attention to by Dr. Arendzen in J.T.S. for October 1901, iii. 74; he suggests that a marginal note in the Greek original or a comparison with the Didaché may account for the codices being of equal extent.)

The obvious anachronism of C. in I. 3 ("which are written in the Gospel") is indecisive, because C., like the other MSS., professes to give our Lord's words. But the addition of C. in I. 4 about the kings in the East (see Note, p. 145), of which the Copto-arabic translator gives only a reminiscence, points in the direction of independence (see also Notes on p. 146 f.). On the other hand, we cannot assume that I. 10 was written by the Test. Compiler because it is omitted in C., for it, or something in its place, must have been in the original of C., which professedly has a lacuna here. This is important when we consider the place of writing (see pp. 42–45). The only things which point in the other direction are that the authorship of the C. fragment is ascribed to Clement, and that it professes to represent our Lord's words. This, however, only shows that the Test. Compiler did not invent the Clementine authorship, which we know from other sources; and it is quite possible that the Compiler's idea of using our Lord's authority instead of that of the Apostles was not original with him, but was borrowed from this C. form of the Prelude.

On the whole, then, it seems probable that the Apocalyptic Prelude I. 2–14a existed in its present form before it was added on to the Church Order which follows. We may perhaps assign it to about the year A.D. 300, or even a good deal earlier, if the Trèves fragment is derived from it. Possibly it was one of the "Apocryphal books" about Antichrist that St. Cyril of Jerusalem speaks so slightingly of in his Catechetical lectures (xv. 16).

If this be the case, we have yet to ask, who added it to the Church Order? The absence of the enlarged Prelude I. 1–18 in any form, and similarly of the concluding chapters of Book II., from any other Church Order, makes us think of the Test. Compiler. There is no good reason for connecting the Prelude with the supposed "Montanistic Church Order," from which the Test. Compiler is thought to have borrowed. It seems rather as if he had wished to make an "improvement" on the Apostolic authorship of other Church Orders, by prefixing the (already existing) Prelude, by adding his own chapters to join it on, and by ascribing the whole work to our Lord. In the absence, therefore, of evidence to the contrary, we may suppose that the Prelude was added by him. Harnack seems to have reached this conclusion.

PREFACE. Probably "Thomas, Matthew, John" are here selected because the two last were Apostles and Evangelists, and St. Thomas was expressly invited to touch the risen Lord (St. John xx. 27). In II. 26 we have "John, Andrew, Peter," and in II. 27, "John, Peter, Matthew." Note that St. John comes in all these lists, and that in Ap. C.O. § 1, "John, Matthew, Peter, Andrew" come first, St. Thomas later, and St. John expressly (§ 3) "speaks first." We see here, as often, the influence of Ap. C.O. on Test. The preface and first chapter are probably the work of Test. Compiler himself.

Chapter 1

Those who through you know and do.] Cf. I. 30 and St. John xvii. 20; also A.C. viii. 1 (Lagarde, 231^7), "those who believe through us" [the Apostles].

Chapter 2

In St. Mark xiii. 3, St. James and St. Andrew unite with St. Peter and St. John in asking this question.

Chapter 4

Lovers of gold.] C. has a remarkable addition *after* this: "Kings then there shall be reigning in the East, inglorious, thoughtless, not grown up, boys, lovers of gold" (*sic*, a second time). The passage may well have been omitted by homoioteleuton, whether by Test. Compiler or by his translator, James of Edessa. It is probably a real part of the Prelude; cf. the mention of the West just below. Dr. Arendzen suggests Alaric as the king of another race, Arcadius and Theodosius II. as the boy kings in the East; but he notes that "every one of them shall try to destroy the life of his fellow" would not be applicable to them. His supposition would necessitate a date about 410 for these chapters. But surely there is no reason for these historical investigations. It is clear that the writer had a vivid imagination, and could invent without merely chronicling what was already past.—Copto - arab. similarly adds after "allied in counsel": "there shall arise in the East those who do not follow the precept." As this last translator treats Test. with the utmost freedom, we cannot argue from this that he had the C. passage in his original; his words may have been inserted because of the "West" just below, but he may have had an independent knowledge of the Prelude, apart from the *Testament.* He inserts his addition in a different place from C. The concurrence of S. M. and B. in omitting the passage of C. makes it unlikely that it occurred, at least, in James of Edessa's translation.

Chapter 5

Gold shall be honoured.] Rahmani conjectures "only gold." Arendzen suggests inserting "not," but C. omits it as well as the other MSS.; he translates (alternatively) "gold shall become dear."

Robbery], lit.: prey of robbers. The Syr. of M. is *PRADA*, of B., *PRDA*, = praeda transliterated ? S. reads *PDRA*, for which Lagarde suggests that as ἐφέδρα, *a siege*, does not suit, ἐπιδρομή, *an attack*, was the underlying word. But the reading of M.B. is more likely.

Chapter 7

Young women newly wedded.] Dr. Arendzen (J.T.S. ii. 407) suggests that the Greek was νεόγαμοι, which C. took wrongly as masculine, though it correctly gives "bring forth."

Chapter 8

The reward of their praise (p. 55).] The underlying Greek word would be δόξα. Lagarde thinks that James of Edessa should have rendered it by "opinion." C. agrees with James here.

Many shall be afflicted (p. 56).] From the reading of C., " and so on," Arendzen conjectures that the Greek had καὶ τὸ τέλος or καὶ τέλος, *and at last*, and that C. thought this meant "and so on," and put another καὶ after it to join it to the next sentence.

She that travaileth.] The words of Micah are often interpreted of the B.V. Mary, but here apparently of the mother of Antichrist. Cf. Keble, *Lyra Innocentium*, Judas's Infancy.

Chapter 11

His left (eye) blue black.] Blue eyes and fair hair are considered to be very unlucky by Mohammedans and by many Eastern Christians; any one possessed of the latter invariably dyes it. The Trèves fragment has "gaudens," a slip perhaps for "glaucus"; but see above, p. 142.

He hath two pupils.] It is not improbable that in Rahmani's Syriac text the masculine (he) is a misprint for the feminine (it). If it is masculine in the MSS., the gender may be due to ὀφθαλμός being masculine in Greek. The Trèves fragment and C. show that the pronoun refers to "the eye," not to Antichrist. Dr. James quotes Pliny, N.H. vii. 16, as showing that a double pupil is the sign of the evil eye (*Apocrypha Anecdota*, p. 187).

The sickle of desolation.] This is only the reading of a marginal note of S., but it is found perhaps in the Trèves fragment ("fallax dilectionis" for "falx desolationis"? see p. 142), and is confirmed by C., which reads: "his little finger large as a sickle, that is the sickle of desolation." M.B. omit "This is the sickle of desolation," probably not understanding the phrase. S. has "the tower of desolation," reading *MGDLA, tower*, for *MGLA, sickle* (see p. 142).—The passage gives to Antichrist a sickle, as in Rev. xiv. 15 the Angel has one (cf. what follows in I. 12). Perhaps the "sickle of desolation" is a reminiscence of the "abomination of desolation" in St. Matt. xxiv. 15 (the Syriac word for "desolation" being the same here as in Pshitta of St. Matthew); Test. seems to connect that passage with the prophecy of 2 Thess. ii. 4.—The Trèves fragment adds at the end of this chapter: "And many as it were Christ will stand by," from the next chapter.

CHAPTER 12

The harvest is ripe . . . own works.] C. reads: the time for reaping [or: he that reapeth] is at the gates (*i.e.* ἐπὶ πύλαις, rightly for ἐπὶ πολλοῖς, *to many*, S.M.B.), and they shall be reaped and he shall praise their deeds. The reading "at the gates" is almost certainly correct, but the error ἐπὶ πολλοῖς must have been a very early one, for the Trèves fragment has it (p. 142).

CHAPTER 15

The *Testament* is probably intended to supply what our Lord is not *recorded* to have said. This chapter, with the last part of the preceding and with the three which follow, seems to be the work of the Test. Compiler himself (see Note on Apocalyptic Prelude, p. 143). There is no such connecting link in the Egyptian Heptateuch between the Apostolic Church Order, which is its first book, and the Egyptian Church Order, which is its second. In Hauler's Verona fragments there is such a connexion, though only of a few lines. Compare with Test., "of what sort he ought to be who standeth at the head of the Church," Hauler (103[4]), "that they may know how those who are over the Church ought to be delivered and kept (?, tradi et custodiri). Hauler has only the germ, which Test. expands in its own manner.

Chapter 16

Martha and Mary and Salome.] The idea is taken from the Ap. C.O. 26-28, which introduces Martha and Mary in order to throw some slight on women's ministry. Test. adds Salome and takes away the slight, as antagonistic to its enthusiastic advocacy of the same. Indeed, the chapter seems to be inserted in order to emphasise the teaching that women are among "those who minister" in the Church (I. 15).

Chapter 17

The Compiler, by a bold adaptation of Rev. i. 3, audaciously puts his "Testament" on a level with the Apocalypse.

Chapter 18

Cast not pearls before swine.] Quoted in A.C. iii. 5, of widows being forbidden to teach mysteries to outsiders.

My commandments and this tradition.] So the Syriac; but there seems to be a mistake here, and a letter (="and") is wrongly inserted. If so we must read: "But this tradition shall be spoken and given to those who are firm and fixed, and do not fall away, who keep my commandments, [to the end] that they, keeping them, may abide." Rahmani has "tradition" twice; it is only once in the Syriac.

The third order.] Perhaps the same as the "third heaven" of 2 Cor. xii. 2. The "rest" is perhaps the "refreshment" (ἀνάπαυσις) of the disembodied state of the faithful departed. See Note on p. 195; and cf. I. 35, II. 15, and (in a rather different sense) I. 44, all these passages being the Compiler's own work.

Chapter 19

DESCRIPTION OF THE CHURCH BUILDING. The Arabic Didascalia, § 35, has this chapter; it seems to be much shorter than Test., but Funk only summarises it. Ar. D. then goes on (§§ 36-39 incl.) to Test. I. 20, 21, 22, summary of 23, and 28. The chief differences are given in the Notes. These are the last chapters of Ar. D., for at the end of its § 39 we read, "The Didascalia is ended, the doctrine of our Fathers the Apostles, consisting of 39 chapters." Apparently these are the only chapters which correspond to Test. (see Introduction, pp. 33, 34).

THE CHURCH WITH THREE ENTRANCES. The word in

Syriac for "Church," as in other languages, stands for both the building and the congregation of the faithful.—In A.C. ii. 57 is a description of the church building. It has porticoes (τὰ παστοφορεῖα) to the east; it is oblong and turned to the east. It is like a ship, the bishop like the helmsman, etc. (Lagarde, 84[16], 84[20], 86[2]). The description of the church in the Ethiopic Didascalia (Platt, § 10) is very similar. The doors in Ar. D. 35 are on south, west, and north; in the Copto-arab. translation of Test. they are, south, west, and "towards the sea." For the type of the Trinity, see Note on p. 157. The three entrances seem to lead, not into the church itself but into the courtyard.

THE DIACONICUM. In Ar. D. 35 the offerings are *not* to be seen; this chamber is called (according to Funk's summary) the Sacristy.

THE BAPTISTERY. (1) *The dimensions.* In Ar. D. 35 also we find an oblong baptistery, not found elsewhere. All other known early examples are circular or octagonal (Dict. Chr. Ant., s.v. "Baptistery"). But the dimensions in Ar. D. are different; they are 24×12, "as a symbol of the four and twenty elders [of the Apocalypse; perhaps in Ar. D. there were twenty-four presbyters in the Church, see Note, p. 192], and . . . the twelve Apostles." (2) *The twenty-one prophets.* The number may be made up by adding to the four major and twelve minor prophets, Samuel, Nathan, Elijah, Elisha, and another (David, or Baruch, or St. John Baptist). Note that Rahmani's "complete *number* of the prophets" is a paraphrase only; there is no "number" in the Syriac, and the resemblance to the "inter prophetas completum numero" of the Muratorian fragment vanishes on inspection. (3) *The one entrance and three exits.* The symbolism is noteworthy. The candidates enter to the font confessing the faith which was before the Gospel, of the One God; in the font they will confess the three Divine Persons whom Christians know to exist within the one Divine Essence, and so they will leave the baptistery professed believers in them.

THE HOUSE OF THE CATECHUMENS. Apparently a chamber is meant opening on to the church, though there is nothing in the text to decide at what part of the structure this chamber was, whether as a narthex at the west end opposite the altar, or as a "side chapel" in the church. Not mentioned in Funk's summary of Ar. D.

THE ALTAR, SANCTUARY, AND BISHOP'S THRONE. (1) The Syriac word for "altar" is constantly used, like θυσιαστήριον, in two senses—alike for the Holy Table and for the Sanctuary. (2) *The throne by the altar.* Rahmani conjectures "on the east"

(Syr. *MDNḤA* for *MDBḤA*); cf. the various reading in I. 41. In Ar. D. 35 we read that on the east is a "ksrdstirin," by which Funk supposes an apse and presbytery is meant, and this makes Rahmani's conjecture probable. (3) *The arrangement.* Cf. Rev. viii. 3, where the "golden altar" is before the throne. This apparently is the arrangement here, the Holy Table being set some little way in front of the bishop's throne, perhaps at the chord of the apse. Such a position has been common both in East and West; in the orthodox Eastern Church to this day the ordinary position of the Holy Table is some distance away from the east wall. In the East Syrian (Nestorian) churches, however, the altar is built into the east wall, or, in the older buildings, into a recess in the east wall. In A.C. ii. 57 (Lagarde, 85¹) the bishop's throne is in the middle, the presbyters on either side, the women apart and silent. Cf. A.C. viii. 12 (Lag. 248¹⁸). (4) *The orientation.* This was not universal. In Constantine's Church of the Resurrection at Jerusalem, the Holy Table was at the west (Dict. Chr. Ant., s.v. "Church," p. 369*b*). (5) *The division of the presbyters.* In Ap. C.O. 18 there is the same arrangement, but *twelve* are mentioned on each side; the twenty-four presbyters clearly there refer to the Revelation, and we note that the passage is put into the mouth of St. John; also in Ap. C.O. those on the right are more honourable (see Note on the "holy phials," p. 200). In Ar. D. 35 the presbyters sit on the right; the left side is for those that follow them; in the middle is the throne for the president (προστάτης). The root-idea of dividing the presbyters is found in 1 Tim. v. 17. (6) *The three steps.* This arrangement, whose Trinitarian symbolism is obvious, was not infrequent in the mediaeval churches of the West. Scottish examples occur in the cathedrals of Elgin and Brechin, and in the little chapel of Hermitage in Liddesdale.

THE TWO PORCHES FOR MEN AND WOMEN. This seems to refer to the church proper; the "porches" (στοαί) would be aisles divided by pillars from the central portion of the nave. Constantine's basilica at Jerusalem is said by Eusebius (*Life of Constantine*, bk. iii., Dict. Chr. Ant. p. 369*a*) to have had two such "porches" (δίττων στοῶν).

LIGHT FOR A TYPE. Cf. the offering of a lamp in II. 11. This is a very favourite piece of symbolism in the *Testament*; no idea is more frequent than the opposition of light and darkness. The exact meaning of the symbolism, however, is not very clearly defined. We might take it as expressive of watchfulness, the loins being girded, the lights burning

(St. Luke xii. 35). But more probably in the sense that Christ is the Light of the world; namely, that as light expels darkness, truth came by Him (St. John i. 17). In Him all Christians are the light of the world (St. Matt. v. 14). The preference evinced by our Lord (St. Luke xxii. 12) and the Apostolic Church for an "upper chamber" and the "many lights" which illuminated that one at Troas (Acts xx. 8) may have been due in part to a similar feeling for a symbolism at once obvious and instructive. The choice certainly served to bring into sharper prominence the difference between Christianity and those Eastern pagan cults, such as that of Mithras, which chose caverns underground instead of upper chambers, and "loved the darkness rather than the light, because their deeds were evil" (St. John iii. 19; cf. Rom. xiii. 12; Col. i. 13; 1 Thess. v. 5, etc.). At the same time practical purposes were not lost sight of. The light is "also for reading."

THE SANCTUARY VEIL. Ar. D. mentions in addition a screen round the altar. The veil is mentioned by St. Athanasius, *Hist. Arian.* 56 (see Brightman, L.E.W. 506^{17}), and in the Canons of Hippolytus 188, 210 (but these sections are thought by Achelis to be interpolations in C.H.). The Test. rule of "pure linen" (Ar. D. similar) may contain a reference to the "pure offering" of Malachi i. 11. See Note on p. 168. Veils have been common at least ever since the fourth century. The Eastern Churches of the present day show three stages. In the Armenian Churches, which are most modernised, a veil is drawn before the altar; the Orthodox have a screen, usually of wood (the iconostasis), with veiled entrances in the middle and at the sides; the Eastern Syrians (Nestorians), the most conservative of Orientals, have a solid wall reaching to the roof, with a single opening in the middle closed by a veil and sometimes by doors.

THE PLACE OF COMMEMORATION (not in Ar. D.). The "commemoration" is probably the deacon's litany (cf. I. 35), in which benefactors would be mentioned. Note the high place of the readers, which is a mark of early date; they are allowed to "name the benefactors by way of commemoration," that is, probably, to say the litany (see Note on p. 204). This mark of early date (for this section) makes it improbable that the "chief deacon" mentioned in the same section (see below) is the later "archdeacon."—James of Edessa uses the word "commemoration" in *his own* writings in the sense of the Great Intercession for the Church after the Invocation in the Eucharistic Liturgy (Brightman, L.E.W. 492^{10}).—In *Pere-*

grinatio Silviae (see Introduction, page 14) the *Bishop* at Jerusalem "commemorates" at the morning service. He "recites the names of those whom he wishes to commemorate." In the same work the deacon "commemorates" at vespers (4 p.m.) and the children answer Kyrie Eleison (Bishop J. Wordsworth gives some extracts in English from this book, on the Day Hours at Jerusalem, in his *Ministry of Grace*, pp. 348–350).— In Test. the place of commemoration is a place to *receive* the offerings; the "house of the offering" seems to be a place to keep them in.—With the mention of naming the donors, compare A.C. iii. 4 (Lagarde, 98^{23}), "tell them [who receive alms] who is the giver, that they may pray for him *by name*." See also Test. II. 16 (p. 132).

THE CHIEF DEACON is twice mentioned in this chapter; but not yet as belonging to a separate order, as an archdeacon. In I. 34 *s.f.*, the same deacon is referred to as one "who is considered among them [the deacons] to be most earnest and best in governing," and therefore chosen as guest-master; but he is not there called a "chief deacon." The Greek original could not have had ἀρχιδιάκονος in this present chapter, or James of Edessa would have rendered it by the usual Syriac transliteration of that word. The use of the name ἀρχιδιάκονος seems not to date, as far as we know, from before the Council of Ephesus, A.D. 431 (Dict. Chr. Ant. p. 135*b*). But Theodoret (*H.E.* i. 26) speaks of Athanasius as the leader of the chorus of deacons (ὁ τοῦ χοροῦ τῶν διακόνων ἡγούμενος). In Test. the "chief deacon," besides entertaining strangers, helps the priest to write the names of the offerers. It is not correct to speak of the *Testament* as mentioning archdeacons. For the bearing of these passages on the question of date, see Introduction, p. 36. The Ar. D. does not mention the chief deacon.

THE PLACE OF THE LECTION. In Ar. D. it is to the north, also outside the "altar" (sanctuary). The arrangement seems to be somewhat like that of some Eastern churches of the present day. The Eastern Syrians have a sort of platform (roughly corresponding to the σολέα of ecclesiastical Greek) outside the sanctuary wall, and from it they read the lections. This platform, which they call the *bema*, is separated from the nave by a dwarf wall. The Western Syrians also have a platform outside the sanctuary wall, called (Rahmani tells us, p. 154) QSṬRUMA (= κατάστρωμα, which in classical Greek means the deck of a ship).

THE HOUSE OF THE BISHOP]. In Ar. D. it is "above the church to the north of it."

THE WIDOWS THAT SIT IN FRONT. See Note on p. 198.
THE GUEST HOUSE. The systematic support by the Church of "the strangers sojourning among us" is mentioned by Justin Martyr, *Apol.* i. 67. Cf. p. 99.

CHAPTER 20

Let the bishop be appointed.] The Syriac word for "appointed" has no reference to the imposition of hands. It is often used of ordination of clergy, but also of any appointment or election, *e.g.* of an emperor. It seems to refer to the whole action from election to ordination inclusive. The corresponding word in Greek, which is probably here underlying the Syriac, namely, κατάστασις, is the most common word for ordination as a complete act. See Brightman in J.T.S. i. 273, 274, for a collection of instances. See below, p. 186, and often.

QUALIFICATIONS OF A BISHOP. These are not given in C.H., Eg. C.O., or Eth. C.O.; very shortly in A.C. viii. 4 and ii. 2 (the latter referring to the Pastoral Epistles, as does Test.). But it is mentioned in all that the bishop must be chosen by all the people: C.H. 7; H. 103[7]; Eg. C.O. 31 (Tattam, p. 32); Eth. C.O. 21; A.C. viii. 4; contrast canon 13 of Laodicea.— Ar. D. says nearly the same as Test. as to the qualifications.

MARRIAGE OF BISHOPS. (1) *Other Church Orders, etc.* None of the earlier Orders which are of the same family as Test. have anything about the marriage of the clergy; C.H. 7, Eg. C.O. 31, Eth. C.O. 21, and H. say nothing about it. But Ap. C.O. 16 in the Syriac (Introduction, p. 11) has: "It is a good thing if he be without a wife, but if not that he should be *from* one wife (cf. p. 154). The form of Ap. C.O. which appears in the Egyptian Heptateuch (*i.e.* prefixed to Eg. C.O.) softens this down by adding that he is to abide with a wife having children (Tattam, p, 18). A.C. ii. 2 have, "*having been* the husband of one wife, and monogamous, ruling well his own house ... if he have or had a holy and faithful wife, if he has brought up children well," etc. In A.C. viii. 4 the bishop's marriage is not referred to, but his household (οἶκος) is mentioned. A.C. show no preference for celibate bishops, but rather the other way. In Ap. Can. 6 or 5 (*cir.* 400 A.D.?), bishops, presbyters, and deacons are forbidden to put away their wives for religion (in canon 40 or 39 the bishop is not prevented from leaving property to his wife or children); so Antioch in Encaen. can. 24, in A.D. 341 (Hefele, *Councils*, ii. 73, Eng. trans.). Both Ap. Can. 17 and A.C. vi. 17 forbid digamists to be clerics. The Synod of Gangra

(Hefele, ii. 329), the date of which is uncertain, but which was held against the Eustathians about the time of the Council of Laodicea, probably in the latter half of the fourth century, says (can. 4) that married priests may offer the sacrifice (the Eucharist). In the Ethiopic Didascalia (Platt, § 3), which exhibits a much shorter form of the Didascalia than A.C. i.–vi., a bishop need not be a widower; "a man that hath married one wife, a woman befitting him, who can govern his house, who hath brought up his children in purity." The Ar. D. is less ascetic than Test. The bishop may be married, though a celibate is preferred; he need not be a widower. The phrase about widowhood is: "that he may not be painfully seized by the evils of widowhood," a phrase which could easily have come from the parallel in Test., but could not have suggested it. (2) *Marriage after ordination* is not explicitly forbidden in the Church Orders, but the tone of the books which mention marriage at all is against it. It was first forbidden by civil law by Justinian in A.D. 528 (*Cod. Just.* i. 3, 41, quoted by Bishop J. Wordsworth, *Ministry of Grace*, 224). Hippolytus (?), in his *Refutation of Heresies*, ix. 12, disallows post-ordination marriage, but Pope Callistus allowed it; the Councils of Ancyra in A.D. 314 (can. 10) and Neo-Caesarea in A.D. 315 (can. 1) forbid it, the latter for presbyters, and the former for deacons unless they have given notice of marriage before ordination (Hefele, i. 210, 223). (3) *Interpretation of* 1 Tim. iii. 2 *as referring to widowers*. We are not here concerned with the true interpretation of this verse, but with the meaning given to it by the writers of the Church Orders, etc., which refer to bishops' marriage. Probably the Syrian Ap. C.O. at least interpreted the passage of widowers; that the bishop's wife must be dead (see p. 153). This is the most natural interpretation of "from one wife." The Test. Compiler inserts here a reference to sympathy with widowhood. In I. 33 of deacons he does not definitely say, but only hints, that it is good if they be celibates; but he goes on to say that at any rate a deacon must be one who is "*from the marriage of one wife* . . . He should not have children, but if he is *from a wife* or [S.: and] have children," etc. These latter phrases seem to be an echo of Ap. C.O.; and they look as if Test. Compiler understood St. Paul to mean that bishops and deacons must be widowers. On the other hand, as far as we know, *deacons* at least have never been obliged in the East to be widowers or celibates. The point of view may be illustrated by the Pshiṭta version of the passage. [We may note in passing that the

Pshiṭta has qashîshâ (= presbyter) for ἐπίσκοπος, and "presbyterate" for ἐπισκοπή in 1 Tim. iii. 1, 2, Tit. i. 7 (to suit Tit. i. 5); but here it is not a question of what Bible text James of Edessa had before him, but what the Test. Compiler was thinking of.] In the Pshiṭta of 1 Tim. iii. 2, 12, widowership is probably implied: "and he *was* the husband of one wife" (ver. 2 and Tit. i. 6); "such as *had* one wife" (ver. 12). This might have led us to suspect that the suggestion of widowerhood is due not to the Test. Compiler, but to James of Edessa, influenced by his Syriac Bible; but the Ap. C.O. "from one wife," and the parallel passage in Ar. D., show that this can hardly be the case, and that the Test. Compiler wrote a somewhat similar phrase in his Greek. But here, as elsewhere, he *hints* more than he explicitly commands. He would like his clergy to be more ascetic than he thinks that he is likely to persuade them to be. For the marriage of presbyters, see Note to I. 29, p. 186.

CHAPTER 21

BISHOPS' ORDINATION ON SUNDAY. So Eg. C.O. 31, A.C. viii. 4; Ar. D. 36 says nothing about it; Eth. C.O. 21 has "Sunday" according to Achelis, but Ludolf gives "in die *Sabbati*" (p. 323). C.H. 7 have: In ea . . . hebdomade in qua ordinatur, *in that week when he is ordained;* Rahmani (p. xxxvi.) suggests that it should be: in eo sabbato, *on that Saturday,* as Ludolf, the Arabic for "Saturday" and "week" being pronounced alike.

The neighbouring presbyters and bishops.] This is a sign that Test. was not only meant for a small and insignificant sect (p. 24). A.C. viii. 4 have a similar phrase, "with the presbyterate and the bishops who are present," and so H. 103[10], Ar.D., etc.

Having washed their hands.] In A.C. viii. 11 (Lagarde, 248[8]) there is a lavabo at the Offertory. Not in the parallels except Ar. D.

The presbyters . . . in silence.] So Eg. C.O. 31 (Tattam, p. 32), Eth. C.O. 21, H. 103[13]. Ar. D. substitutes "the whole congregation," and C.H. 9 are similar.

THE DECLARATION SAID BY ALL THE BISHOPS. The usage in Test. is the same as in Ar. D. (but there "the first bishop among them" says the prayer, words which show some trace of a primacy), and appears to be halfway between two opposite customs—that of all the bishops saying the prayer of consecration or ordination (there is no difference in the nomenclature at this early date), and that of only one bishop saying it. In Hauler 103[17] one bishop "asked by all," says, all others being silent: "O God and Father of our Lord Jesus Christ," etc., and lays on a hand. In C.H. 9, 10, all (not only the bishops) pray for him, saying: "O God, strengthen him whom Thou hast prepared for us"; then "one of the bishops and presbyters" (unus ex episcopis et presbyteris) is chosen to lay on a hand, and prays: "O God and Father," etc. [For a discussion of the curious phrase just mentioned, see Bishop J. Wordsworth, *Ministry of Grace*, 128.] In Eg. C.O. 31 all pray silently for the Holy Ghost, and the chief (or chosen, πρόκριτος) of the bishops lays on hands (or hand, see below), and prays (the words of the prayer not given); all the bishops, however, have previously laid on hands, praying *silently* for the descent of the Holy Ghost. But in Eth. C.O. 21 (Ludolf, p. 323), which has much affinity with Test., all the bishops lay on hands and *each one* says the prayer: "O God and Father" (see also below on I. 23, p. 165). In A.C. viii. 4 three bishops are selected, the rest of the bishops and presbyters praying in silence, the deacons hold open the Gospels on the ordained's head; "one of the first bishops with two others standing near the altar . . . says to God . . ." What do the two bishops do? Do they lay on hands? This is probable, though imposition of hands is not mentioned. Do they also say the prayer? Perhaps from the *other* bishops being expressly bidden to be silent we may infer that they do repeat the words. The fourth canon of Nicaea throws no light on the question, as it only says that three bishops must come together for the ordination (χειροτονία), which need not at all mean that all three must lay on hands, but ensures that no bishop be appointed except when three bishops of the neighbourhood have met; yet this canon may have suggested to A.C. the number "three." All the above Church Orders imply a number of bishops being present. The formula in Test. (which Copto-arab. varies slightly) is almost the same as that still used in the West Syrian Ordinal (Rahmani, p. 29). The declaration seems to be the work of Test. Compiler himself.

Chosen in the Spirit (p. 65).] In Ar. D., "in the Name of Father, Son, and Holy Ghost."

The Church which alone hath the principality, and which is not dissolved,] i.e. the monarchical and indissoluble Church. Ar. D. has "one and immaculate Church." This has been noted as a non-Montanistic feature, but see p. 16.

Holy revelations.] See Note on I. 29, p. 186. This is omitted by Ar. D.

The Trinity.] So A.D.; cf. Eg. C.O. baptismal formula of submission given in Note to II. 8; found in Test. I. 19, 21, 23 (thrice), II. 7; in C.H. 2 (bracketed by Achelis), where see Achelis' note (p. 38); he quotes Hippolytus *c. Noet.* c. 14; 53, 16.

THE ORDINATION PRAYER IN OTHER CHURCH ORDERS. It is not given in Eg. C.O.; C.H. 11–18 have a prayer from which we may, by omitting the italic portions as not being in the other Church Orders, conjecturally restore that of the supposed original "Lost Church Order." The prayer in C.H. is:

O God, Father of our Lord Jesus Christ, Father of mercies and God of all comfort, who dwellest in the heights and lookest on humble things, who knowest all things before they are; Thou who hast constituted the bounds of the Church,[1] by whose power (imperio) it is that *from Adam* there should remain a just race (var. lect., genus sublime) *in the manner* (ratione) *of this bishop*, who is great Abraham,[2] who hast constituted prelacies and principalities[3] (praelaturas et principatus),[4] *look on N. Thy servant*, giving Thy power (virtutem) and effectual (efficacem) Spirit,[5] whom Thou gavest to the holy Apostles through our Lord Jesus Christ, Thy only Son, to them who founded the Church in every place to the honour and glory of Thy holy Name. Forasmuch as Thou[6] knowest the heart of each one, grant to him[7] *that without sin he may see* (videat) *Thy people*, that he may be worthy to feed Thy great [and] holy flock. *Cause also that his life may be an example* (mores ejus sint superiores) *to all the people without any falling away. Cause also that he may be envied by all for (his) excellence*, and receive his prayers and offerings, which he shall offer to Thee day and night, and may they be to Thee a sweet savour. Give also to him, O Lord, the episcopate, and a mild (clementem) spirit, and power to forgive sins; and give him the ability (facultatem) to loose all bonds *of iniquity of demons, and to heal all diseases; and bruise Satan under his feet quickly*, through our Lord Jesus Christ, by whom be glory to Thee, with Him, and the Holy Ghost, for ever, Amen.

[H. 103, Eth. C.O. 21 (Ludolf, p. 323), and Const. H. 2 have very nearly the same prayer, omitting the italicised words. The principal variations are here noted:

[1] H., Eth. C.O., Const. H. add: through the word of Thy grace. Test. has in its own manner personified "word."

[2] H.: the race of the just men, Abraham; so Eth. C.O. and Const. H., but with "from Abraham."

[3] H.: princes and priests; Eth. C.O.: judges and priests; Const. H.: rulers and priests.

[4] H. adds (Eth. C.O. and Const. H. similar): and didst not leave Thy holy [place] without a ministry, and from the beginning of the world wast pleased to be preached (*or* to preach) in those whom Thou hast chosen.
[5] For "effectual spirit" and the following words, see below, p. 159.
[6] H. and Eth. C.O. (not Const. H.) insert "Father" as Test.
[7] The endings in H., Eth. C.O., and Const. H. are very like each other, but the order of C.H. is a good deal altered; thus H. has: grant to this Thy servant whom Thou hast chosen to the episcopate, to feed Thy flock, and to perform the chief priesthood (ἀρχιερατεύειν, Const. H.) to Thee, serving without blame night and day, constantly to reconcile (ἱλάσκεσθαι, Const. H.; cf. A.C. viii. 5) Thy face and to offer the gifts of Thy holy Church, to have in the spirit of the chief priesthood (τῷ πνεύματι τῷ ἀρχιερατικῷ, Const. H.) power to forgive sins according to Thy command, to give lots according to Thy precept, to loose every bond according to the power which Thou gavest to the Apostles, to please Thee in mildness and a pure heart, offering to Thee a sweet savour, through, etc. Eth. C.O. has "priesthood" for "chief priesthood," "ordines" for "lots," and "may *see* Thy face" (cf. Test.) for "reconcile." These Church Orders are an interesting link between C.H., or rather the "Lost Church Order," and the *Testament*.]

The Ar. D. has some differences, though in the main it is the same as Test., having the passage interpolated before "O God and Father." It adds to "Name of Thee and of Thy Only-begotten" the words "and of Thy Holy Ghost" [which might well be added by a writer coming after Test., but could hardly have been omitted by Test. if Ar. D. had preceded; Test. had a clear conception of the personality of the Holy Spirit (Introduction, p. 20), and would be very unlikely to omit this phrase if he had it before him] for "after the pattern of Thy heaven" it has "as a pattern of the virgin Church in heaven." It gives thrice the name of the ordained; for "princes for Thy people" it has "president of the priests"; it varies the phrase about the "princely Spirit" (see p. 159); for "Father who knowest the hearts" it reads "O God, who triest the hearts and reins," as if conscious of the incongruity of applying "who knowest the hearts" (καρδιογνώστης) to the Father when in the Acts it is the epithet of our Lord [in A.C. ii. 24 (Lagarde, 49[9]) and iii. 7 (Lagarde, 104[7]) it is applied to our Lord, but in A.C. viii. 5 (Lagarde, 238[15]), the parallel to this passage, it is used of the Father, as here]; it omits "to stand at the head of the priesthood," and is more full in the clauses about the erring people, and has some other minor variations. On the whole, the Ar. D. prayer is probably derived from Test., and not *vice versâ*.

The prayer in A.C. viii. 5 is very much longer than C.H., Eth. C.O., etc., and is largely interpolated.

THE ORDINATION PRAYER IN THE TESTAMENT (p. 65).
(1) The *preamble* [down to " O God and Father "] is probably
the work of the Test. Compiler; it is not in the parallels,
except Ar. D. It seems to be an expansion of the "Omni-
potens" with which Eth. C.O. (unlike C.H. and H.) begins
(so Ludolf, p. 323, but Achelis, p. 42, has omitted it).—(2) *Thy
princely Spirit*, etc. Evidently the Greek had ἡγεμονικόν. The
Syriac word used by James of Edessa is found in the Syriac
version of Clement of Rome's quotation from Ps. li. (Clem.
Rom. xviii. 12); but the Pshitta in that psalm renders "thy
glorious Spirit." The parallels in this prayer have: C.H.
(Achelis), efficacem; Const. H. and A.C. viii. 5, ἡγεμονικόν;
Eth. C.O. (Ludolf) and H., principalis; Ar. D., Almighty.—
(3) There is a curious variation in the words which follow:
which Thou didst deliver to Thy beloved Son Jesus Christ.
Eth. Co., H., and A.C. viii. 5 (Lagarde, 238^{12}) are similar to
Test. But Ar. D. has " whom Thou hast given to Thy holy
Church through Thy dear Son," and so Const. H. and C.H.
(but with "Apostles" for "Church"); and the modern Coptic
and Abyssinian omit the reference to our Lord here.—(4) *Day
and night:* so pp. 68 (but see below), 91, and so also C.H. 16;
but Eth. C.O. 21, Hauler 105^{14}, Const. H. 2, and A.C. viii. 5
have "night and day." The latter phrase seems to allude to the
Eastern division of time, in which a new day begins at sunset;
the former to the Roman division, in which a new day began at
midnight (cf. Test. II. 12, 19). The biblical usage varies, St.
John preferring the former, St. Mark and St. Paul the latter,
St. Luke being indifferent (Wordsworth, *Ministry of Grace*,
p. 305). The Test. usage would point, perhaps, to a connexion
with Asia Minor (cf. p. 45), but that Test. is inconsistent with
itself, passages on pp. 68, 106, 133, 136, showing the opposite
custom. For the context, cf. Acts xxvi. 7, Rev. vii. 15; but
" ministering " in Test. would be λειτουργοῦντα, as Const. H. and
A.C., whereas Acts and Rev. use λατρεύειν.—(5) *Thy powerful
Spirit, to loose*, etc. This is not the same word as before (Syr.
mshalṭâ); perhaps the Greek was βασιλικόν (cf. Ar. D., "royal
Spirit") here. But Const. H. has ἀρχιερατικόν, *high-priestly*.

DOXOLOGIES TO THE PRAYERS IN THE TESTAMENT. The
general form is "*through* whom (the Son) glory be *to* the
Father, *with* the Holy Ghost (I. 21, 23, 30, 32, II. 5, 9, 16;
and, omitting the Holy Ghost, I. 38, 43). We have, however,
in the beginning of the Eucharistic thanksgiving (p. 72), " that
we may praise Thee and Thy Only-begotten Son, and Thy
Holy Ghost, now and alway and for ever and ever " [but see

p. 249], and at the end of that chapter (p. 77), "glorified in Father and in Son and in Holy Ghost"; also (I. 26), "praised is the kingdom of the Father and of the Son and of the Holy Ghost"; in I. 41, "to Thee [be] praise and to Thine Only-begotten Son, ... and to the (var. lect., Thy) Holy Ghost"; and in I. 43, "in Thy Father, and in Thee, and in the Holy Ghost is our hope for ever." That the general form is as above is instructive in an anti-Arian document. The form "to the Father, through the Son, in the Holy Ghost," is the unvarying one in Sarapion, and Mr. Brightman (in J.T.S. i. 92) deduces an early date for that prayer-book from the words. For though that form is found occasionally in St. Athanasius, yet in Egypt Didymus (*de Trin.* i. 32, 34, iii. 23, quoted by Brightman) treats it as simply heretical. It occurs in A.C. viii., but that writer's semi-Arian bias would fully account for this. That one so violently anti-Arian as the Test. Compiler should ordinarily use it, implies an early date.

BISHOPS AS HIGH PRIESTS. The name "high priest" (ἀρχιερεύς) is not actually used in this chapter; but it is implied by phrases like "head of the priesthood," and it is used expressly in II. 21. It is not found in Sarapion. It is in C.H. 200 ("a principe sacerdotum"), the passage corresponding to Test. II. 21. And in the bishop's ordination prayer H. mentions "chief priesthood" (not Eth. C.O.; see above). Probably the earliest explicit use of the name "high priest" in this connexion is in Tertullian, *de Bapt.* 17; he says "the high priest (summus sacerdos), who is the bishop, has the right of giving baptism" (Migne's *Tertullian*, vol. i. 1326). Thenceforward the expression became common. St. Clement of Rome (I. 40) has the germ of the idea; he compares the Christian ministry to the Jewish: "Unto the high priest his proper services have been assigned, and to the priests their proper office is appointed, and upon the levites their proper ministrations are laid [cf. A.C. ii. 25, Lagarde, 54^5, H. 37^{12} ff.]. The layman is bound by the layman's ordinance." St. Justin Martyr (*Dial.* 116) says of the Christians: "We are the true high priestly race of God" (ἀρχιερατικὸν τὸ ἀληθινὸν γένος ἐσμὲν τοῦ θεοῦ).

THE KISS OF PEACE. So the parallels; Eg. C.O. 31 (Tattam, p. 32), Eth. C.O. 21, H. 106^3, C.H. 19. In A.C. viii. 5 it comes after enthronisation, which is not mentioned in Test. or the above parallels, though it is alluded to in C.H. 30, 32. In Copto-arab., at the end of the ordination prayer, there is a rubric directing the bishops to give the kiss of peace to the new bishop.

LAYING ON OF HANDS, SINGULAR OR PLURAL. The usage varies, though the singular (laying on of one hand) is by far the commoner custom. The following is a conspectus:

(1) *Bishop's ordination.* Test. here and Eg. C.O. 31 (according to Lagarde, but not according to Tattam) plural, and so Eth. C.O. 21 (but there all the bishops lay on hands throughout, and all say the whole prayer); but C.H. 10 and H. 103[17] singular. Laying on of hands not mentioned in A.C. viii. 4.

(2) *Presbyter's ordination.* Test. I. 30, H. 108[19], Eth. C.O. 22, and A.C. viii. 15 singular; C.H. 30 do not say, but "all is like a bishop's ordination"; Eg. C.O. 32 plural (so both Tattam and Lagarde), yet in a reference to a presbyter's ordination in Eg. C.O. 33 the singular is used.

(3) *Deacon's ordination.* Test. I. 38 singular (but Codex S. plural), and so C.H. 38, Eth. C.O. 23, and "Gallican Statutes" 4 (Wordsworth, *Ministry of Grace*, p. 166 n.); but Eg. C.O. 33 plural (twice mentioned; so both Lagarde and Tattam), and so A.C. viii. 16, H. 109[15].

(4) *Minor orders.* No laying on of hands in Test. or earlier parallels. In A.C. viii. 18 ff., for deaconesses and subdeacons plural, for readers singular.

(5) *Benediction of catechumens.* Test. singular in I. 27 (but there it merely represents χειροθεσία), and expressly in II. 5, 16, 20. In Eg. C.O. 45 plural (cf. confessors: Note on p. 197).

(6) *At exorcism before baptism.* Singular in Test. II. 7 and Eg. C.O. 45; plural in C.H. 108, but only there a stretching out of hands.

(7) *Confirmation.* Singular in Test. II. 9, C.H. 136, Eg. C.O. 46. The reading in H. 111[8] is doubtful.

CHAPTER 22

HOURS OF PRAYER FOR THE BISHOP. We note that they begin in the *evening* as the first hour of the whole twenty-four (see II. 24 and Note on "day in night" on p. 159).—Test. has "the twelfth hour [of the day] at the lamp [lighting]"; the parallel phrase in Ar. D. has "at the beginning of the night." Thus Test. identifies the twelfth hour (6 p.m.) as the lamp lighting. Silvia, who visited Jerusalem in winter, describes the tenth hour as the "lamp lighting" (see Note on II. 24, p. 238).

I have said unto you.] Ar. D. has "the Lord hath said"; it seems to have purposely removed the "Testament" pretence.

THE BISHOP'S FASTS. The *eighteen exalted entrances*, or steps, are identified in Test. with the three weeks' fast after Ordination, that is, six to each week, Sunday being expressly excepted. But why eighteen? Clearly Ar. D. did not understand (see below). It is possible that the Test. Compiler had before him some devotional work under this name, just as a modern devotional book has been entitled *The I will's of Christ*. If we examine the Gospels to find such entrances, we shall find very few in St. Matthew or St. John, but, curiously enough, St. Luke yields exactly eighteen. Thus (1) Entrance to Samaria and Galilee on the way to Jerusalem, xvii. 11; (2) to Jericho, xix. 1; (3) to Zacchaeus's house, xix. 6; (4) to Bethphage and Bethany, xix. 29; (5) to Jerusalem on Palm Sunday, xix. 38; (6) to the Temple on Sunday, xix. 45; (7) to the Temple on Monday, xxi. 37; (8) to the Temple on Tuesday, *ib.*; (9) to the Temple on Wednesday, *ib.*; (10) to Jerusalem for the Passover, xxii. 14, cf. ver. 10; (11) to the Mount of Olives, xxii. 39; (12) to Caiaphas, xxii. 54; (13) to the Council, xxii. 66; (14) to Pilate, xxiii. 1; (15) to Herod, xxiii. 7; (16) to Pilate the second time, xxiii. 11; (17) to Golgotha, xxiii. 33; (18) to Paradise, xxiii. 46, cf. ver. 43. Thus it is possible to conjecture a reference to a devotional work founded on St. Luke.

In Ar. D. 38 these eighteen entrances were not understood, and they are reduced to three (death, resurrection, ascension), connected with the three days' fast a week all the year round. The explanation is not happy, as the last two entrances in Ar. D. are not entrances *to the Passion*. But the fact that Ar. D. explicitly explains the entrances, however mistakenly, and that Test. assumes that his readers will understand without explanation, points to the latter being before the former. Test. could never have increased three to eighteen without explaining why; but we can well understand that Ar. D., not understanding eighteen, reduced them to the three which he could easily explain.

The food mentioned in Ar. D. (bread, oil, etc.) is "for that year during which he fasts." Ar. D. is apparently speaking of a year's fast after ordination, and *perhaps* this is the meaning of Test., in which case "the rest of the time" means "after the first year." In the three weeks' fast, Ar. D. says expressly that nothing is to be eaten till the Saturday. It omits the clause about the Eucharistic Cup; Copto-arab. does the same, and also omits "whether he be well or ill." Both Ar. D. and Copto-arab. also make an exception to the three weeks' fast when the bishop is "consecrated in the days of the Fifty (Pentecost)," and say that the fast is to be broken on Saturday. Note that Ar. D. has exactly the same obscure phrase about the three days' fast each week that appears in Test.—The "wine of the Holy Thing" in Test. (p. 69) is probably "wine such as is provided for the Eucharist." See I. 31, pp. 95, 188.

We notice that Test. does not say on which days the bishop is to fast. Wednesday and Friday are not mentioned, as they are in Ar. D. 38. Particular fast days are not laid down in Test. except two before Easter. Now Wednesday and Friday are mentioned as fasts, about 120 A.D. (?), in the "Didaché" or *Teaching of the Twelve Apostles*, and we find many early references to those days; they were observed diligently in Egypt, but, if Bishop Wordsworth's conclusion from the evidence be correct (*Ministry of Grace*, p. 327), the practice of fasting on these days was not used, or else was dropped, in the rest of the East, until it was somewhat vehemently taken up at the end of the fourth century by Epiphanius and others. It is found in A.C. v. 15 (Lagarde, 145^{19}); and Ap. Can. 69 (68) says that a clerk not observing these days, unless let by sickness, is to be deposed. The absence, then, in Test. of any reference to these days is an early and non-Egyptian characteristic.

BISHOPS NOT TO EAT MEAT. So in Ar.D. 38. This rule still obtains among both East and West Syrians (Nestorians and Jacobites), the former, at least, insisting that the bishop shall not have eaten meat during the whole of his lifetime, nor yet his mother during her pregnancy. Contrast Ap. Can. 51 and 53 (50 and 52), which expressly allow meat to bishops, and also wine, though not to excess (cf. A.C. viii. 44).

DAYS FOR THE EUCHARIST. Test. says that the Eucharist is to be celebrated only on Saturday *or* Sunday and on a fast day. From the directions at the beginning of I. 23 it is probable that we must, by the omission of a single letter (Aleph), correct *or* into *and;* Ar. D. 38 says "Saturday and Sunday," and adds "festivals which fall on week days, unless the festival fall on Wednesday or Friday," but perhaps it allows the Eucharist on these days after 3 p.m.; Copto-arab., with reference to the last point, says merely "festivals occurring in the week." In A.C. ii. 59 (Lagarde, 90^8) Saturday and Sunday are specially appointed for divine service; but in the parallel passage in H. 44^{14}, Sunday only is mentioned. In C.H. 201 the bishop may celebrate the Eucharist "as often as he wishes to enjoy the mysteries"; that a celebration and not only a reception of the Holy Communion is intended, is seen by the mention of "white vestments, more beautiful than [those of] all the people, especially splendid." In Ar. D. 38 daily communion is prescribed for the bishop, but this would probably be by reservation; see Note on II. 25, p. 239.

The question of a Saturday Eucharist is an obscure one. Mr. Brightman (in J.T.S. i. 92) observes that Sarapion only provides for a Sunday Eucharist, as Prayer 19 is entitled "The First Prayer of the Lord's Day"; but this seems hardly to be conclusive. He says that the observance of Saturday was coming into use in the East in 375, and was already established in Egypt in 380. Saturday was regarded as a fast in the West (see canons 23, 26, of the Council of Elvira in Spain, *cir.* A.D. 305), but as a feast in the East, where feeling was influenced by opposition to the Marcionites, who were stringent in making it a fast.—If for "a fast day" we read "Wednesday and Friday," as in other parts of the world in the fourth century, the Test. rule would give exactly the communion usage of St. Basil, who speaks of Sunday, Wednesday, Friday and Saturday as days when he communicated, though, he says, some received daily (*Ep.* 93 *ad Caesariam*). St. Basil's seems to have been a common practice, but it does not follow that there would be an Eucharist on each of these days (see p. 239).

THE BISHOP INSTRUCTING ON THE EVE (lit., in the evening). This means the evening before, which is still reckoned as the evening of the day itself in the East. See above, Note on I. 21 (p. 159), "day and night."

THE CATECHUMENS ADMONISHED WITH MEDITATIONS OF THE PROPHETS AND APOSTLES. Perhaps we should render "Apostle," *i.e.* St. Paul. The "Apostle" is constantly used in later times for the liturgical Epistle.

CHAPTER 23

THE EUCHARISTIC LITURGY

PROBABLE ORDER OF SERVICE AT DAWN. (None of it is appointed to be said daily, the Eucharist expressly not daily.)

Three "hymns of praise," or prayers, with two antiphons between them (I. 26).

Psalms and four O.T. canticles (I. 26).

Preface and concluding "hymns of praise," with two antiphons between them (I. 26).

The "prayer is completed" (I. 27; see Note on p. 193).

The lections; and instruction by bishop or presbyter (I. 27).

Prayer (extempore?) and dismissal of catechumens (I. 27).

Deacon's litany, the bishop "completing the prayer" (I. 35).
Mystagogic instruction on festivals (I. 28).
Deacon's short "admonition" (I. 23).
Preface and Eucharistic thanksgiving (I. 23).
Benedictus qui venit, etc., and communion (I. 23).
Thanksgiving after reception (I. 23).

LITURGIES OF OTHER CHURCH ORDERS, ETC.

(1) *The Canons of Hippolytus* 20-29 do not give a liturgy, but say that the deacon brings the offerings, and the new bishop lays his hand on them with the presbyters, saying, The Lord be with all, etc., and Sursum Corda, after which he says the prayer and finishes the Offering ($\pi\rho o\sigma\phi o\rho\acute{a}$?). They then refer to the prayer over the oil and first fruits, if any, ending with the Gloria Patri in the form "Glory to Thee, Father and Son and Holy Ghost, for ever and ever, Amen."

(2) *The Egyptian Church Order* 31 (Tattam, p. 32) also gives no Liturgy, and only says that the deacons bring the offering to the new bishop, who lays his hand on it with the presbyters, and says, giving thanks, The Lord be with you all, etc., and Sursum Corda, and so he prays the rest which follows according to the order of the Holy Offering.

(3) *The Ethiopic Church Order* 21 gives the anaphora in full. The Ethiopic and Latin are in Ludolf, pp. 324 ff., and an English translation in Brightman, L.E.W. pp. 189 ff. It is a shorter form of the Testament Liturgy. Note especially that the presbyters say the eucharistic prayer with the bishop [cf. p. 156 for all the bishops joining in the ordination prayer in Eth. C.O.; in all these orders the bishop offers with the presbyters (but in Copto-arab. this rule is somewhat altered); and cf. the rule of Test. that the people are to say "Remembering Thy death" with the bishop (p. 73), and also another passage on p. 75]. In the Eucharistic thanksgiving Test. begins as Eth. C.O., but interpolates after "Proclaimer of Thy purpose" down to "Thou, Lord, didst send Thy Word" (a long interpolation, p. 72), after which it follows Eth. C.O. almost word for word, with very slight variations and interpolations [note Test. and H. "fix the boundary" = Eth. C.O. "establish a covenant," which Abyss. Anaphora of our Lord (see p. 247) follows, against Test.]. Eth. C.O. does not have "for the forgiveness of sins," or St. Paul's words, or the phrase about the cup and the type, but gives our Lord's "This is My blood" (p. 73). In "Remembering Thy death" Test. follows Eth. C.O. almost

exactly to "serve Thee in priesthood," after which the latter
gives the Invocation, quite different from Test., mentioning
the Holy Spirit, but saying nothing about transforming the
elements (see p. 174, Note on the Invocation). Eth. C.O. has
no Intercession for the Church; it has a prayer over oil,
prayers for communicants, Sancta Sanctis, "One is the Holy
Father," etc., "The Lord be with you," etc., and communion,
but does not give the words of administration (cf. Test.); then
it adds the thanksgiving after reception and the blessing.
Test. does not follow Eth. C.O. after the Invocation, but the last
part of the Eth. C.O. Invocation, "fulfilling with the Holy
Ghost . . .," is almost word for word like the end of the Intercession in Test., "that they may be filled . . . for ever and
ever" (p. 75). One may conjecture that Eth. C.O. originally
had nothing after the blessing of the oil; see Hauler, below.

(4) *Hauler's Verona fragments* give an Anaphora almost
exactly like the preceding to the end of the blessing of the
oil; the rest is omitted. H. does not say that all the presbyters are to say the Eucharistic prayer with the bishop as
Eth. C.O. does, and we note a similar difference in the ordination
of a bishop (Note on I. 21, p. 156). A few differences may be
noticed. In the Eucharistic thanksgiving, where Test. has
"Thy Word . . . by whom Thou madest all things, being well
pleased with Him," H. has "Thy inseparable Word by whom
Thou madest all things, and (who) was well pleasing to Thee,"
and Eth. C.O. has "the Word from Thee, in whom Thou
madest all things by Thy will"; and in the following sentence
H. is nearer to Test. than to Eth. C.O.; it has (lower down)
"lighten the just" like Test., where Eth. C.O. has "lead forth
the just." In the Invocation, which follows Eth. C.O. closely,
H. has before "fulfilling with the Holy Ghost" the words
"gathering (them) together into one, give to all the saints
who receive, for fulfilling . . ."; compare the words of Test.
which immediately precede. H. has the benediction of oil as
Eth .C.O. (nearly), and adds a blessing of cheese and olives. It
then goes on immediately, without a lacuna, to the ordination
of a presbyter. On the whole, H. is interesting as a connecting link between Eth. C.O. and Test., though it is much nearer
to the former.

(5) *The Arabic Didascalia* in its parallel chapter (38) does
not give a Liturgy, but describes it. Besides the German
of Funk, Brightman gives an English translation of this part
from an Oxford MS. (L.E.W. 510, 511). It adds incense
when the *presbyter* brings the elements; the bishop goes thrice

round the altar with incense, and the presbyter then takes the censer through the congregation (Silvia mentions incense in the pre-anaphoral service; cf. also Ethiopic Didascalia, Platt, § 14). Ar. D. mentions psalmody, "sections from the Apostolic word" by the deacon "and a section from the Psalms"; then the Gospel. It goes on to speak of the prayer for the Church, which is more developed than Test.; the sick, travellers, the needy, are mentioned; prayers are offered for the fruits of the earth, for kings, rulers, the departed, benefactors, catechumens, the universal Church, the bishop and clergy, and the whole congregation (see p. 176, Note on the Intercession). It also mentions the waving of fans by the deacons [cf. A.C. viii. 12 (Lagarde, 248^{22}), and the (later?) Egyptian Liturgy given by Brightman, L.E.W. 461–463, and perhaps Test. II. 10 *q.v.*], and linens (?) "like the wings of the cherubim." A sanctuary veil is mentioned, and bishop, presbyters, deacons, subdeacons, the reader, and widows "who are deaconesses and have spiritual gifts," stand within.

(6) *The Abyssinian Anaphora of our Lord* (given in Ethiopic and Latin by Ludolf, 341–345; see Appendix I.) is taken with some variations from Test. It has an Invocation of the later form. It is specially interesting as being the connecting link between the modern Abyssinian and Coptic Liturgies and the Testament, to which they, through it, are greatly indebted.

(7) *In the Copto-arabic translation of Test.* the text of the Liturgy has been somewhat altered and modernised; the Sanctus is introduced, an Invocation addressed *to the Holy Ghost* (so Rahmani), long diptychs, and the Lord's prayer before communion have been inserted.

(8) *The Apostolic Constitutions,* book viii., have a very much more elaborate Liturgy than the older forms, but as it is so well known it need not be described here at length; after diffuse dismissals of catechumens, etc., follow the litany, kiss of peace, lavabo, deacon's short admonition, the bringing in of the elements, Sursum Corda with benediction, an Eucharistic prayer, very long, with Sanctus, the words of Institution, Oblation, an Invocation of the later form, and a long Intercession, then a Benediction, Short Litany, Sancta Sanctis, Benedictus qui venit and Hosanna, Communion, Thanksgiving after reception, and Dismissal. See Introduction, p. 33.

(9) *St. Cyril of Jerusalem* gives the following as the order of service at Jerusalem in 348 (*Cat. Lect.* xxiii.; he delivered these lectures while yet a presbyter). The clergy wash their

hands; kiss of peace; Sursum Corda and preface with Sanctus; Invocation [no mention of our Lord's words, nor of the oblation, but see Note, p. 170, on the former]; Intercession for quick and dead; the Lord's prayer; Sancta Sanctis and communion (no fraction mentioned); thanksgiving after reception.

(10) *Sarapion, cir.* 350 A.D., gives a Liturgy as used (presumably) at Thmuis in the Nile Delta; he writes the parts said by the bishop in full, but not the deacon's or people's part. The Sursum Corda is referred to; then follow the preface with Sanctus, the Oblation with recital of our Lord's words, Invocation of the Logos, addressed to the Father, Intercession, fraction, prayer, and communion, with a benediction, a post-communion thanksgiving, and an oblation of oil and water.

The above descriptions show the essential unity of structure in all these early liturgies.

HOURS OF THE EUCHARIST. In Test. it is to be over by sunrise (I. 26, p. 78), to begin before dawn. So Pliny in his letter to Trajan (*ante lucem*), Tertullian *de Cor. Mil.* 3 (*antelucanis coetibus*, but Bishop Wordsworth thinks that this is exceptional, and that generally it was in day light), St. Cyprian *Ep.* 63, 16 (*mane*). See Wordsworth, *Ministry of Grace*, 317.

THE SANCTUARY VEIL, WHY CLOSED (see also page 151). The allusion here is difficult (p. 70). The mention of the veil suggests Exod. xxxiv. 30, 33 (where the Israelites' fear to approach the shining face of Moses might be the "erring of the ancient people") and 2 Cor. iii. 13; but in neither of these passages is there any mention of an offering. [It may be noted that the Syriac word here used for a veil is not the same at that employed in the Pshiṭta to denote the veil on Moses' face; it is the same as that used for the veil of the tabernacle.] Perhaps Test. means that the reason there was for it under the Law—which he states—subsists under the Gospel; though, if that be his doctrine, it is not easy to reconcile it with St. Matt. xxvii. 51, and Heb. x. 20. Can he mean by the "ancient people" the Corinthian Christians of the first age, whose excesses led St. Paul to put things "in order" at the celebration of the Eucharist (1 Cor. xi. 17–34)?— St. Augustine often contrasts the openness of the Gospel with the secrecy of the Law, as symbolised by the taking away of the veil and the rending of the veil of the Temple; cf. *Hom. in N.T.* 24 (74), 5; 87 (137), 6; 110 (160) 6.

WIDOWS WITHIN THE VEIL. Test. and Ar. D. alone allow them inside the veil. The Council of Laodicea (can. 44) says that "women may not approach near the altar." The Test. arrangement would point to a very large number of widows, as they on the one side of the Sanctuary correspond to deacons, readers, subdeacons, and deaconesses on the other. We note the inclusion of deaconesses, though they are expressly excluded from the "priesthood" later on in this chapter (p. 76).—*Those with gifts.* Cf. Ar. D. (above), "widows who are deaconesses and have gifts." In both, "gifts" ($\chi\alpha\rho i\sigma\mu\alpha\tau\alpha$, the supernatural gifts of the Holy Ghost, 1 Cor. xii. 4) are taken for granted as going on in the writer's time. See I. 47 for the parallels.

DEACON'S ADMONITION BEFORE THE SURSUM CORDA (p. 70). Copto-arab. has slightly modernised this. For "despise the prophets" it has "reject the divine Scriptures." For "Let us not despise the cross" it has "Whoso is ashamed to confess the cross of Christ, let him depart." It also omits some clauses.—The whole "admonition" bears a strong resemblance to the old-fashioned "Fencing" or "Debarrings" once common in Scotland. — In the last two clauses, "Lift up your hearts to offer, . . . let us receive the grace," the twofold character of the Eucharist is recognised; "offer" answering to our Lord's "This do," etc., and "receive" to "Take eat," etc.—The word "admonition" in the Syriac is not the usual word for the deacon's Litany or Ectene in Syriac literature.

BENEDICTION BEFORE SURSUM CORDA (p. 71). This benediction in the various liturgies takes two forms: (A) "The Lord be with you," or the like; (B) "The grace of our Lord Jesus Christ," etc., as 2 Cor. xiii. 14. Test. has A with the Egyptian rite alone among Eastern liturgies; C.H. also have A (which is based on the salutation of Boaz to his reapers and their reply, Ruth ii. 4); and we thus see a connexion between Test., Egypt, and Rome; also the following have A —Eth. C.O. 21, H. 106[7], St. Mark in Greek (Brightman, L.E.W. 125), modern Coptic (Br. 164), modern Abyssinian (Br. 228); so of Westerns, Roman, Ambrosian (Hammond, L.E.W. p .322). On the other hand, the following have B—the Antioch Liturgy as shown in St. Chrysostom's writings (Br. 473), A.C. viii. 12 (Lagarde, 248[27]), St. James in Greek and Syriac (Br. 49, 85), all three East Syrian (Nestorian) Liturgies now extant (Addai and Mari, Theodore, Nestorius), St. Basil, St. Chrysostom, and the Armenian (Br. 321, 384, 435), early Byzantine (Br. 529); and note especially that James of Edessa in his own writings (*Letter to Thomas the Presbyter*, Br. 491) has this B form, and expressly calls attention to the difference between his custom and that of the "Alexandrine fathers"; also the Egyptian

Anaphora (Sahidic Eccl. Canons 65, Tattam, p. 118), which Brightman conjectures to be an adaptation of A.C. viii. (Br. xx.[31]), has B; and it is found in the Mozarabic alone of Westerns (Hammond, L.E.W. 321). We see then that in this respect, as we cannot suppose Test. to be an Egyptian document (see Introduction, p. 44), it stands in a peculiar position.

THE SANCTA SANCTIS (p. 71). Its position after the Sursum Corda is peculiar, as is the response which Test. adds, analogous to that of Sursum Corda. It is found in Eth. C.O. just before communion (but perhaps this part of Eth. C.O. is a later addition, see above, p. 166), and so in Cyr. Jer. xxiii. 19; in A.C. viii. 12 (Lagarde, 259[13]) it comes just before the "One Holy" and the "Benedictus qui venit."

ABSENCE OF SANCTUS. It is omitted in Eth. C.O. and H. as in Test. It occurs in fourth century liturgies, however—in Sarapion and A.C. viii.12 (Lagarde, 254[4]), and in St. Chrysostom's writings (Brightman, L.E.W. 474[14]). The germ of it is in Test. in the words "Thou, Lord, the Founder of the heights ..." (p. 72). It will be observed that seven of the angelic orders are there enumerated. The inclusion and conjunction among them of Raiments and Lights remind us of Ps. civ. 2. See I. 28, p. 85.

WORDS OF INSTITUTION. (1) We notice that Test. omits, though it refers to, our Lord's words over the Cup. This cannot be for reverence, as the words over the Bread are given. Justin Martyr quotes them even in an apology to the heathen (*Apol.* i. 66), but not there as part of the service. It is perhaps more than a curious coincidence that whereas here in Test. the words over the Cup are omitted, in II. 10 the words in administering the Cup are not given (see Note, p. 222), and that in II. 8 our Lord's baptismal formula is omitted, no words for baptizing being given. The Ethiopic translation of Test. supplies the omission here (in I. 23) with the words, "Also the cup of wine which He mixed, He gave to His disciples, saying, Take drink it all of you. This is My blood which is shed for you." The omission in Test. is no mistake of the manuscripts, as Rahmani suggests, for it occurs in the derived Abyssinian Anaphora of our Lord (see Appendix I., p. 247).

(2) There are perhaps other instances of the omission. St. Cyril of Jerusalem does not mention our Lord's words in the service at all. The argument from silence is precarious in what is only a description of the service, and the omission of our Lord's words is somewhat discounted by the omission of the Oblation also. On the other hand, (*a*) St. Cyril describes the preface rather fully, the mention of heaven, earth, sea, ...

angels, archangels, etc., yet says nothing of any recital of the work of redemption, and his "then" (εἶτα) after the Sanctus is rather strong; he says, "*then*, having hallowed ourselves by these spiritual hymns" (the Sanctus), "we call upon (παρακαλοῦμεν) God, who loveth man, to send the Holy Spirit . . ."; and (*b*) later on, in defending the intercession for the dead, he says, "We, when we offer to Him our supplications for those who have fallen asleep, . . . offer up Christ, sacrificed for our sins, propitiating our merciful God both for them and for ourselves," thus perhaps referring to the Oblation (*Cat. Lect.* xxiii. 6, 7, 10). Certainly St. Cyril *comments* elsewhere on our Lord's words (xxii.), but not in connexion with the service; yet his words there seem to have a liturgical reminiscence. Brightman (L.E.W. 469, Note 11) calls attention to the phrase "His undefiled hands and feet" (xx. 5) as corresponding to St. James's Liturgy, Greek and Syriac.

(3) Our Lord's words are omitted altogether in the oldest of the three East Syrian anaphoras (Addai and Mari, probably of the first part of the fifth century; they occur in the two later anaphoras). With the omission must be compared the early form of Invocation in that Anaphora (see Note on the Invocation, p. 175). It has been thought that the words have always been recited as a tradition, though not written; but there is no evidence for this, and the omission must be considered significant, as this anaphora seems to represent a type earlier than that of the great fifth century anaphoras, and was the product of a far-distant Church not greatly influenced by the liturgical changes of its Western neighbours until its third anaphora (of Nestorius, so called, which depends much on Byzantine work) was composed.

(4) On the other hand, the words of our Lord are found in full in Eth. C.O., H., Sarapion, A.C. viii. 12 (Lagarde, $255^{25\text{ff}}$.), and in St. Chrysostom's writings expressly (Brightman, L.E.W. 474, 479), and Test. has accordingly *omitted* what he had before him. It will thus be seen that the theory of Mr. Ffoulkes (*Primitive Consecration of the Eucharistic Oblation,* chap. v.), that the early liturgies had only the Invocation, without our Lord's words, considering the latter as properly represented by the words of administration of the elements, and that the A.C. writer first inserted them in the interests of Arianism, is not well founded. But we may not improbably deduce from the evidence the conclusion that in the fourth century (as among the Orthodox Easterns very generally now) the recital of our Lord's words was regarded as a historical state-

ment prefatory to the Oblation and Invocation; it is to be noted that wherever they occur they precede the Invocation, there being no pre-Reformation authority, as far as is known, for placing them *after* it. We may probably further infer that the "Western theory of consecration," that the only essential words are "This is my Body, etc. . . . This is my Blood," etc., all prayers and invocations being but edifying additions, is not that of the fourth century. As the Bishop of Salisbury points out (*Ministry of Grace*, p. 382), it is difficult "to get free from the presupposition that a certain form of words is necessary to consecration," but it is probable that we shall be led to the conclusion that the Eucharist, Confirmation, and Holy Orders have no fixed and certain form, according to ancient ideas.

(5) *St. Paul's words* (1 Cor. xi. 26) *introduced into the Words of Institution.* This is not uncommon. Test. introduces them in the curious form, "When ye shall do this ye make My resurrection." There is no such introduction in Eth. C.O. or H. or Sarapion; but it is found in A.C. viii. 12 (Lagarde, 256¹), and in the Abyssinian Anaphora of our Lord (which, however, changes the Test. words " My resurrection " to " commemoration of Me "). It is found in many later liturgies: "Ye do shew My death and confess My resurrection and ascension till I come" (St. Mark, Brightman, L.E.W. 133); "Ye do confess My resurrection, ye do make My memorial till I come" (Coptic, Br. 177); "As often as ye do this, make ye memorial of Me [and the people answer: We show Thy death, Lord, and Thy holy resurrection, we believe Thine ascension, etc.]" (Abyssinian, Br. 232); "This be ye doing till I come, for whensoever ye eat . . . ye commemorate My death till My coming" (East Syrian, "Liturgy of Nestorius"); cf. "This be ye doing *whensoever ye come together* for My memorial" (East Syrian, "Liturgy of Theodore").

(6) *The Cup . . . a type of the blood.* So in II. 10 (p. 128), "the bread . . . for a type of My body . . . the cup . . . a sign (or shewing forth) of blood and of the laver." Not in Eth. C.O. or H., parallel passages to this, but H. and Eg. C.O. have it in the parallels to II. 10, and there are many examples of the expression. Tertullian (*Adv. Marc.* iv. 40, Migne, vol. ii. col. 491), in maintaining the reality of our Lord's body, calls the Eucharistic bread "the figure (figura) of" Christ's "body," and says that unless the body were real it could not have a figure. Cf. also the Pfaffian fragment (of Irenaeus?) quoted on p. 174 in the Note on the Invocation. Sarapion, § 1, in giving the Words of Institution, has: "This bread is the likeness (ὁμοίωμα)

of the holy body, ... we have offered also the cup, the likeness of the blood." So St. Cyril of Jerusalem (xxiii. 20) says: "When we taste we are bidden to taste not bread and wine, but the sign (ἀντιτύπου) of the body and blood of Christ"; in xxi. 1 he calls oil the "sign" of the Holy Ghost in Confirmation; in xx. 6 he says that baptism is the "sign" of the sufferings of Christ. We may also compare an early fragment of the Latin Canon of the Mass (Pseudo-Ambrose *de Sacramentis* iv. 5, qu. by Wordsworth, *Ministry of Grace*, 82): "this oblation ... which is the figure (figura) of the body and blood of our Lord Jesus Christ." Also (besides the parallels to II. 10) Eg. C.O. 60 (Tattam, p. 80) has, "If thou hast ... partaken of (the Cup) *like* as of the blood of Christ," etc.; and Hauler, 117[23], "Thou hast received (the Cup) as it were the antitype of the blood of Christ."

THE OBLATION. (1) *Remembering therefore*, etc. (p. 73). In Eth. C.O., and probably in parallel liturgies, these words are the corollary of "This do in remembrance of Me." But in Test. (even in the interpolated form of the Ethiopic translation, for which see above, p. 170) this last phrase is absent, and "Remembering therefore" is out of place. This is another instance (we shall see a third in the Note on the Invocation, and yet another in the omission of milk and honey in II. 10) where Test. has omitted what was before it in its authorities, not seeing the connexion between what it omitted and the words which it retained. We note that Sarapion also omits "This do," etc., but then he also omits "Remembering therefore," and after reciting our Lord's words, continues: "Therefore we also have offered the Cup," etc. Mr. Brightman (in J.T.S. i. 96) remarks that the Byzantine Liturgy of St. Chrysostom alone of the great rites omits "This do," etc.

(2) *The people repeating this passage with the priest* (cf. p. 165, for the Eth. C.O.). The text does not say how much the people are to repeat; probably from "Remembering therefore." In analogous cases in East Syrian MSS., a large red asterisk shows how much is to be repeated, but in them it is the *priest* who is to say the passage twice, a favourite custom.

(3) *Text of the concluding passage*. "We have brought this drink and this food of Thy holiness [to Thee]" (p. 74). In the translation the reading of B. has been followed, and it is supported by the Abyssinian Anaphora of our Lord, which reads (p. 247): "We give Thee this gift; not food nor drink do we offer to Thy holiness. Cause that it," etc. M., followed by Rahmani, has: "Bring this drink and this food of Thy holiness

[to us]," making the Invocation begin at "Bring." But this scarcely makes sense. The Invocation in B. is still addressed to the Holy Trinity, the imperative being feminine in Syriac to agree with "Trinity." An emendation of the Syriac might be suggested, namely, to read "to Thy holiness" instead of "of Thy holiness," by the change of one letter (L for D), as in the Anaphora of our Lord.

THE INVOCATION OR EPICLESIS (p. 74). The Test. Invocation is remarkable for two things—(1) that it is addressed to the Holy Trinity, the Son being named first in the preceding sentence; and (2) that it does not pray expressly for the Holy Spirit to transform the elements, but asks that they may be beneficial to the communicants.

1. *The Invocation, to whom addressed.* We may notice that "Invocation (ἐπίκλησις) *of* a Person" may mean either praying *for* Him to come, or praying *to* Him. But in the expression "Invocation of the Holy Trinity" we must apparently understand Invocation addressed *to* the Three Persons. Irenaeus uses the word ἐπίκλησις as well known in his day: he speaks of the Invocation of God, or of the Father, or of the Holy Ghost, or of the Holy Trinity, and also uses the word Invocation by itself, absolutely. The Pfaffian fragment, ascribed to Irenaeus (but this is more than doubtful), has: "We invoke the Holy Ghost to declare this sacrifice both the bread the body, the cup the blood of Christ, that they who receive the antitype may obtain remission of sins and everlasting life" (see Ffoulkes, *Primitive Consecration of the Eucharistic Oblation*, p. 62). Here the Holy Ghost seems to be addressed. In St. Cyril of Jerusalem the evidence is not quite clear. In *Cat. Lect.* xxiii. 7 the Father is apparently addressed: "We call upon the merciful God to send forth His Holy Spirit"; but in xix. 7 the Holy Trinity: "Things also hung up at idol festivals . . . which are polluted by the invocation of unclean spirits. . . . For as the bread and wine of the Eucharist before the holy invocation of the adorable Trinity was simple bread and wine, while after the invocation the bread becomes the body of Christ and the wine the blood of Christ, so in like manner such meats belonging to the pomp of Satan . . . become profane by the invocation of the evil spirit." The "invocation of the unclean spirits" must mean invocation addressed *to* the unclean spirits, and so the "invocation of the Trinity" must mean invocation addressed *to* the Trinity. In xxii. 3 we read of the "invocation of the Holy Ghost" in the Eucharist; here the meaning seems to be prayer *for* the Holy Ghost. On the whole, St. Cyril

seems to support the *Testament*. The Council of Hippo, in North Africa, in 393 (can. 21, Hefele, *Councils*, ii. 398, Eng. trans.), forbade such invocations addressed to any but the Father. "In prayer, no one shall address the Son instead of the Father, or the Father instead of the Son, except at the altar, when prayer shall always be addressed to the Father. No one shall make use of strange forms of prayer without having first consulted well-instructed brethren." Bishop J. Wordsworth (*Rev. int. de théol.* 1900, p. 471) suggests that this was prompted by the *Testament*. For the order of the three Persons in the latter, cf. Ignatius (*Magnes.* 13), "in Son and Father and in Spirit," and 2 Cor. xiii. 14. The Ignatian passage is omitted by the interpolator (who is the same as the compiler of A.C.), but that would be accounted for by the Arian leanings of the latter, and therefore there is no good reason for supposing, with Bishop Wordsworth (C.Q.R. April 1900), that it is not genuine. —In Eth. C.O. and H. and (though less explicitly) in Sarapion the Father is addressed. In St. Chrysostom's writings (Brightman, L.E.W. 474) the priest "calls the Holy Ghost to come and touch the oblations" (τὰ προκείμενα); here, as in the Pfaffian fragment, the Holy Ghost seems to be addressed. In *De Sacerdotio*, iii. 4 [179], St. Chrysostom speaks of the priest bringing down, not fire like Elijah, but the Holy Ghost.

2. *What is prayed for in the Invocation.* In the later forms, at least, the prayer is for the descent of the Holy Ghost to transform the elements that the communicants may receive a blessing. Sarapion is unique in asking God to send His holy Word to come (ἐπιδημησάτω, a favourite word with him) on the elements, "that the bread may become (γένηται) body of the Word," "that the cup may become blood of Thy Truth," with a prayer for the recipients. Sarapion has not a very clear hold on the personality of the Holy Ghost. Justin Martyr (*Apol.* i. 66) appears to call the Holy Ghost the Word of God. "As Jesus Christ was made flesh by the Word of God, ... so the food which has been given thanks over (εὐχαριστηθεῖσαν) by prayer of the Word (or: prayer for the word?) which is from Him (δι' εὐχῆς Λόγου τοῦ παρ' αὐτοῦ), etc. Tertullian also seems to confuse the Word and the Spirit of God (*adv. Praxeam* 26, Migne, vol. ii. col. 212).—All other known anaphoras seem to ask definitely for the Holy Ghost; but Eth. C.O., H., St. Chrysostom's writings (*ubi supra*), and the East Syrian Addai and Mari (see above, p. 171) have no prayer for the transforming of the elements, only one for the communicants. The Invocation of the last named is, "May Thy Holy Spirit, O my Lord, come

and rest upon this oblation of Thy servants, and may He bless it and hallow it, and may it be to us, O my Lord, for the pardon," etc. The later East Syrian anaphoras have Invocations of the ordinary later type. Eth. C.O. and H. have not even "bless it and hallow it." The Test. Invocation deliberately omits a reference to the Holy Ghost which was in its predecessors. On the other hand, A.C. viii. 12 (Lagarde, 256[13]) have: "Send down upon this sacrifice Thy Holy Spirit, ... that He may declare (or make, ἀποφήνῃ) this bread the body of Thy Christ, and this cup the blood of Thy Christ, that they who partake," etc. And the Egyptian Anaphora, derived apparently from A.C., has: "Let the high priest pray over the oblation that the Holy Ghost may descend on it, making the bread the body of Christ, and the chalice the blood of Christ" (Sah. Eccl. Can. 66, Tattam, p. 122; Brightman, L.E.W. 462). Also the Anaphora of our Lord, while retaining the Test. Invocation, clumsily adds another of the later type. [See an interesting article by Dr. Swete on *Early Eucharistic Belief* in J.T.S. iii. 161 (published since the above was written).]

It would seem that after the rise of the Macedonian controversy the invocation of the Holy Ghost became universal, probably as a protest against the Pneumatomachi. As the Test. writer is very precise as to the personality and divinity of the Holy Ghost, we may conclude that his liturgy was written before the controversy arose. It is otherwise inconceivable that he would have erased an already existing petition for the Holy Spirit.

THE INTERCESSION (p. 74). The earlier anaphoras have either no Intercession or little developed ones. Eth. C.O. and H. have none; in Sarapion this feature is but little developed, but he recites the names of those prayed for, departed [and living?]. The Test. Intercession is simple, whereas that in Ar. D. is much more elaborate (see note above, p. 167; this is another sign of the priority of Test.). St. Chrysostom describes a rather elaborate Intercession at Antioch (Brightman, L.E.W. 474). It would seem, however, as if the Intercession was developed earliest in Jerusalem, for St. Cyril's description is very full, for the first half of the fourth century. He mentions prayers for the common peace of the Church, for the tranquillity of the world, for kings, soldiers, allies, the sick and afflicted, and all who need; the departed are commemorated, "first patriarchs, prophets, apostles, and martyrs, that at their prayers and intervention God would receive our petition; afterwards also on behalf of the holy fathers and bishops who have fallen asleep before us," and for all the faithful departed (*Cat. Lect.* xxiii. 8, 9).

THE BENEDICTUS QUI VENIT (p. 75). (1) Its *position* in Test. before communion is noteworthy. So in A.C. viii. 12 (Lagarde, 259[17]). In the modern Coptic it comes just before the communion of the women. It is not found in Eth. C.O. (which also has no Sanctus), nor in St. Mark (Greek), nor in the modern Abyssinian. It is joined to the Sanctus (perhaps a later arrangement) in most of the great liturgies (St. James, Greek and Syriac, all three East Syrian, and St. Basil, St. Chrysostom, and the Armenian). It is not joined to the Sanctus in Sarapion, but it is not mentioned elsewhere, as not belonging to the priest's part. It is not mentioned in Cyr. Jer. (2) *The past tense* ("that hath come"). In the Gospel passages of the Pshiṭta, as usually read, the present is used, but Pusey and Gwilliam (*Tetraevangelium Sanctum*, Oxford, 1901) give as a variation "came" in St. Matt. xxi. 9 from the margin of a ninth or tenth century MS. (Massora 2), and from the text of a sixth century Vatican MS., which also has the past tense in St. Luke xiii. 35. Thus we cannot be sure that James of Edessa had a past tense before him in his Greek copy of Test.; he might have been influenced by the biblical phrase which was familiar to him; in his description of the Liturgy of his own day, in his letter to Thomas the presbyter (Brightman, L.E.W. 490 ff.), he does not mention the Benedictus. With the "hath come" we may perhaps compare the Syrian interpretation of Maranatha (an Eucharistic watchword, connected in Didaché, x. 6, with the Hosanna) as meaning "The Lord hath come." As A.C. (*ubi supra*) has "cometh" in the Benedictus, it is not unlikely that the past tense is due to James. (3) There is no *Hosanna* in Test., as there is in A.C. viii. 12 (*ubi supra*). It is not mentioned in Sarapion nor in St. Cyril of Jerusalem.

COMMUNION. (1) *The rule about not communicating* (p. 76). Cf. Lev. xv. 16, 19, and A.C. vi. 27 (Lagarde, 189[25ff.]), where it is denied that the Jewish ceremonial law remains, though the Jewish moral law is upheld by quotation as for all time. The A.C. writer says that mere physical pollution cannot separate any one from prayer, only moral pollution can do so. (2) *Communion of the clergy*. We notice that all the clergy from bishops to subdeacons, including widows, but not deaconesses, are called "priests." It may be remarked here that there are two Syriac words equivalent respectively to ἱερεύς, sacerdos, and πρεσβύτερος, presbyter, the former denoting office and duty, the latter denoting rank, and usually confined to the second order. In this translation "priest" renders the former, and "presbyter" the latter. In Syriac the abstract word "priesthood" denotes the ministry in all its grades; thus St. Ephrem Syrus, who was a deacon, says that he was of the "priesthood." (3) *Communion of the people.* The communicant apparently says the prayer while holding the Holy Loaf in his hand, before consuming it. For the words of administration and the administrators, see pp. 222–224. The Syriac word for "babes" means either infants or children under five (so II. 8, 19, and elsewhere). The prayer said by the communicants is almost exactly the same as that now said by the priest in the modern Coptic (Brightman, L.E.W. 185^{25}), and by the faithful in the modern Abyssinian (Br. 241^7). Note the "Amen" before it in the Coptic, and the double "Amen" after it "to apply to the body and the blood." Cf. modern Abyssinian, in Br. 241^4, 241^{39}. (4) *The Lord's Prayer.* It does not occur in Test. But in the communicants' prayer there is a clear reference to it. It is absent also from Eth. C.O., Sarapion, and A.C. viii., but Brightman (J.T.S. i. 97) thinks that it is implied in Eth. C.O. and Sarapion. It was used at Jerusalem in St. Cyril's time in the Liturgy (*Cat. Lect.* xxiii. 11–18); he comments on it (omitting the doxology) and places it directly after the Intercession, before the Sancta Sanctis and Communion. St. Chrysostom mentions the Lord's Prayer, but his language (*in Gen.* xxvii. 8) does not necessarily imply that it was said publicly as part of the service, though that is probable (Brightman, L.E.W. 480, note 28). In Didaché (viii. 3) it is to be said (in private?) thrice daily. The doxology in the Test. communicants' prayer, such as it is, is a variation of the common doxology of the Lord's Prayer, and illustrates the way in which it crept into the text of St. Matt. vi. 13; the doxology of the Lord's Prayer seems to be still more clearly alluded to at the end of the post-communion thanksgiving of Test.

THANKSGIVING AFTER RECEPTION (p. 77). For the phrase "helmsman of souls," see the description of the church in A.C. ii. 57, noted above on I. 19 (p. 149).

ABSENCE OF VESTMENTS, TRISAGION, FRACTION. (1) *Vestments.* In I. 34 the deacon is ordered to wear a white vestment, but not at the Church service. Eucharistic vestments are referred to in C.H. (see p. 163). (2) *The Trisagion* (Holy God, Holy Mighty, Holy Immortal, have mercy on us), afterwards such a favourite feature, was probably not introduced into the Byzantine Liturgy till A.D. 434–446 (Brightman

L.E.W. 531[11]). We find it first at Chalcedon (*ib.* 590). (3) *The Fraction.* This is a more remarkable omission. It is not in Cyr. Jer., but it is in Sarapion and in the baptismal Eucharist of Eg. C.O. and H., for which see p. 221 f.

CHAPTERS 24, 25

PRAYER OVER OIL AND WATER. This prayer is quite different from those in Eth. C.O. and H. They have no reference to "gifts of healing" (but generally to strengthening and sanctifying) or to the Paraclete. The Test. prayer seems to be the work of the Test. Compiler, or, as the use of the name "Paraclete" (here only in Test.) suggests, perhaps of the supposed Montanist Church Order which he used. The name "Paraclete" is used in A.C., *e.g.* in the bishop's ordination prayer (viii. 5, Lagarde, 237[31]), where it is an interpolation by A.C., not being in Const. H. or C.H. or Eth. C.O. there. So in A.C. ii. 26 (Lagarde, 55[1]), etc.—The oil and water are for the *sick.* In Sarapion 5 there is a "prayer concerning the oils and waters" that are offered, with a reference to healing as Test. In Sarapion 17 the water is to be drunk ("that it may be to those who *partake* . . ."), and so in A.C. viii. 28 (Lagarde, 266[30]: "water for *drink* and cleansing"), where the bishop or presbyter blesses oil and water, mentioning the power of healing and putting evil spirits to flight. But in some cases it was poured or sprinkled (Brightman in J.T.S. i. 261). Test. does not say which. Sarapion 17 mentions the blessing of oil, *bread,* and water for the sick. We notice that the healing of the soul as well as of the body is referred to in Test. and elsewhere as in St. James v. 14, 15.—For the use of the name "the Lord" of the Holy Spirit, see pp. 40, 201, 241.

CHAPTER 26

THE PRE-ANAPHORAL PRAYERS. This chapter, which shows an enthusiastic love of prayers addressed to our Lord, is apparently the work of the Test. Compiler. There are a great many of these prayers in Sarapion, but they are quite different from those of Test. For characteristic phrases of Test., see Introduction, p. 21 ff.

Hymn of praise.] This word is used for the canticles as well as for those prayers which offer praise. For some instances of East Syrian "hymns of praise," see Maclean, *East Syrian Daily Offices,* p. 156, etc.

We praise Thee, etc.] This response is an instance of antiphonal singing, in which the minister says a verse and the people answer with another; cf. the Gloria Patri and Ps. cxxxvi. See below, p. 181.

That cannot be injured (p. 80).] Compare the rule about Communion, pp. 137, 239.

In Thine own person (p. 80).] Syr. qnûmâ. In the Eutychian and Nestorian controversies of the fifth century, the Eutychians maintained one qnûmâ and the Nestorians two qnûmâs in our Lord, while both taught one Parsôpâ.

Four hymns of praise (p. 81).] The hymns of Moses would be Exod. xv. 1–21 and Deut. xxxii. 1–43; the hymn of Solomon, the Song of Songs; those of the Prophets, the Song of Isaiah (Isa. xii.), the Song of Hezekiah (Isa. xxxviii. 10–20), the Song of Habakkuk (Hab. iii.), the Song of Hannah (1 Sam. ii. 1–10), and the Song of the Three Children (Apocryphal part of Daniel; cf. Test. II. 24). See Bona, *Div. Psalmod.* xvi. 12, as to songs from Scripture used in the Latin Church, and the reason he gives why the Song of Solomon is not used.

Three deacons, three presbyters (p. 81).] See p. 192. This number, of course, does not mean the whole number in the city. For the choir, see below.

The applied Sursum Corda with Benediction (p. 82). Test. applies this from the Eucharist to the other offices; at the beginning of this chapter there is also a reminiscence of the Sursum Corda. The East Syrians similarly apply it in the baptismal office.

The Tormentor of darkness, the Ray of light (p. 83).] If the reference is to St. Matt. viii. 29, the "darkness" would be the powers of darkness, Satan and his angels. Compare Milton's "Of the eternal, co-eternal *Beam*."

Who adornest all (p. 83).] The same thought is found in a prayer in the (thirteenth century) Pontifical of Bishop David de Bernham of St. Andrews.

THE CHOIR (p. 81). It is not very easy to reconcile the notices here and in II. 11, 22, either as to the composition of the choir or as to the method of antiphonal singing. Some features, however, are prominent. (1) The singers are not yet a separate "order" (a mark of early date), whereas in A.C. iii. 11 (Lagarde, 106[20]) they are distinctly so ($\dot{\psi}\delta o \acute{\upsilon}\varsigma$); so in Ap. Can. 43 (42) and 69 (68); and at Laodicea (can. 23) cantors are not allowed to wear a stole, a sign that they wished to do so and were pushing their claims as an order. The "boys" are mentioned in all the three Test. passages; cf.

Silvia's account of the boys answering Kyrie Eleison to the litany (p. 152). But here *male* virgins besides deacons and priests are mentioned, while II. 11 only refers to the boys, and II. 22 only adds *female* virgins. (2) *Method of singing.* We should not expect any mention of instrumental music. This was not introduced till at least the seventh century, and then in the West. The notices of *antiphonal singing* in Test. at once attract our attention. That in some form or other this method of singing was used by the Christians from the earliest ages, is clear from Pliny's letter to Trajan ("saying to one another in turn"); and this we should have expected from the example of the Jews. There are, however, two methods of antiphonal singing: (1) that in which one singer says a portion, and the others answer; and (2) that in which two choirs answer each other. The latter was the Jewish custom, and it is common in Christian Churches to this day, both in the West, where it is the usual custom, the choirs being divided into the sides of the dean (decani) and of the precentor (cantoris); and in the East, especially, for example, among the East Syrians, who name their daily office book "Before and After," from the "first" and "second" choirs which alternately begin the singing. But in Test. there seems to be no certain trace of this method, unless it is referred to in II. 22 in the one case of psalms said in *private houses*. In the first clause of II. 22 the other method is prescribed: "In answer to him who singeth the psalms ... let the virgins (fem.) and boys respond and sing." This is probably the method here, in I. 26. The people adopt it in the response "We praise Thee" (see p. 180), and perhaps in the psalms and canticles the choir do similarly, one singer saying a clause and the rest responding with the next; and so in II. 11. The people do not join in the psalms and canticles, but in II. 11 they join in with Hallelujah. In A.C. ii. 57 (Lagarde, 85^{13}) one sings the psalm and the people answer (ὁ λαὸς τὰ ἀκροστίχια ὑποψαλλέτω). The first method of antiphonal singing is attributed by Socrates (*H.E.* vi. 8) to St. Ignatius of Antioch, and may have been common in that city. For a full discussion of the subject, see Bishop J. Wordsworth, *Ministry of Grace*, 203, 341.

CHAPTER 27

Let the prayer be completed.] See Note to I. 35, p. 193.

THE LECTIONS. There are none except at the Eucharist, save as noted in II. 18, and so in Silvia and A.C. The words "the prophets and the rest" must include the "Apostle" (St.

Paul); see the latter specially mentioned in the instruction of catechumens in I. 22, II. 1; and it is probably intended by the "New [Testament]" in II. 4. In I. 31, however, only the Prophets and Gospel are mentioned in the catechumens' teaching (p. 95). For the readers of the lections, and for the position of the order of "readers," see pp. 203 f.

PREACHING. We note that, though the Mystagogia is not to be said before every Eucharist, yet there is to be always teaching before the mysteries (cf. the reason in I. 28). So the Western Reformers insisted on a sermon at the Sacraments. The "bishop or presbyter" teaches in Test.; in A.C. ii. 57 (Lagarde, 86[1]) each one of the presbyters exhorts, and then last of all the bishop, whose special work it was to preach. Bishop J. Wordsworth (*Ministry of Grace*, 164 f.) thinks that presbyters' preaching in the fourth century was more common in the East than in the West, and a revival. He mentions as evidence for apostolic times, 1 Tim. v. 17; for the second century, Pseudo-Clement (2 Clem. *ad Cor.* xvii. 3); for the fourth, the Council of Ancyra in 314 (can. 1), Silvia, A.C. as above, and St. Chrysostom (*Hom.* 2 *in verbis Esaiae*). Sozomen tells us that preaching was uncommon at Rome (vii. 19).

DISMISSAL OF CATECHUMENS. In A.C. ii. 39, 41, the penitents as well as the catechumens leave the church after the lections (in A.C. viii. there are elaborate dismissals). Penitents in A.C. are restored with laying on of hands. In Test. they are not mentioned as a class (see p. 194).—For the "laying on of the hand" in the sense of a benediction, cf. II. 5, 6, 20. The underlying Greek word is $\chi\epsilon\iota\rho o\theta\epsilon\sigma\iota\alpha$, which, with its Syriac parallel, is constantly used both for an actual contact and for a mere stretching forth of the hand in blessing; *e.g.* cf. A.C. viii. 36–38, where $\chi\epsilon\iota\rho o\theta\epsilon\sigma\iota\alpha$ is used for a benediction. Note that $\chi\epsilon\iota\rho o\tau o\nu\iota\alpha$, on the other hand, is used both of laying on of hands in ordination (*e.g.* in A.C. viii.) and of the election or appointment of the clergy.

CHAPTER 28

THE MYSTAGOGIA. The Arabic Didascalia has this in its last chapter (printed below in Appendix II.), but in a different form, on the whole shorter than the Test. form, though the Address of Death is slightly longer. The principal differences are, the alteration of the triple division of Adam in Test. into body, soul, and spirit (p. 85 ?), the omission twice of the phrase about our Lord descending into Hades in His soul (pp. 85, 87); it omits or alters the antitheses "passible yet not passible, Son yet not created, incomprehensible yet comprehensible" (p. 86), but retains "dead yet alive."; it omits about our Lord's hiding Himself from the armies of heaven (p. 86), but adds that He placed Himself in union with the Virgin's body; it omits about our Lord's self-emptying, and alters "the dead race of Adam in all its kinds" (or properties, see p. 185) to "Adam and his race" (p. 86); it alters "through it the whole nature of mankind, always bearing it (the cross), is made inseparable from God" (p. 87), to "who (or which?—the cross) at all times standeth on the highest grade of perfection." It retains, however, the personification of Thought, Intelligence, so characteristic of Test., and the reference (p. 86) to the blood and spirit of our Lord being our life and holiness (but in this case with a slight change). The Address of Death is slightly enlarged in Ar. D. Not improbably this address was familiar in many different forms, quite apart from the Mystagogia (see p. 185); and the Ar. D. writer would naturally insert the form which he knew. The strange conclusion in Test., identifying the Spirit with the "Voice" of God through whom our Lord gives thanks to the Father, is shortened and altered in Ar. D. into an equally strange form which has reminiscences of Test., and which could have hardly been the original of the latter, but which could well have been derived from it. In Ar. D. Jesus thanks "*the Word of God, the Father*," for the *speech* through which the world was made; "that is *the word* that *through the Spirit* is in Us, which speaketh with Thee alone . . ." The Bishop of Salisbury (*Rev. int. de théol.* 1900, p. 461) thinks that the Ar. D. form is the older. It is certainly shorter; and, had we been dealing with a prayer, this would be suggestive of priority. It will be noticed (compare the section on the theology of Test. in the Introduction, p. 18 f.) that Ar. D. has not got the clauses which Dr. Wordsworth marks as Apollinarian, and the inference which appears to be most probable is that the Ar. D. writer omitted phrases which by the time that he wrote (though not in the time of the Test. Compiler) had become discredited as tainted with Apollinarian heresy. In the concluding section Ar. D. certainly appears to be later; it is difficult to conceive the Test. Compiler evolving his conclusion from the short section of Ar. D. And as the preceding chapters of Test. are almost certainly earlier than Ar. D. (cf. pp. 154 f., 158, 161 f., 167, 176), we conclude that Ar. D. is derived from Test., and not *vice versâ*.

THE TESTAMENT MYSTAGOGIA. Rahmani's version is a paraphrase. In the Syriac there is no "ille est," "ipse est," etc.; the whole of the first part down to "Provision, Drink, and

Judge" is one sentence, probably depending on "we confess."
—*When said.* The Mystagogia is clearly meant to be said on Easter Even and Easter Day (in addition to Epiphany and Pentecost), and not on every Saturday and Sunday, though the Syriac would be patient of the latter interpretation. Cf. the times for the widows' "giving praise" in I. 42 (p. 109).

Dead Adam (p. 85).] Adam seems to be taken for man as he was in Adam, as in the Epistle to the Romans.

Who in His (human) soul descended in the Godhead into Sheol (p. 85).] The Syr. has mnaphshâ = Lat. animatus, perhaps = Gk. ἔμψυχος, *i.e.* endowed with a soul. We might render it "the animated one." See the Introduction (p. 17) for the alleged Apollinarian theology of Test. The phrase seems to mean that our Lord, who had laid aside His body, was still clothed with His human soul, which was (as Test. proceeds to state) continuously united to His Godhead.

Of one will with Him.] We may perhaps render "in concord with him" (Payne-Smith, *Thesaurus Syriacus*, 4083, quoting St. Ephrem). The Ar. D. has here "one shepherd," which (if it be translated from or influenced by the Syriac) might have come by mixing up the Syr. *R'IA, shepherd,* with *R'INA, mind.* If so, perhaps the Greek here had ὁμόνοια.

The Angels' Crown, etc. (p. 85).] The angelic hierarchy here somewhat resembles that in I. 23 (p. 72), but it is not so numerous. Probably there was no fixed scheme of a hierarchy in the Compiler's mind, as later there was of the ninefold order corresponding to the nine divisions of the priesthood, a favourite Syrian idea.

Passible (yet) not passible, etc. (p. 86).] Quoted by Bishop Wordsworth as Apollinarian. Note that A.C. viii. 12 (Lagarde, 255[11]), where the tendency is all the other way, has a passage not unlike this: "The Judge judged, the Saviour condemned, the Impassible was nailed to the Cross, and He who by nature is immortal died, the Life-giver (ὁ ζωοποιός) was buried that He might loose from suffering and take forth for Himself (ἐξέληται) from death those for whom He came (παρεγένετο), and break the bonds of the devil (cf. Test.). C.H. 196 has also, "that the impassible Lord of the universe suffered for us"; but this is bracketed by Achelis.

Who giveth light (p. 86).] This is Rahmani's conjecture (*i.e.* Syr. *DMNHR*); if so, the MSS. have left out a letter, as they read *DMNH.* The Ar. D. has "who maketh glad." Possibly, therefore, we should read *DMNIḤ,* "who delightest in."

Cast into ignorance the opposing hosts (p. 86).] Alike the good angels and the fallen ones are here described as kept in ignorance of the Incarnation. The ignorance of the devil was a common theme in early Christian times; cf. Ignatius, *Eph.* xix. 1.

Immortality instead of death (p. 86).] The meaning may be that we may be made worthy to pass from death to immortality. It is very doubtful if there is any reference to St. John v. 24. Ar. D. has "that we by His death might have a title to freedom from death and wake up in the real world."

The dead race of Adam in all its kinds (p. 86).] Lit., by kinds. The Syr. word for "kinds" is εἶδος transliterated. Bishop Wordsworth renders "in its properties." He remarks that Apollinarius represents our Lord as continuing ἐν τοῖς ἀνθρωπίνοις ἰδιώμασι, *in His human properties*, even after His Ascension (C.Q.R. April 1900). For the Ar. D. parallel, see p. 183. εἶδος was one of the Greek words on which James of Edessa wrote a commentary (Dict. Chr. Biog. iii. 333).

Come to birth as man, though He is God (p. 87).] Compare the Christmas hymn—

> "Man is worshipped by Angels,
> And God comes to birth."

The mystery which is revealed ... as it is (p. 87).] The literal translation is given in the text. Rahmani's paraphrase perhaps gives the real sense, "which once was hidden, but now the mystery is opened, and is plain to the faithful, not as it seems to be, but as it is."

By this (cross) *ask for yourselves* (p. 87).] The meaning seems to be: Make your petitions depend upon the cross. We might render: Ask this for yourselves; or: Seek to this (cross, as an oracle); or: Ask of this.

The Address of Death (p. 87).] The subject of our Lord's descent into Sheol and the "harrowing of Hades" was very common in early Christian literature. There is something like the Test. passage in the apocryphal Gospel of Nicodemus, xv.–xvii. inclusive. Compare especially Test., "flesh bound by me," with Nic. xvii. 11, xviii. 4, "suffereth no corruption," with Nic. xvii. 3 (Hone's sections). The descent into hell was made much of by the Marcionites. It is also mentioned in the legend of Addai (Thaddeus) preaching to Abgarus, as given (literally translated from Syriac) by Eusebius (*H.E.* i. 13) in its older form: "Thaddeus said ... I will preach ... concerning the coming of Jesus, how He was born, ... and His abasement and humiliation, and how He humbled Himself, and died, and abased His divinity, and was crucified, and descended into Hades, and burst the bars which from eternity had not been broken, and raised the dead, for He descended alone, but rose with many, and thus ascended to His Father."

Things that were on the left hand, etc. (p. 88).] There is a connexion between this allusion to the Judgment and the honourable position given to the older presbyters in I. 19 (cf. p. 150).

After He rose on the third day (p. 88).] If B.'s reading "before" be right, we might compare the thanksgiving which follows with Jonah's psalm out of the belly of Sheol.

CHAPTER 29

PRESBYTERS' MARRIAGE. Nothing is said about it; bishops and deacons are only mentioned in this connexion (I. 20, 33), perhaps because in the Pastoral Epistles only "bishops" and deacons are referred to. In Ap. C.O. 18 it is suggested that presbyters should not be married. Test. seems, however, to hint at more than he actually enjoins. He would prefer celibacy for all the clergy, but feels that he cannot press it. He makes no provision for the support of the children of presbyters or bishops, as he does for those of deacons (I. 33).

REVELATIONS EXPECTED. This has been noted as a Montanistic feature. They are mentioned frequently: I. 21, p. 65 (bishops); 23, p. 74; here (presbyters, and gift of healing added); 31, p. 92 (presbyters and bishops); 32, p. 97 (prophetical utterances by any one); 40, p. 106 (to the saints about widows, and to the widows themselves). In I. 47 gifts of healing, knowledge, and tongues are to be expected by any Christians (p. 114).

CHAPTER 30

APPOINTMENT OF THE PRESBYTER. κατάστασις would be the underlying Greek word. See p. 153.

PRESBYTERS ASSISTING AT THE ORDINATION OF A PRESBYTER. This is not in C.H. 30 or A.C. viii. 15 (Lagarde, 261[30]). But it is in Eg. C.O. 32 (so Tattam and Lagarde), Eth. C.O. 22, H. 108[20], and the "Gallican Statutes" 32. Bishop Wordsworth conjectures that the introduction of the custom into the Roman Ordinal was from Gaul (*Ministry of Grace*, p. 58). In the Roman Ordinal the bishop lays on hands first alone, and afterwards with the presbyters. See Note on I. 38, p. 195.

ORDINATION PRAYER FOR PRESBYTERS. In C.H. 30 the prayer

is said to be the same as that for ordaining a bishop; only "the name of bishop" and "episcopate" are to be changed to "presbyter" and "presbyterate" [*not* sacerdos, sacerdotium], and enthronisation is omitted. The Eg. C.O. 32 (Tattam, p. 34) says likewise, "Let him pray over him, according to the form which we have spoken of concerning the bishops.". But Eth. C.O. 22 has a separate prayer, very simple, and the germ of Test. It is as follows (Ludolf, p. 337):

O my God, Father of our Lord and Saviour Jesus Christ, look on this Thy servant, and bestow upon him the spirit of grace and the counsel of holiness, that he may govern Thy people in integrity of heart. As Thou lookedst upon the chosen people [the Israelites],[1] and commandedst Moses to choose elders whom Thou filledst with the same spirit which Thou didst give to Thy servant and minister (famulum) Moses. Now, O my Lord, give to this Thy servant grace which hath never failed, preserving for us the grace of Thy Spirit and our fitting portion, supplying in us Thy worship in the heart (cultum tuum in corde), that we may sincerely celebrate Thee, through Thy Son Jesus Christ, in whom be praise to Thee, and power to Father and Son and Holy Spirit in Thy holy Church, both now and always and for ever and ever. Amen.

Hauler (108[23]) has an almost exactly similar prayer. But note: (1) Eth. C.O. "govern Thy people"=H. "to help the presbyters and to govern Thy people"=Test. "to help and govern Thy people (so A.C. viii. 15); (2) Eth. C.O. and H. and A.C. viii. 15 have "commandedst Moses to *choose* elders," so that Rahmani's conjecture that we must correct the "ask" of Test. into "choose" is probably right, James of Edessa having taken ἐκλέγειν wrongly in the former sense rather than in the latter; (3) H. and Test. have simply "bestow Him on Thy minister," which, as Eth. C.O shows, refers to Moses; (4) neither Eth. C.O. nor H. has the Test. "made disciples by Thee," a confusion of persons being characteristic of Test.; (5) the close is slightly different in all three, the prayer being for "us" in Eth. C.O. and H., for the ordinand in Test.

A.C. viii. 15 have a separate ordination prayer very like Test. Sarapion's, however, is different. We notice that in Eth. C.O. and Sarapion the name "presbyter" is not mentioned, in H. only incidentally; in Eth. C.O., H., Test., no priestly function is mentioned, and none but reconciliation in Sarapion. A.C. mention τὰς ἱερουργίας (sacrifices or priestly duties) on behalf of the people (Lagarde, 262[22]).

For the phrase "Spirit of the presbyterate," see page 195. The idea is taken from the mention of the spirit in the case of Moses' elders (Numb. xi. 17, 29). The words "who doth

[1] Ludolf's bracket.

not grow old" represent a paronomasia which is often found, as in St. Clement of Rome (*ad Cor.* i. 3), perhaps in Hermas, *Vis.* ii. 4, and in Ap. C.O. 18 (Tattam, p. 20): "It behoves the presbyters that they should be in the world after the manner of old men," etc. But this is not in the Syriac Ap. C.O. (Arendzen in J.T.S. iii. 69). Cf. p. 202. Polycarp, *Phil.* v. 2.

CHAPTER 31

The Copto-arabic translation has altered and modernised this chapter much, and has omitted several things in it. The chapter seems to be the work of the Test. Compiler.

PRESBYTERS' FASTS. See Note on I. 22, p. 162.

PRESBYTER TO VISIT HIS PARISHES (p. 92). This is παροιχίαι translated; cf. II. 27, 1 Pet. i. 17. The word is used in the sense of "diocese" in A.C. viii. 10 (Lagarde, 245^7, singular; 245^{13}, plural), and A.C. ii. 58 (Lagarde, 88^9, 88^{15}), and Ap. Can. 14, 15 (13, 14).

PRESBYTERS' OR BISHOP'S FOOD AND RAIMENT (p. 92). Note that the Sermon on the Mount is here specially applied to the clergy.

TARES IN THE WHEAT (p. 93). It would almost seem from this that the writer regards the Christian dispensation as that "end of the world" in which, in the parable, God is to send forth His angels, and perhaps that these angels are the clergy. The prefixing of the Apocalytic prelude "on the End" lends some probability to this hypothesis. Otherwise, in the face of the parable, this is presumptuous in the extreme.

In the day of the Lord, the Word, etc. (p. 93).] Perhaps "The Lord, who Himself is the Word of God, and thus the Judge of those that hear," is the meaning. But not improbably the Greek had "The word will be demanded of him," though the Syriac gender is wrong for this.

Let him confirm . . . with the word of teaching (p. 95).] Copto-arab. inserts instead of this: "Let the presbyter have the power of a bishop in all things except ordination and consecration of holy places and the altar; and therefore a presbyter should exercise the works of virtue which also a bishop should exercise." Copto-arab. also omits the paragraph, "Let him fast . . . care for his work."

Let him receive of the cup (p. 95).] That is (perhaps) ordinary wine, but such as is used for the Eucharist. See p. 163. The text is translated literally, but Rahmani suggests, it may be rightly: "If it is proper that he should receive wine of the cup, let so much suffice him as . . ." This requires an extra letter (*D*).

CHAPTER 32

PRESBYTERS' DAILY HYMN OF PRAISE. This chapter is apparently the Test. Compiler's own work, and is modelled on I. 26. There appears to have been no fixed time for these prayers, but each presbyter would say them "at his own time," with some of the faithful to respond. As there were to be twelve presbyters, they would be repeated twelve times. At any rate they are not part of the public dawn service (see Note to I. 23, p. 164); the pre-anaphoral part of the latter is only appointed to be said when the Eucharist is celebrated— that is, not daily. Compare II. 24 (see Note, p. 236 f.) on the Hours of prayer. There nothing is laid down as to what prayers are to be said at those times. It would appear that these latter prayers were less formal and were not fixed. Daily services are more developed in A.C. vii. 47 and viii. 34–39. We find there fixed Psalms and the Gloria in excelsis. There is no table of psalms or lessons, however. Cf. A.C. ii. 59. In the treatise *De Virginitate*, of the end of the fourth century, much is added: fixed psalms, Nunc Dimittis, Benedicite. For Silvia's description of daily service at Jerusalem, see Note, p. 238. At Rome daily public service was not introduced till at least the fifth century; and Bishop Wordsworth (*Ministry of Grace*, 347) thinks that daily public morning and evening prayers were not known even in the East till the third quarter of the fourth century. This is only an argument from silence, but the evidence of Test. favours it, for it lays down no formal public daily prayers for all men.

LOVE FEASTS (p. 96). Lit., "rests," the same word as in 2 Pet. ii. 13, Jude 12. In other writers it also means funeral feasts; cf. C.H. 169, A.C. viii. 42–44 (Lagarde, 276[3] ff.).

A reward for saying prophetical words (p. 97). See I. 29, Note on Revelations, p. 186. Copto-arab. omits this sentence.

CHAPTER 33

S. numbers this 37, and the last part of our § 31 is numbered by S. 35 and 36, the number 35 going straight on from 14; the numbers 15–34 are omitted, whereas no notice is taken by S. in its numbers of our § 32 being omitted. This would show that S. is copied from a MS. which had not our § 32, since S. did not invent its own numbers.

DEACONS' MARRIAGE. See pp. 153 ff., 186, especially for the phrase "from a wife." Deacons' marriage is expressly allowed (but once only) in Ap. C.O. 20.

A handicraft.] Copto-arab. adds: "which may keep him from works of piety."

CHAPTER 34

For proclamation (p. 98).] Lagarde suggests ἐπὶ τροφῇ, but he does not like it. "Proclamation" does not make good sense, and S. did not understand it. It may be permissible to conjecture *L'BDTA, for service,* instead of *LSBRTA, for proclamation,* as *R* and *D* are constantly interchanged in Syriac. It will then agree with Eg. C.O. 33 (Tattam, pp. 34, 36), "he shall not be ordained for the priesthood, but for the service of the bishop," as in Test. I. 38, where see Note (p. 195).

THE DEACON THE COUNSELLOR OF THE WHOLE CLERGY (p. 98). Eg. C.O. 33 (Tattam, p. 36) says that he is *not* the counsellor (σύμβουλος) of the whole clergy; Eth. C.O. 23 says he is not appointed to be the teacher of all the ordained; H. 109[20] says he is not partaker of counsel in the clergy. Test. deliberately here extols deacons, and separates this precept from the beginning of I. 38, with which it is connected in the other Church Orders. The tendency to disparage deacons found in much fourth century literature is not found in Test. But see II. 10, and p. 223.

THE DEACON THE MYSTERY OF THE CHURCH (p. 98). Lagarde, σύμβολον or μυστήριον. Perhaps the former is what James of Edessa read, but he may have mistaken it for σύμβουλος. In that case the Test. Compiler would mean "the counsellor of the whole clergy, yes, the counsellor of the Church." Lagarde compares A.C. ii. 28 (Lag. 57[7]), which speaks of the presbyters as the counsellors (σύμβουλοι) of the bishop and the crown of the Church. For they are the senate and council (συνέδριον καὶ βουλή) of the Church. Copto-arab. reads: "that he may accomplish those things which the rule orders him (to do), with reference to the bishop and presbyter, that he may warn them about the things which are necessary, that he may be faithful as regards the mysteries of the Church." The translator evidently did not understand how a deacon could be a "mystery."

DEACONS BURYING THE DEAD. See p. 235.

DEACONS KEEPING ORDER. See pp. 133, 232. Copto-arab. transfers these rules to the chapter about the Liturgy (I. 23).

DEACONS AND THE SICK. See p. 234. Cf. A.C. ii. 32, 44, iii. 19, where they are *to tell the bishop,* and so Eg. C.O. 33

(Tattam, p. 36), unlike Test., which leaves them with a larger discretion. Later there were special officials who visited the sick, especially in pestilence; they were numerous at Alexandria, and were called parabolani ($\pi\alpha\rho\alpha\beta o\lambda\alpha\nu\epsilon\hat{\iota}\varsigma$). Their office ceased soon after Justinian. In the fifth century they became a somewhat turbulent body, and they distinguished themselves for their violence at the Robber Synod of Ephesus in 449 (Dict. Chr. Ant. 1551; Wordsworth, *Ministry of Grace*, 196). Deacons gradually endeavoured to extend their power, and to devolve their minor duties on subordinates. It is a mark of early date of Test. that so many menial works are given to deacons.

CHIEF DEACON ENTERTAINING STRANGERS (p. 99). See Note on I. 19, p. 152.

THE STOLE (p. 99). This is probably the first mention of this vestment in known Christian literature. Here it is used by the chief deacon (cf. I. 19) in the guest house, presumably as a badge of office. It is not mentioned as being used in service time. Outside Test., stoles are first mentioned at the Council of Laodicea in Phrygia (can. 22, 23), the date of which is uncertain, but which was probably held in the last half or last quarter of the fourth century. Those canons forbid subdeacons to wear them; they were evidently not then new things, and the reference is to their use in service. Their use in Test. merely as a badge of office, and only by the chief deacon (the other deacons and the subdeacons had not yet put forward a claim to wear them), would seem to point to a date earlier than Laodicea. We notice that the deacon wears the stole on one shoulder, as is the case at the present day.

NUMBER OF THE CLERGY. This will be a convenient place to consider the numbers of clergy in the different ranks. Test. here (p. 99) enumerates twelve presbyters, seven deacons, fourteen subdeacons, thirteen widows who sit in front. Copto-arab. says there are not to be more than twelve presbyters in the Church, seven deacons, four subdeacons and readers, three widows, and singers (it does not say how many of the last). The twelve presbyters would correspond to the Apostles, or to half the elders of the Apocalypse (cf. pp. 149 f., 200). The seven deacons are as in Acts vi. Test. omits here (but not elsewhere) readers, and we are perhaps (like Copto-arab.) to include them in the subdeacons. Rahmani conjectures from Copto-arab., and also from the number (three) of widows in Ap. C.O. (see below), that we are to amend the Test. " fourteen and thirteen " to " four and three." But this is unlikely, as from the arrangement at the altar (see pp. 70, 169) there must have been a very large number of widows. The following is a summary of the different orders, and is indebted for some of the references to the *Ministry of Grace*, p. 152 ff.:

(1) *Presbyters*. Ap. C.O. 17, 18, mentions three, but refers to the twenty-four of the Apocalypse; perhaps three is meant to be the minimum, twenty-four the proper number in the whole city. There were thirty-six (or forty-six) at Rome in 251, according to Cornelius' list in his letter to Fabius of Antioch (Eusebius, *H.E.* vi. 43); Wordsworth suggests thirty-six as nearly half of Moses' elders; but it is possible that it is the half of the seventy-two disciples of our Lord—"Seventy-two disciples" being a common substitute for "the Seventy" in Syriac literature, and also, *e.g.*, in the Abyssinian Anaphora of our Lord (see p. 249)? The late and untrustworthy Eutychius, Arab patriarch of Alexandria in the tenth century, mentions twelve presbyters in that city in early times, and the number is highly probable. St. Ignatius compares the presbyters to the Apostles' college, and they may have numbered twelve at Antioch (*Trall.* iii. 1); A.C. ii. 26 (Lagarde, 55^6) and H. 37^{26} also liken the presbyters to the apostles.

(2) *Deacons*. Seven in Cornelius' list at Rome in 251, also at Neocaesarea in 315 (can. 15, referring to the Acts). So Prudentius, ii. 18, v. 157. But Ap. C.O. 20 in Syriac (Arendzen, J.T.S. iii. 71) names three, quoting St. Matt. xviii. 16; Tattam's version (p. 22) reads with less probability, "let the deacons be appointed by three testifying," etc.

(3) *Subdeacons*. Seven in Cornelius' Roman list in 251. Not mentioned in Ap. C.O. At Constantinople, later, there were seventy (Dict. Chr. Ant. 1939).

(4) *Readers*. As to their numbers we have no information. Not in Ap. C.O. Cornelius mentions fifty-two "exorcists and readers."

(5) *Widows*. In Ap. C.O. 21 three (see below on I. 40, p. 198).

We note that there were in the East no acolytes, of whom Cornelius mentions forty-two at Rome in 251; and that in Test. there are no exorcists or doorkeepers as separate classes. Cornelius has no deaconesses, virgins, nor psalmists (singers).

CHAPTER 35

THE DEACON'S LITANY

This chapter is omitted in the Copto-arabic translation; it

is apparently in the main the Test. Compiler's own composition. For the word "admonition," see p. 169.

THE DEACON THE EYE OF THE CHURCH (p. 99). Cf. A.C. ii. 44 (Lag. 73^8), where the deacon is to be the hearing, eye, mouth, heart and soul of the bishop.

THE LITANY. (1) The ectene or litany is said in Test. before the Eucharist, as in all later rites; in the West, in mediaeval times, it took the form of the procession before Holy Communion; but in the East a litany is said at other services, in the evening as well as in the morning. In Silvia a litany is said at the "lamp lighting" service at 4 p.m. (see pp. 152, 238).

(2) *The modern Abyssinian Litany* is clearly derived from this *Testament* one. See Brightman, L.E.W. lxxvi. and 206–208, where it is given, and note especially the petition for late comers, as in Test. I. 36. The Abyssinian has "martyrs" for Test. "confessors," "widows and celibates" for Test. "presbyteresses" (for which see p. 199), omits deaconesses and catechumens, but adds singers, virgins, and ascetics; it has "excommunicated" for the Test. "persecuted," and adds several clauses. The petition for late comers is inserted at the end, thus: "Let us draw nigh and ask the Lord that He may hear and accept our prayer. For our thanksgiving we beseech that the Lord write our petition in the book of life, and the eternal God remember us in the resting place of saints in His own light. For those of our brethren and sisters who lag behind we beseech that the Lord grant them to have a fervent desire and turn away from them the bondage of this world, and give them a good conscience and love and good hope. For the sake of the body and blood of the Son of God, so be it, so be it."

(3) No response of the people is given in the Test. Litany, but from the example of Silvia and of later litanies we cannot doubt that they said "Lord have mercy" after each clause.

BISHOPS RIGHTLY DIVIDING THE WORD OF TRUTH (p. 100). So frequently of bishops: *e.g.*, A.C. viii. 10 (Lagarde, 245^{11}), and later litanies; so again in A.C. ii. 43, viii. 12 (Lag. 72^{16}, 256^{26}). Here James of Edessa doubtless translates direct from the Greek. The Pshitta has "preaching." For *Length of days* (p. 100), cf. A.C. viii. 10 (Lag. 245^{19}). Except for these two points the A.C. Litany differs greatly from Test.

THE BISHOP COMPLETING THE PRAYER (p. 102). Compare the presbyter or bishop beginning the prayer a little before (p. 100). Cf. I. 27. Can this mean giving a blessing before and after the litany, or is it left to the bishop (or presbyter) to pray extempore? In A.C. viii. 11, there is a long prayer after the deacon's litany said by the bishop (Lag. 246[30]). In the Liturgy of Addai and Mari (see p. 35) the deacon "completes" (says a bidding prayer?—Brightman, L.E.W. 271).

Chapter 36

LATE COMERS. (1) Instead of "that of the dawn," S. reads "the beautiful one." Lagarde understands it thus: "If any come late to the service, either when the Στῶμεν καλῶς, *let us stand upright* (lit., beautifully), is being said, or when the offering is being offered . . ." according to a marginal gloss in S. But the Στῶμεν καλῶς does not occur in the Test. Liturgy; and though no doubt this was what the S. scribe, or at least the S. glossator, understood by "the beautiful one," M.B. probably have the original reading. By the "hymn of praise of the dawn" we must then understand the pre-anaphoral prayers. (2) Lagarde renders "let him beseech" (instead of "let us beseech") as if these words were part of the canon. But the new context of our § 35 shows that this is wrong. (3) The words about late comers are inserted by Copto-arab. in the chapter about the Liturgy (I. 23). It says that before the Liturgy the *subdeacon* is to shut the doors. For these words in the modern Abyssinian Litany, see p. 193.

Chapter 37

This seems to be the work of Test. Compiler. Copto-arab. omits almost all of it.

TREATMENT OF POST-BAPTISMAL SIN. "Let not the deacon bring him in, . . . even if he repent." This has been treated by Bishop Wordsworth (*Ministry of Grace*, 30) as an example of extreme severity, and as Montanistic. The only parallel instance in the Catholic Church would be the ultra-rigorist Council of Elvira in Spain, *cir.* 305 A.D. But this seems to be a mistaken interpretation of Test., and has nothing else to bear it out in the rest of the work. The meaning appears to be merely that the deacon is not to have the power of dealing with the case. Much discretion is given to the deacon (cf. especially Note on p. 190), but in this case the matter is taken out of his hands.

PENITENTS. This is almost if not quite the only reference to them in Test. There are no *stations* of penitents. See Introduction, p. 37.

A work.] This is a characteristic phrase (Introduction, p. 22). Cf. A.C. ii. 61 (Lagarde, 92⁴): "Let such an one know that the handicrafts (τέχναι) of the faithful are activities (ἐπέργια), and that godliness is a work," but the context is different. So A.C. ii. 27 (Lag. 55¹⁷): "If any one does anything apart from the bishop, he does it in vain, for it will not be reckoned to him as a work."

LAST PARAGRAPH. Copto-arab. says: "If the deacon accomplish these [works of piety], let him not neglect the sacred ministry of the Church, which belongeth to his degree and which placeth the fear of God always before his eyes, and inciteth love to the places of the rest of God" (cf. I. 18 *s.f.?*, and Note on p. 148).

CHAPTER 38

THE DEACON NOT APPOINTED TO THE PRIESTHOOD. (1) This phrase itself would be sufficient to show that Syriac was not the original language of the *Testament*. See Note on the Communion of the Clergy in I. 23 (p. 178). (2) This passage is found in the *Other Church Orders*. C.H. 33, 34 say (but not in reference to the bishop alone laying on the hand) that a deacon does not belong to the *presbyterate* but to the diaconate, as [becomes] a servant of God. Let him minister to the bishop and presbyters in all things, not only at the time of the Offering, and minister to the sick. Eg. C.O. 33 (Tattam, pp. 34, 36) says that the bishop alone lays hands on the deacon, because the latter is not ordained for the *priesthood* (Lagarde, ἱερείαν) but for the service of the bishop, that he may do those things which he shall command him. It goes on about his not being the counsellor of the clergy (see p. 190). So Eth. C.O. 23 and H. 109¹⁸; both these agree with Eg. C.O. in referring to the "spirit of the presbyterate" which the deacon does not receive, and which Test. (I. 30) refers to in the ordination of a presbyter, where the others do not mention it. [Test. personifies it, and refers to it also in I. 35.] H. also fills a gap in Eth. C.O. (Ludolf) here, and adds that the presbyter receives and does not give the "common and similar spirit of the clergy" (communem et similem cleri spiritum), and therefore does not ordain the clergy, but at a presbyter's ordination he "seals" (consignat) when the bishop ordains; then the presbyters lay on hands in addition (superimponant manus). We may compare C.H. 47, which say that a confessor, though he does not receive the *form* of the presbyterate, yet has got its *spirit* (see next chapter). In H. 40⁸ and the Ethiopic Didascalia (Platt,

§ 16), it is said that the deacon does service for presbyters as well as for the bishop. The Statuta Ecclesiae Antiqua, § 4 (qu. by Wordsworth, *Ministry of Grace*, 166, who calls them the "Gallican Statutes"), give the same reason for the bishop alone ordaining a deacon—"because he is consecrated not to the priesthood (sacerdotium), but for service (ministerium). The eighteenth canon of Nicaea says that deacons are the servants (ὑπηρέται) of the bishop.

ORDINATION PRAYER FOR A DEACON. The prayer in C.H. 39–42 is quite different; it alludes to St. Stephen. Sarapion's prayer, which again is different, alludes to the seven deacons. Eg. C.O. gives no prayer, as in the case of the other ordinations. Eth. C.O. is deficient here (Ludolf breaks off just before the prayer). H., however (which breaks off in the middle of the prayer), gives us what seems clearly to be the original of the first part of the Test. prayer, as follows (110[9]):

O God, who didst create all things and didst ordain (perordinasti) [them] by the Word, Father of our Lord Jesus Christ whom Thou didst send to minister Thy will, and to manifest to us Thy desire (desiderium), give the Holy Spirit of grace and earnestness (sollicitudinis) and diligence (industriae) to (in) this Thy servant whom Thou hast chosen to minister to Thy Church and to offer . . . [lacuna].

Note that Test. has personified, in its usual manner, the "desiderium" of H. into "Thy Thought, Thy Wisdom, Thine Energy." The converse change would be very unlikely, and here we have an almost certain indication of the priority of H.

CHAPTER 39

CONFESSORS IN OTHER CHURCH ORDERS. (1) C.H. 43–47 give, perhaps, the original of the later Orders. A confessor before the judgment seat who is punished and is then released deserves the grade of the presbyterate in God's sight, not according to episcopal ordination, for his confession is his ordination; but if he becomes a bishop, let him be ordained. If any one having confessed is not tormented, he is worthy of the presbyterate, but let him be ordained by the bishop. Such an one, if a slave, if tormented, is a presbyter to the flock, he has the spirit of the presbyterate (see Note, p. 195); let the bishop therefore omit that part of the prayer [of ordination?] which relates to the Holy Spirit. Whatever else may be thought of this *dictum*, it is at least quite intelligible, which is more than can be said of the Test. passage. (2) Eg. C.O. 34 (Tattam, pp. 36, 38) agrees generally with the first part of the above, but omits about the torture. It says that they shall not lay hands (pl.) on him for a *service* (cf. Test. "the diaconate") or priesthood, for he hath the honour of priesthood by his confession. If appointed a bishop, he is to have hands (plural) laid on him. It goes on to say that if a confessor is not brought before rulers, or bound or imprisoned or condemned unjustly, but has been insulted ... and privately punished and has confessed (Christ), being worthy of every sacerdotal office, he is to be ordained. The bishop is to give thanks as aforesaid, but he need not be tied down to the exact words so long as he prays in an orthodox manner. (3) Eth. C.O. (Ludolf) and H. are wanting here.—We see that Test. has softened down the assertion of C.H. that confessorship is ordination, and omits the rather slighting reference to episcopal ordination, as does Eg. C.O. The last part of the Test. chapter seems to mean the same as Eg. C.O., but without the latter it would be impossible to make sense of it. (4) A.C. viii. 23 (Lagarde, 264^{23}) say much the same that Test. (I. 46) says of virgins. A confessor is not ordained; it is of his own will (γνώμη) and endurance; but he is worthy of great honour; if he is wanted for a bishop *or a presbyter or a deacon*, he is to be ordained. A self-asserting confessor is to be cast out.

When the shepherd advanceth,] or "reacheth forth [his hand]." But the former interpretation agrees with the same phrase in II. 1 (p. 116, "make progress") and with Eg. C.O. (Tattam, p. 38), "if when he *again prays.*"

For the *relative position of confessors*, see on I. 45 (p. 203).

But let him not pray, etc.] Copto arab. omits this last sentence, probably because the translator, not inexcusably, failed to understand it.

PERSECUTION. See Introduction, pp. 35, 36.

CHAPTER 40

WIDOWS. This and the following three chapters seem to be the work of the Test. Compiler, perhaps working on the supposed "Montanist Church Order."

WIDOWS IN OTHER CHURCH ORDERS. These do not develop the subject nearly so much as Test. (1) In C.H. 59 widows are to be honoured for abundant prayers, care of the sick, and frequent fasts. (2) In Eg. C.O. 37 (Tattam, p. 40) a widow is to be appointed "for prayer"; nothing is said of her teaching women. (3) A.C. have much fuller notices of widows. In viii. 25 (Lagarde, 265^6 ff.) it is said that a widow is not to be ordained, but if she has long lost her husband and lived well she may be admitted to the widows' list ($\chi\eta\rho\iota\varkappa\acute{o}\nu$). For ii. 57 see p. 199. In iii. 6 (Lag. 100²²), as in Test., women are not allowed to teach in the church. In iii. 7 (Lag. 104¹³) widows are subject to deaconesses. They are chiefly for receiving alms and praying for the donors. In ii. 26, iii. 6, 14 (Lag. 55¹², 101⁸, 108¹), a widow is called "the altar of God," as in H. 37²⁸ and Polycarp, *Phil.* 4; so in Test. her prayers are the "sacrifice and altar of God." In iii. 3 the widow must be "pious, having brought up her children well, and having entertained strangers without blame." (4) In Ap. C.O. 21 two widows are appointed for "prayer for every one who is in temptations" and for thanksgiving, and one for visiting sick women; so Tattam (p. 24). But the Syriac (Arendzen in J.T.S. iii. 71) adds, "for revelations and instructions concerning what is required"; Hauler 95²⁷ only adds "for revelations about whatever is necessary" (cf. the Test. words in this chapter about "widows visited by the spirit"). But on the whole Ap. C.O. discourages widows as much as Test. encourages them, with an argument (§§ 24–28) from which it logically would follow that women ought not to communicate, though it does not say so. For the revelations, see Note on p. 186.—In Test. widows receive support when necessary for themselves and their children, but they are appointed for ministry and are among the clergy; though they do not receive laying on of hands they are appointed by special benediction, unlike deaconesses. They are not allowed to speak in the church (so Eg. C.O. 37, Tattam, p. 40; and A.C. as above).

MONOGAMY OF WIDOWS is implied in Test., but not absolutely stated. Second marriages for *women* were little liked, or at least monogamy was approved, in all early ages. St. Paul testifies to this, but he directs younger [widows] to marry, 1 Tim. v. 14 R.V. Copto-arab. expressly mentions monogamy, and like St. Paul mentions sixty as the age for admission.

WIDOWS WHO SIT IN FRONT. Cf. I. 19, 41, 43, II. 4, 8, etc. The Greek was no doubt $\pi\rho o\varkappa\alpha\theta\acute{\eta}\mu\varepsilon\nu\alpha\iota$. That this was a recognised technical expression is seen by I. 19, where we read "widows who *are called* $\pi\rho o\varkappa\alpha\theta\acute{\eta}\mu\varepsilon\nu\alpha\iota$." We notice that in Test. there are no other widows, as an *order*, than these "who sit in front." The same expression occurs at the Council of Laodicea in Phrygia (can. 11), where the appointment of these widows is forbidden for the future (Hefele, *Councils*, ii. 305, Eng. trans.). "The appointment of the so-called presbyteresses ($\pi\rho\varepsilon\sigma\beta\acute{\upsilon}\tau\iota\delta\varepsilon\varsigma$), or they that sit in front ($\pi\rho o\varkappa\alpha\theta\acute{\eta}\mu\varepsilon\nu\alpha\iota$), shall not take place in the Church." This can hardly be only intended to forbid the appointment taking place within the walls of a church, but must, as Hefele shows, forbid the appointment altogether. Certainly these canons were not universally binding; but this prohibition in Laodicea is evidence that these widows (προκαθή-μεναι) were dying out, at any rate in Phrygia, probably all over the East. We therefore conclude that Test. dates some considerable time before the Council of Laodicea, which probably belongs to the last quarter of the fourth century.

PRESBYTERESSES (I. 35, II. 19) AND WIDOWS WHO SIT IN FRONT. Are these the same? We may almost certainly assert the affirmative in Test. In I. 35, in the litany, presbyteresses are mentioned between deacons and subdeacons, as in these chapters (living confessors are apparently not mentioned by name as a class in the litany). In II. 19 widows and presbyteresses are indeed mentioned separately, but probably there the "widows" mentioned first are ordinary widows, as they follow the married women; the presbyteresses mentioned afterwards would be the "widows who sit in front." At Laodicea they clearly are the same (see above). But it does not follow that this nomenclature was universal. The very words "that are called" at Laodicea and in Test. I. 19 would imply perhaps the contrary. In Syria it would seem that there were other professed widows than the presbyteresses. In A.C. ii. 57 (Lagarde, 86[20]), the virgins, widows, and presbyteresses (πρεσ-βύτιδες) are to sit in front, in the congregation, however. The Bishop of Salisbury points out (*Ministry of Grace*, 271, note 18) that the "presbyteress" of A.C. iii. 5 (Lagarde, 100[20]) replaces "widow" of the earlier Didascalia. The "widows" of A.C. ii. 57 would be professed widows, but the "presbyteresses" a higher class of professed widows. Epiphanius, *Haer.* 79, 4 (quoted in *Ministry of Grace*, 275), distinguishes between πρεσβῦτις and πρεσβυτερίς or ἱέρισσα, allowing the former as an elder widow, but not tolerating the latter names or functions.

PRESBYTERESSES (WIDOWS) AND DEACONESSES. In Test. these are quite distinct (see I. 23, 35, 40). The former bear to the latter somewhat the same relation that presbyters bear to deacons. Yet deaconesses are less important in proportion than deacons; they are expressly not included among the clergy, whereas widows are (see Note on the Communion of the Clergy in I. 23, p. 177). There is a somewhat close parallel to Test. usage in the *Acts and Martyrdom of Matthew*, § 28, a recension of Gnostic Acts (Dict. Chr. Biog. i. 30a; Dict. Chr. Ant. 2036b), where a king's wife is ordained as πρεσβῦτις, and his son's wife as a deaconess. There is no benediction of deaconesses in Test. In Ar. D. 38 widows are identified with deaconesses (p. 167). Neither widows nor deaconesses are mentioned in Sarapion. In A.C. their relation is entirely reversed (p. 198). There are no deaconesses in C.H. nor in Eg. C.O.

WIDOWS TAKING DEACONS WITH THEM. So in A.C. ii. 26 (Lagarde, 54[25]) deaconesses are to do nothing apart from the deacon.

THE FIGURES OF THE SOULS. This has been noted as a Montanistic feature. Bishop Wordsworth (C.Q.R. April 1900) compares Tertullian, *de Anima*, 9 *s.f.* (Migne, vol. ii. 702). This work was written by Tertullian after he became a Montanist; he ascribes to the soul a certain corporeality. Dives had a tongue in Hades, Lazarus a finger, Abraham a bosom; the souls of the martyrs were *seen* by St. John in the Spirit. But though there is a general likeness of this Test. passage to Tertullian, the resemblance is not very close.

THE HOLY PHIALS AND THE TWELVE PRESBYTERS. This passage seems to be explained by Ap. C.O., which here, as often, has left its mark on Test. In Ap. C.O. 18 we read: "All ... said ... There are twenty-four presbyters, twelve at the right and twelve at the left. John said: Well do ye remember [the Apocalypse here ascribed to St. John the Apostle?] my brethren; for those at the right, when they have received the vials (so Syr., but Tattam, p. 20, has "censers") from the archangels (Tattam, "angels"), offer to the Lord, but those at the left bear rule over (Tattam, "shall be sustained by") the multitude of the angels." Then earthly presbyters are spoken of. In Rev. v. 8 each of the twenty-four elders has a harp and golden vials full of incense, which is the prayers of the saints. But Ap. C.O. seems to limit the vials to the twelve on the right hand, who are more honourable than those on the left. It expressly makes the earthly presbyters on the right hand have the honoured office of caring for those who labour at the altar, while the presbyters on the left hand have the care of the multitude of the people. Test. seems to follow this interpretation of Rev. v. 8, and we note that it makes the twelve presbyters "praise my Father who is in heaven": they (in the words of Ap. C.O.) "offer to the Lord." Nothing short of this very highest honour is to be the ideal of the widow. Rahmani conjectures that James of Edessa read φιάλη for φυλή, and that we should render: "go to meet the holy bands; of these are the twelve presbyters."

But, in view of what has been said, this is very improbable. The passage is obscure also in Copto-arab.

CHAPTER 41

ENTRANCE OF THE ALTAR. See Note on I. 19, p. 149.

CONSUBSTANTIAL. This is used of the Holy Ghost, and is undoubtedly ὁμοούσιος in the Greek. But James of Edessa does not use the ordinary Syriac equivalent for that expression, "son of the nature of"; he translates it more literally for himself, transliterating οὐσία into Syriac. This word at once shows us that the book cannot be of Rahmani's early date; indeed, he notes it as an interpolation. See section on Theology in the Introduction (p. 16), and Note on the Eg. C.O. parallel to Test. II. 8, p. 214. For declarations of fathers in the middle of the fourth century as to the consubstantiality of the Holy Ghost, see Dr. Swete in Dict. Chr. Biog. iii. 121.—In the Creed in the Antiphonary of Bangor (Irish, between 680 and 691), the Holy Ghost is described as "having one substance with the Father and the Son" (unam habentem substantiam). It does not use the same words regarding the Son.

This passage of Test. joins to the word "consubstantial" the phrase "Maker of life" (ζωοποιός), used at the General Council of Constantinople (381 A.D.); so in I. 24 it uses "the Lord" as in the Creed of that Council. But in that Creed the word "consubstantial" is not used of the Holy Ghost. Thus it is not probable that Test. is quoting from the Creed in using "Maker of life." The substantive comes from 2 Cor. iii. 6: "The Spirit giveth (lit., maketh) life" (ζωοποιεῖ). ζωοποιός is used in the Creed in the *Ancoratus* of Epiphanius (374 A.D.), and Epiphanius, in introducing it, bids his readers "tell (your children) that this is the holy faith, ... as the Church received it from the holy Apostles of the Lord to keep." And so A.C. (see p. 184). Thus ζωοποιός was certainly used before Constantinople. Epiphanius (*Ancoratus*) also calls the Holy Spirit "the Lord." For the bearing of these phrases on the date of Test., see pp. 40, 241.

CHAPTER 42

THE TEMPLE, *i.e.* in the nave. This is still the East Syrian name for the nave of a church. Copto-arab. omits the prohibition.

BATHING AT PASCHA. This was a common practice on Maundy Thursday. In II. 6 the catechumens *bathe themselves* on that day. The Council of Elvira (*cir.* 305 A.D.; can. 48) forbade priests or clergy to wash the feet of the newly baptized. Pseudo-Ambrose (*de Sacramentis*, iii. 1; Hefele, *Councils*, i. 158, Eng. trans.) says that this was the custom at Milan, but not at Rome. Probably the usage may be connected with our Lord's washing His disciples' feet on that day. Bishop Hefele (*Councils*, i. 158, Eng. trans.) points out that in the Gallican Church there was a pedilavium of the newly baptized.

THE DAYS OF PENTECOST. See Note, p. 218, on Pascha.

CHAPTER 43

FIRST PRAYER SAID BY WIDOWS. Copto-arab. turns this into a night prayer for the whole of the faithful, by a slight change. Test. says it is to be said "quietly"; cf. I. 40, where the widow may not speak in church. In the word "Rejuvenate" (p. 110) we may see an allusion to presbyteresses (cf. p. 188).

CHAPTERS 44, 45

READERS AND SUBDEACONS. For their position, see below. At Laodicea and in A.C. a subdeacon is called ὑπηρέτης. In Test. there is no laying on of hands for either subdeacon or reader (see I. 45). But both are to be appointed on Sunday. Copto-arab. omits this, and in it the exhortation to a subdeacon begins: "I say to thee, N., pay attention in the fear of God that thou minister under the presbyters and deacons, and follow justly the precepts of the Gospel."

PROMOTION. We note that this is spoken of for subdeacons and readers; and the promotion of catechumens to being baptized Christians is mentioned. But there is no reference in Test. to promotion of deacons or presbyters. In A.C. viii. 22 (Lagarde, 264[21]) promotion is spoken of for readers, and in viii. 17 (Lagarde, 263[10]) for deacons. The reference both in Test. and in A.C. is to 1 Tim. iii. 13. There is no reference to the promotion of subdeacons or readers in Eg. C.O. 35, 36 (Tattam, pp. 38, 40). On the other hand, the Council of Sardica, *cir.* 347, says (can. 10, if genuine) that a bishop must have been a reader, deacon, and presbyter in succession. The fear was of the sudden promotion of a rich or influential man.

NAMING THE CANDIDATES. In Test. the bishop *says* the name in appointing both subdeacons and readers. In Eg. C.O. 36 (Tattam, p. 40) we read of the subdeacon, "he shall be named." But Eg. C.O. contains no prayers for ordinations or appointments of the clergy in any of their grades. The "name" is not mentioned in A.C. viii. 20, 22 (Lagarde, 263 f.).

RELATIVE POSITION OF THE MINOR ORDERS, AND READERS OF THE LECTIONS. In Test. there are traces of two features of ecclesiastical organisation which were obsolete in the fourth century, namely, the high position of the reader, and his privilege of reading the Gospel. (1) There is an inconsistency in Test. as to the reader's position. In I. 23 twice, in the arrangement at the altar and at the communion of the clergy (pp. 70, 76), he comes before the subdeacon. In the latter passage widows come before either, as in the present chapters. But in I. 35, and here, the subdeacon comes before the reader. In ancient times the position of the reader had been a high one, but at Rome in 251 he had fallen far below subdeacons (see Note on the number of the clergy on p. 192). In C.H. 48, Eg. C.O. 35 (Tattam, p. 38), he is above the subdeacon (49 of C.H., on subdeacons, is bracketed by Achelis as an interpolation; but in § 48 the reader comes after the deacon; in the passage C.H. 217, "subdeacons" must clearly be altered to "deacons," as Achelis points out; if he is correct, the uninterpolated C.H. did not mention subdeacons at all). In Ap. C.O. 19, 20, he comes even before the deacons; this Church Order does not mention subdeacons. In Tertullian (de Praescr. 41, Migne ii. 69) the reader comes after the deacon. On the other hand, in A.C. viii. 20–23 subdeacons come first, ordained (unlike the other Church Orders) by laying on of hands; then readers, also ordained by laying on of hands. We may notice also that in C.H., Eg. C.O., and Test., confessors come before them both; whereas in A.C., confessors, virgins, and widows come after subdeacons and readers. Widows in Eg. C.O. 37 come after readers and subdeacons (Tattam, p. 40); in Ap. C.O. 21 (Tattam, p. 24), after readers and deacons; but in Test. they come before subdeacons and readers. Bishop Wordsworth (*Ministry of Grace*, 189 n.) says that in Eth. C.O. 27 readers come before subdeacons, but after widows. This part of Eth. C.O. has not yet been published. This is another mark of affinity between Test. and Eth. C.O. Hauler's fragments are wanting here; but note subdeacons in H., both in the Didascalia and in the Church Order (40^7, 116^{21}).

(2) *Reading of the lections.* At one time the reader was allowed to read the liturgical Gospel. St. Cyprian says that he did so in his time (*Epp.* 38, 39), although by his time he had already fallen in rank below the subdeacon. Bishop Wordsworth (*Ministry of Grace*, 191 n.) suggests that the

phrase "minister of His words" in Test. I. 45 points to the reader's reading the Gospel in old times. In I. 27 the presbyter or deacon reads the Gospel, the reader the Prophets [and Apostle, see Notes on pp. 181, 210]. As the reading of the Prophets went out, the office of reader seems to have gradually gone out also. In I. 45 only "the book" is given him, whereas in C.H. 48 the Gospel is given to him; in Eg. C.O. 35 the "book of the Apostles" is given him; in Const. H. § 11, merely a book, as in Test. In A.C. viii. 22 (Lagarde, 264^{11} ff.) the prayer for a reader refers to his reading the holy Scriptures and "Thy laws," and mentions Ezra; the passage ii. 57 (Lag., 85^7, 85^{17}) gives the same rule as to the Gospel and Prophets as Test., and mentions the Acts and Pauline Epistles, but it merely says "they are read," and does not say by whom; perhaps by the reader. In Ar.-D. 38 the deacon reads the "Apostolic word" and also the Gospel. In Justin Martyr (*Apol.* i. 67) the reader is apparently distinct from the President and deacons. When the reader ends, the President prays and preaches, and the deacons give communion. In the Diocletian persecution the readers were much persecuted because they had charge of the books; subdeacons are also mentioned at that time (Wordsworth, *ubi supra*, 189). From the fourth canon of the first Council of Toledo (Hefele, *Councils*, ii. 420, Eng. trans.), we learn that subdeacons read the Epistle and Gospel in Spain up to 400 A.D., and that readers and doorkeepers were classed together as not being able to do so. Among the Eastern Syrians (Nestorians) to the present day the bishop, or failing him the presbyter, reads the Gospel. In the fifth century, at Alexandria, the archdeacon exclusively read the Gospel (Isid. Pel. *Ep.* i. 136); elsewhere deacons, in some places presbyters, but on great occasions bishops, read it, as at Constantinople (Brightman, L.E.W. 507, note 5).—There are no benedictions of minor orders in Sarapion, but in the preanaphoral prayer numbered twenty-five the following are prayed for in order: the bishop, presbyters, deacons, subdeacons, readers and interpreters, solitaries and virgins, etc. Nothing is said about the reading of the lections.

(3) Two further points in Test. illustrate the old position of readers. In I. 19 the reader is allowed (as an alternative to the *chief* deacon) to say the "commemoration," that is probably the litany, or the suffrages of the litany on behalf of offerers (p. 151). Also in I. 45 the reader is to be "with much experience." This is not found in the other Church Orders, except in Ap. C.O. 19 (which, as we have seen, places the reader

above the deacon). There the reader must have been "proved by a great trial" (Tattam, p. 22 note), words that are much more emphatic than those used of deacons. In C.H. 48 the reader must have the "virtues of a deacon."

With regard to the prohibition of laying hands on confessors, widows, subdeacons, readers, etc., Bishop Wordsworth justly remarks (*Ministry of Grace*, 286) that prohibition of a thing generally means that some one wanted to do it. In A.C. viii. 18 ff., deaconesses, subdeacons, and readers are ordained by the laying on of hands.

After I. 45 Copto-arab. adds a chapter about the appointment of a singer.

CHAPTER 46

VIRGINS, MALE AND FEMALE. In Test. they are not an order, and nothing is said of any breach of their vows. Their condition is of their own choosing, or free will ($\pi\rho o\alpha i\rho\epsilon\sigma\iota\varsigma$). But still they are used for teaching, catechising, visiting, and singing (here and I. 26, p. 81). Their prayers for the faithful are recognised as especially fruitful, and are given in exchange for the alms of the people. There are no communities of celibates in Test., and no profession nor formal vows are mentioned, nor is the metaphor of female virgins being brides of Christ used. Virgins are not to have a hand laid on them, and so also we read in Eg. C.O. 38 (Tattam, p. 40) and A.C. viii. 24 (Lagarde, 265³). But C.H. 51 allow laying on of hands if a mature age is reached. C.H. seem to speak only of men, Eg. C.O. only of women. Here in Test. virgins' veils are mentioned. But this is not a ceremonial veiling. Virgins are put on a par in this respect with married women. Cf. II. 4.

CHAPTER 47

GIFTS OF HEALING, KNOWLEDGE, TONGUES. See Note on p. 186. This chapter is omitted in Copto-arab.—C.H. 53, 54, say that if any one wishes to be ordained because he has the gift of healing, he is not to be ordained until it is made clear that the gift is of God. Eg. C.O. 39 (Tattam, p. 42) says that if any has received the gift of healing by revelation he is not ordained, for his trustworthiness is shown by the result; here Test. introduces the characteristic phrase "the work." A.C. viii. 25 (Lagarde, 265¹⁵) say that an exorcist is not ordained, ... he who receives the gift of healing is shown by God through revelation, the grace within him being evident to all. But if he is needed as bishop, priest, or deacon, he is ordained (cf. A.C. on Confessors, in Note on I. 39, p. 197). Thus Test. adds the gifts of "knowledge and tongues" from 1 Cor. xii. 1–10; the others speak only of the gift of healing. See Note on I. 23 (p. 169).

BOOK II

CHAPTER 1

"NEW COMERS" IN OTHER CHURCH ORDERS. (1) C.H. 60-64 give a very short form of this chapter; new comers to be examined as to the reason for their coming; if this is good, they are to be asked as to their trade, and be taught by the *deacon*, and learn *in church* to renounce Satan. If any be the slave of a heathen, he may only be baptized with his master's consent; let him be content that *he is a Christian*. If he die unbaptized, he is not to be separated from the rest of the flock (cf. Note, p. 211). There is nothing in C.H. about catechumens' marriage.

(2) Eg. C.O 40 (Tattam, p. 42) is also shorter than Test. Note the provision as to marriage. If the "new man" is unmarried, let him learn not to commit fornication, but either marry in the law or abide in the law. Test. hints a little more strongly at celibacy: "if he desire to persevere thus, let him abide in the Lord."

(3) A.C. viii. 31 (Lagarde, 267[23] ff.) say that new comers are to be examined as to reasons for coming, their introducers to bear witness to them; their manners ($\tau\rho\acute{o}\pi o\iota$) and life to be asked about; whether slaves or free; if a slave come, his master is to be asked if he witnesses for him; if not, he is to be rejected until he shows himself worthy to his master. If married, new comers are to be content with their consorts; if unmarried, to learn not to commit fornication, but to marry in the law. Nothing is said about catechumens and celibacy. A demoniac is to be taught piety, but not to be received into communion till cleansed. A.C. is nearer to Eg. C.O. than Test. is.

[Hauler is wanting from the middle of the ordination of a deacon to the middle of the Baptismal Creed.]

Lagarde suggests a lacuna in Test. after "providing for him." But M.B. show that if so it was before the time of James of Edessa.

Chapter 2

FORBIDDEN TRADES AND PROFESSIONS AND MILITARY SERVICE IN OTHER CHURCH ORDERS. (1) C.H. 65–79 have a long list of those who are not to be admitted—idol makers, actors, gladiators, huntsmen, idol priests; and (later on) it excludes fornicators, those who make a gain out of fornication, astrologers, etc. If they do these things after baptism, they are to be expelled until they do penance. A grammarian, a teacher of little boys, if he know no other art to get a living, is to *repudiate the heathen gods whom he teaches*. No man who has *received the power of killing*, or is a soldier, to be received. But those who, being soldiers, are commanded to fight, but have abstained from evil talk, and have not placed crowns on their heads, but "omne signum adepti sunt" [meaning?] . . .(here there is a lacuna; Achelis suggests "may be received"). Any one in office who does not clothe himself with justice to be cut off. Christians are not voluntarily to become soldiers; if compelled, they must beware lest they be guilty of blood; if they have shed blood, they are not to receive Holy Communion till they repent. If a Christian, having lived with a special concubine who has borne him a son, wishes to cast her off and marry, he is a murderer unless he has found her in fornication (contrast Test.).

(2) Eg. C.O. 41 (Tattam, p. 44), headed "Of Actions and Works," does not apparently forbid military service to those who are already soldiers; here also we read "a soldier *being in authority*." It goes on, "he who has the power of the sword" [but Rahmani, p. xxi. n., thinks that this ought to be a governor of a maritime district] "or a city governor *clothed with purple*" [note C.H., above] to be rejected or else cease (from their profession). Catechumens or baptized persons wishing to be soldiers to be rejected because they have despised God. Eg. C.O. has almost the same rule as Test., one which seems to be impossible in practice, that Christians are not to become soldiers. Yet Eg. C.O. probably represents a code actually in existence. The C.H. rule (see above) is hardly less impracticable. For how can a soldier help killing an enemy in war? The Council of Nicaea (canon 12), perhaps referring to the special case of Licinius, who required his soldiers to apostatise, says that soldiers who have given up the military service and return to it are to do penance for many years. The third canon of Arles (A.D. 314) is very obscure; it perhaps forbids Christians to be

gladiators, or it may (but this is unlikely) forbid soldiers to give up their service during peace. It says that those are to be excommunicated "qui arma projiciunt in pace" (see comments of various writers in Hefele, *Councils*, i. 185, Eng. trans.). There seem to have been many contrary opinions in early times on the subject of military service, from that of Tertullian, who treats Christianity as an exclusive sect having no interest in political affairs, to that of those who looked upon Christians as being bound to fulfil the duty of citizens. We know that in the third century there were large numbers of Christians in the army. But, on the other hand, we read of many in the persecutions who renounced their service, even in war, and were put to death in consequence. The Church Orders lean to the stricter view. But we cannot therefore ascribe them to sectarian bodies, who kept themselves aloof from ordinary Christian life; they, like many other teachers, only lay down precepts which it is impossible to follow strictly.—In forbidden trades, etc., Eg. C.O. agrees generally with Test., as to grammarians exactly, as to immoral persons, astrologers, and the like, generally. It says that magicians are not to be brought to judgment ($\varkappa\rho\iota\sigma\iota\varsigma$; cf. Test.), *i.e.* need not be examined as to their fitness for the catechumenate until they give up their trade (cf. "judged" in Test. II. 3). As to concubines, it says that a concubine slave, having borne children to her master and devoting herself to him alone, may hear (come under instruction), but otherwise not. If a man have a concubine, he must cease and marry in the law, or else be cast out. We notice that here, as in Test. and A.C. (see below), two distinct precepts as to concubines are given, one treating of the man and the other of the woman.

(3) A.C. viii. 31 (Lagarde, 268^{12} ff.) agree generally about forbidden trades, but altogether soften down the words about military service. A soldier is to be taught as in St. Luke iii. 14 (note how Test. uses the same text, p. 118). A concubine slave of a heathen who devotes herself to him only may be received, but if she commits impurity with others she is to be cast out. If a believer have a slave or free concubine, he must cease and marry in the law, or else be cast out.

Copto-arab. alters this chapter—(*a*) as to grammarians; if a teacher of heathenism have no other craft, he is to be warned by the priest not to bring forward the names of idols [before his scholars], and so he may be received; (*b*) as to military service and authority; all this is omitted, and also about the catechumen wishing to become a soldier.

Chapter 3

LENGTH OF CATECHUMENATE. C.H. 91 say that a worthy catechumen is not to be hindered by the time, and the teacher is to judge when he should be baptized; no period is mentioned for the catechumenate. Eg. C.O. 42 (Tattam, p. 48) appoints three years, but if any show zeal it is not the time but the character (Lagarde, τρόπος) which is judged. So A.C. viii. 31 (Lagarde, 269⁹) almost word for word.

In Spain at the beginning of the fourth century we find two years named (Elvira, can. 42). St. Cyril of Jerusalem does not mention a period. St. Jerome says (*Ep.* 61) that in his time forty days was the usual period. Later, in 506, the Council of Agde ordered eight months for Jewish converts as an excessively long probation. Thus the evidence shows that there was no fixed or even normal period in early times. Probably both before and after the fourth century the two or three years were not ordinarily maintained as the proper time of the catechumenate.

Chapter 4

KISS OF PEACE, ETC. (1) In C.H. 92, when the teacher has ended his daily instruction, catechumens are to pray apart from the Christians (in C.H. 63 a catechumen wishing to be baptized but prevented is called "a Christian"; see Note on p. 207, above). In C.H. 97, 98, women are to be separated from the men; younger women, virgins on coming to womanhood, to veil themselves like older women with a large covering, not with a thin veil.

(2) Eg. C.O. 43 (Tattam, pp. 48, 50) is shorter than Test. Catechumens are to pray alone when the teacher ceases; women to pray apart whether believers or catechumens. The catechumens are not to receive the kiss of peace when they have done praying; the faithful receive it, the men from men and the women from women. All women are to be veiled, not only with a linen covering.

(3) In A.C. ii. 57 (Lagarde, 87^{13}) the men kiss the men, the women the women; in viii. 11 (Lagarde, 247^{30}) the laymen greet laymen, the women the women. In ii. 57 (Lagarde, 88^{6}) women are veiled for communion.

(4) In Ap. C.O. 27 Syr. (not Tattam or Hauler) women are veiled for communion. Cf. Test. I. 46, pp. 113, 205.

"*The New [Testament]*" here seems to mean the Epistle. See Note on p. 181.—The phrase "new" used absolutely for the

N.T. is not uncommon in classical Syriac. See Payne-Smith, *Thesaurus Syriacus*, col. 1207.

This chapter is almost entirely wanting in Copto-arab.

CHAPTER 5

DISMISSAL OF CATECHUMENS. Copto-arab. has somewhat modernised this and the following chapters; it inserts a prayer for blessing the font in II. 8, and omits in this chapter the passage about a martyred catechumen.

In C.H. 99 the *teacher* lays a hand on catechumens before dismissing them. So Eg. C.O. 44 (Tattam, p. 50) expressly, "whether ecclesiastic or layman." A.C. viii. 31 merely say that the teacher may be a layman if learned and holy, for "they shall all be taught of God" (Lag. 269^{12}). Eg. C.O. refers to the teacher praying, but the prayer in Test. is peculiar to it, and is probably the work of the Compiler.

MARTYRED CATECHUMENS. C.H. 101 say that a martyred catechumen is to be buried with the other martyrs, for he has been baptized in his own blood (cf. Note on p. 207, above, on C.H.). Eg. C.O. 44 (Tattam, pp. 50, 52) says that a catechumen apprehended for the Name of the Lord is not to hesitate concerning martyrdom (or the testimony; Test. gives another turn to this), for if ill-treated "he will be justified in the forgiveness of his sins," for he has been baptized in his own blood.

For the "laying on of the hand," see Note on I. 27, p. 182.

CHAPTER 6

THE COMPETENTES, OR SELECTED CANDIDATES FOR BAPTISM. (1) In C.H. 102–107 they are to be witnessed to as to their life, if they have visited the sick, if they have been meek, etc.; the bishop himself is to approve them; the appointed Gospel for the season (evangelium illius temporis) is read over them, and they are several times interrogated. They are to bathe (see Note on page 201) and eat on [Maundy] Thursday, and to fast on [Good] Friday. A menstruous woman not to be then baptized, but her baptism is to be put off till another day [this is perhaps the meaning of Test.].

(2) In Eg. C.O. 45 (Tattam, pp. 52, 54) they are to be examined, if they have lived chastely, honoured widows, visited the sick, fulfilled every good work; if they that introduce them bear witness to them, they are to hear the Gospel, and

when they are dismissed "let them lay hands upon them *in that day* [the "daily" of Test. is in neither C.H. nor Eg. C.O.]. When the day of baptism approaches, the bishop exorcises each, "that he may know that they are pure. If any one is not good or clean, he is to be put apart that he may not hear the word *with the faithful* [contrast Test. "faithfully"], for a stranger can never be concealed" [contrast Test.]. The competentes are to wash and be made free on the fifth Sabbath (Lagarde rightly, τῇ πέμπτῃ τῶν σαββάτων, *on the Thursday*; cf. Test., "on the fifth day of the *last* week"); to fast on the Friday (Tattam, "on the preparation of the Sabbath"; Lagarde simply τῇ παρασκευῇ, *on the preparation*, the usual name for Friday), but "on the Sabbath" to be assembled, etc. [Test. seems to have read as Tattam, but to have understood it "on the preparation *and* (for *of*) the Sabbath, but on the Sabbath let the bishop assemble them," etc., thus enjoining two days' fast where Eg. C.O. enjoins one.]—Test. seems to have had here νηστεύειν with direct accusative; cf. II. 12, Didaché viii. 1, A.C. v. 15 (Lag. 145[19]), Oxyrhynchus Logia 2.

Chapter 7

EXORCISM OF THE COMPETENTES. In C.H. 108–110 the bishop assembles them on the Saturday (Easter Even), and warns them to kneel facing East, and stretching out his hands over them prays to expel the evil spirit (the words of the prayer are not given), breathes on them and signs them on the breast, forehead, ears, and mouth.

In Eg. C.O. 45 *s.f.* (Tattam, p. 54) they are assembled by advice of the bishop, commanded to pray and kneel; the bishop lays his hand (singular) on them and exorcises strange spirits (the words of the exorcism are not given), breathes on them, seals (signs) their foreheads, ears, mouths, nose (Tattam conjectures that this should be omitted), and raises them up.

The long exorcism given in this chapter seems to be the work of the Test. Compiler. The Syriac used by James of Edessa for "laver" (lit., washing) is a common word for baptism, and is used in the Pshiṭta of Tit. iii. 5; it represents λουτρόν.

DEMONIACS. In Spain, at the beginning of the fourth century (Elvira, can. 29, 37), those who became mad after baptism were debarred from communion till their death or recovery, while those who were mad and unbaptized could not be baptized till their deathbeds.

THE SEAL. This name is frequently used, as here and II. 9, for the *sign of the cross*, both in Syriac and Greek (σφραγίς);

e.g. St. Cyril of Jerusalem (*Cat. Lect.* xiii. 36), says: "Be the cross our seal made with boldness by our fingers on our brow, and in everything; over the bread we eat and the cups we drink; in our comings in and goings out; before our sleep, when we lie down and when we awake; when we are in the way, and when we are still. . . . Despise not the seal, because of the freeness of the gift; but for this the rather honour thy Benefactor." But the "Seal" is also used for the Eucharistic bread (Brightman, L.E.W. Glossary, p. 587), and, as in Test. I. 26, etc., for a conclusion of the service (p. 82).

Chapter 8

BAPTISM IN OTHER CHURCH ORDERS, ETC. (1) In C.H. 111-134 the competentes keep vigil all night with sacred discourses and prayers; at cockcrow they are to stand near flowing, pure, prepared, sacred water of a stream (*sic*, see p. 215). Sponsors are to unclothe the infants, adults unclothe themselves, women unclothe women. *Women* are to lay aside ornaments and unloose their hair, lest any thing *strange of strange spirits* descend into the water with them. The bishop prays over the oil of exorcism, and gives it to a *presbyter* on his left, then prays over the oil of anointing, "that is the oil of thanksgiving," and gives it to another presbyter on his right. The candidate turns to the West (So Test. and Cyr. Jer., but not Eg. C.O.) and says: "I renounce thee, Satan, with all thy pomp (company)." The presbyter anoints him with the oil of exorcism, that every evil spirit may depart from him. Then he gives him to the presbyter who stands over the water, and that presbyter, "performing the office of a deacon," takes his right hand, turns his face to the East in the water. Before he goes down to the water, turning to the East (so Test. and Cyr. Jer., not Eg. C.O.), the candidate says: "I believe and bow myself before Thee and all Thy pomp (company), O Father, Son, and Holy Ghost" (so Test.; cf. Cyr. Jer., not Eg. C.O.). Then he goes down to the water, and the presbyter lays his hand on his head and asks him the Creed (see p. 217) in three divisions, dipping him between each, keeping his hand on his head. *At each time* he says: "I baptize thee in the Name of the Father and of the Son and of the Holy Ghost, who is equal" [Achelis brackets the last three words as an interpolation]. When the baptized comes out of the water the presbyter takes the chrism of thanksgiving, and signs his forehead, mouth, breast, and anoints his whole body and head and face, saying: "I anoint thee in the Name *of the Father and* of the Son *and of the Holy Ghost* (contrast Test., Eg. C.O., and H.). For the continuation of these Church Orders, see the Notes to the next chapter (p. 219 f.).

(2) In Eg. C.O. 46 (Tattam, pp. 54–60) they pray at cock-crow over the water (no blessing of the water in C.H. or Test. as in Eg. C.O., A.C. vii. 43, Sarapion, Cyr. Jer., etc.); the water to be drawn into the font, or flowing into it, unless it be scarce (see p. 215). The candidates undress themselves, the *young* are to be first baptized (cf. Test., "babes"; see page 178), to answer for themselves if they can; if not, their parents answer, or a relation. After the great men (adults) the women, having loosed their hair and laid aside their ornaments (so C.H.; Test. extends this rule to the men also), to be baptized. None to take a *strange garment* into the water. The bishop gives thanks over the oil of thanksgiving and puts it into a vessel; another oil he exorcises over, and calls it the oil of exorcism. A *deacon* bears the oil of exorcism, and stands on the left of the *presbyter*. The presbyter takes hold of each candidate and make him renounce, saying: "I renounce thee, Satan, and all thy service and all thy works." He anoints him with the oil of exorcism, saying: "Let every spirit depart from thee." Then the bishop *or presbyter* receives him unclothed, and places him in the water. The *deacon* goes with him into the water, and teaches him to say the formula of submission: "I believe in the only true God, the Father Almighty, and in His Only-begotten Son Jesus Christ, our Lord and Saviour, and in the Holy Spirit, the Quickener; the Trinity of the same essence (τὴν ὁμοούσιον τριάδα); one sovereignty, one kingdom, one faith, one baptism; and in the holy catholic apostolic Church, and in the life everlasting. Amen." The candidate then repeats: "I believe this," and "he who bestows it" (baptism) lays his hand on his head, dipping him thrice, confessing *these things* each time. *Afterwards* he says the Creed (see p. 217) while still in the water, and again says: "I believe," and they go up, and the presbyter anoints him with the oil of thanksgiving, saying: "I anoint thee with the holy anointing oil in the Name of Jesus Christ" (cf. Test. and H.; contrast C.H.). No formula of baptism is given.

(3) Hauler, 110, 111, begins in the middle of the Creed, after a lacuna. The baptizer lays a hand on the head of the candidate and baptizes, as in C.H. and Test., between each part of the Creed. They go up, and the presbyter anoints him

with the hallowed oil, saying: "I anoint thee with holy oil in the Name of Jesus Christ." No formula of baptism is given.

(4) St. Cyril of Jerusalem describes baptism at Jerusalem in the middle of the fourth century in *Cat. Lect.* xix.–xxi. incl. The candidates enter the outer hall of the baptistery, and, facing west, say: "I renounce thee, Satan, and all thy works and all thy pomp and all thy service." Then, turning to the East, they say: "I believe in the Father and in the Son and in the Holy Ghost and in one baptism of repentance." Entering the inner baptistery, they put off their garments, are anointed with the oil of exorcism all over the body, and then led to the font and asked if they believe in the Father, Son, and Holy Ghost; they descend three times into the water, and ascend again (the formula of baptism is not given). Then they are anointed, and reference is made by St. Cyril in connexion with the anointing to the Christ (xxi. 1–5), "now ye were made Christs by receiving the emblem of the Holy Ghost" (cf. formula of anointing in Test., Eg. C.O., and H.). It does not appear from Cyr. Jer. that any other formal creed was used at baptism; though from the lectures as a whole may be deduced a creed like that of Nicaea.

(5) In A.C. vii. 41–45 the candidate says: "I renounce Satan and all his works," etc. Then he says: "I submit to Christ," and a long creed (turning to the West and East not mentioned) resembling the Nicene, but without the Homoousion and otherwise altered. He is then anointed, the "high priest" blessing the oil. They come to the water, and a long prayer is said to hallow it. The candidate is baptized in the name of the Father and of the Son and of the Holy Ghost; after a prayer for blessing the myrrh, he is anointed with it, and perhaps laying on of hands is indirectly referred to (§ 44, Lag. 227^{13}). The Lord's Prayer is said, to the East, followed by another prayer.—In A.C. iii. 16 (Lag. 111^2) the bishop anoints the baptized with myrrh; cf. ii. 32 (Lag. 60^{12}). The presbyter or bishop baptizes (iii. 16, Lag. 110^{22}), and the deacon receives the men, the deaconess the women.

A comparison of Test. with these other authorities suggests several points:

(*a*) The water in Test. must be *pure and flowing*. So Didaché vii. 1 (ἐν ὕδατι ζῶντι), C.H. 112, Eg. C.O. 46 (but this is not so strict in case of necessity). Hauler is deficient here. Note that in C.H., according to Achelis, the water must be *sea* water. But this seems to be a mistake. As Mr. Burkitt shows in J.T.S. i. 279, it is merely a flowing stream that is ordered.

In C.H. 213 we ought likewise, in all probability, to understand the Arabic rendered by Achelis, "aquam maris undosi," of a river merely. The rule in these Church Orders seems to be that the water is to flow into and out of the font.

(b) It is possible to conjecture, especially when we read the evidence of Cyr. Jer., that the *formula of submission* represents the most ancient expression of the faith, and that the creed is an addition.

(c) In all these authorities except A.C. *the baptismal action is split up.* There is a curious parallel in the East Syrian (Nestorian) rite as used to this day; in it the formula of baptism is divided to suit the triune immersion, and "Name" is said three times: "He immerses him thrice, at the first time saying: N. is baptized in the Name of the Father. They answer: Amen. At the second: In the Name of the Son. They answer: Amen. At the third: In the Name of the Holy Spirit for ever. They answer: Amen."

(d) There is *oil of exorcism* in C.H., Eg. C.O. (H. has a lacuna), Test., Sarapion 15 (but not by that name), Cyr. Jer. Not in Justin Martyr, Tertullian, Cyprian, or Augustine.

(e) There is no *formula of baptism* given in Test. or Eg. C.O. or H., as there is in Didaché vii. 1, C.H., Ethiopic Didascalia (Platt, § 16), A.C. iii. 16, vii. 43 (Lag. 110^{23}, 227^4). None is given in Sarapion, but as that is only a pontifical, it would not be expected there. It is implied, however, in Test. II. 7, p. 124.

(f) *The anointing with chrism after baptism.* In Test., as in C.H., the presbyter applies chrism blessed by the bishop; then in Test. the bishop says an invocation of the Holy Ghost, and lays his hand on the baptized and anoints him again and signs him with the "seal"; in C.H. he prays, lays on a hand and signs; so Eg. C.O. In Sarapion 16 the bishop consecrates the chrism, and no more is said. Bishop J. Wordsworth (*Bishop Sarapion's Prayer Book*, p. 56) conjectures that this was all the bishop had to do, and that the presbyter did the rest, the bishop superintending its application. We notice that in Test. the oil of exorcism and the chrism are blessed at the time of baptism.

(g) *Widows anointing women* in Test. Elsewhere deaconesses do this, as in A.C. iii. 15, Ethiopic Didascalia, § 16 (Platt); in the latter the deaconess anoints the women before baptism, clothes them again afterwards, and the bishop anoints both men and women on the forehead. In A.C. iii. 15 (Lag. 110^{10}) the *deacon* anoints the *forehead* of women; in iii. 16 (Lag. 110^{20}) the bishop anoints the head of either sex.

THE BAPTISMAL CREED. In C.H., H., and Test. this is the Roman Creed; in Eg. C.O. it is of the Nicene type. The first three are placed for comparison in parallel columns:

Testament.	Can. Hipp.	Hauler's Ver. fragm.
Dost thou believe in God the Father Almighty?	Dost thou believe in God the Father Almighty?	[Lacuna]
Dost thou believe also in Christ Jesus, the Son of God, who came from the Father, who is of old with the Father,	Dost thou believe in Jesus Christ, the Son of God,	Dost thou believe in Christ Jesus, the Son of God,
who was born of Mary the Virgin by the Holy Ghost,	whom Mary the Virgin bore of (ex) the Holy Ghost, [who came to save the human race]	who was born of (de) the Holy Ghost of (ex) Mary the Virgin,
who was crucified in the days of Pontius Pilate and died, and rose the third day (lit., to three days); [who] came to life from the dead,	who was crucified [for us] under Pontius Pilate, who died and rose from the dead the third day,	and was crucified under Pontius Pilate, and died and was buried and rose the third day, living from the dead,
and ascended into heaven, and sat down on the right hand of the Father, and cometh to judge the quick and the dead?	and ascended to heaven, and sitteth at the right hand of the Father, and shall come to judge the quick and dead?	and ascended into heaven, and sat down on the right hand of the Father, being about to come to judge the quick and dead?
Dost thou believe also in the Holy Ghost,	Dost thou believe in the Holy Ghost [the Paraclete, proceeding from the Father and the Son]?	Dost thou believe in the Holy Ghost
in the holy Church?		and the holy Church, and the resurrection of the flesh?

For the interpolated passage, "who came from the Father," etc., in Test., see p. 18, and cf. p. 96[10]. The brackets in the middle column are those of Achelis, who considers the passages so marked as interpolations. The last bracketed passage is obviously of later introduction. Dr. Sanday remarks that the "vivus" (living) of Hauler (cf. Test.) is a characteristic of Spanish Creeds, and found also in Nicetas of Romatiana (J.T.S. iii. 4).

The Egyptian Church Order Creed is as follows: "Dost thou believe in our Lord Jesus Christ, the only Son of God the Father; that He became man in a wonderful manner for us, in an incomprehensible unity, by His Holy Spirit, of Mary the holy Virgin, without the seed of man; and that He was crucified for us under Pontius Pilate, and died of His own will once for our redemption, and rose on the third day, loosing the bonds (of death); He ascended up into heaven and sat on the right hand of His good Father on high, and He cometh again to judge the living and the dead at His appearing and His kingdom? And dost thou believe in the Holy good Spirit, and Quickener, who wholly purifieth in the holy Church?"— It will be noticed that the belief in God the Father is omitted, though it is contained in the formula of submission before baptism (see above, p. 214).

In Pseudo-Ambrose, *de Sacramentis*, ii. 7, there is a very short Baptismal Creed: Dost thou believe in God the Father Almighty? [then the baptized is dipped the first time]. Dost thou believe also in our Lord Jesus Christ and in His cross? [then he is dipped the second time]. Dost thou believe also in the Holy Ghost? [then he is dipped the third time]. In this passage the writer refers to the baptized being buried with Christ.

THE FORTY DAYS OF PASCHA (OR LENT). This expression occurs in Ap. Can. 69 (68), "the holy forty days of Pascha," τὴν ἁγίαν τεσσαρακοστὴν τοῦ πάσχα, but there it is a strict fast. In Test. it is a time of prayer and vigil, specially used for the preparation of catechumens for baptism, but it is not a fast. So in Nicaea (can. 5) it is mentioned as a season (the holding of synods is the subject) without reference to fasting. In his early years St. Athanasius only speaks of a *week* of fasting. The custom of fasting for forty days grew in the fourth century; and in 347 St. Athanasius orders a forty days' fast. Throughout Test. "Pascha" does not mean Easter Day, but the season. So "Pentecost" is the whole season of fifty days from Easter Day to Whitsunday (I. 42, II. 12, etc.; cf. Nicaea, can. 20). In I. 28 (p. 90) we have "the *days* of Epiphany and of Pentecost." In Test. the forty days include Holy Week; not so in A.C. v. 13 (Lagarde, 141[10]), where the forty days are a *fast;* cf. Pseudo-Ignatius (who is identical with the A.C. Compiler), *Phil.* 13. At Rome, Socrates (*H.E.* v. 22) mentions three weeks' fast before Pascha, excluding Saturday and Sunday. Duchesne supposes the three weeks were *alternate*. With this we may perhaps compare the East Syrian (Nestorian) custom of specially marking the alternate weeks of Lent as the "weeks of the mysteries."

We notice that the Test. writer is not a Quartodeciman. He specially mentions Sunday as Easter Day.

For the parallel Church Orders, see p. 233.

CHAPTER 9

CONFIRMATION IN OTHER CHURCH ORDERS [continued from the last chapter].

(1) In C.H. 135-140 the presbyter wipes the baptized dry with a cloth, and brings him clothed into the church. The bishop lays his hand on all the baptized, and says a prayer [the words are given, but are quite unlike Test. or Eg. C.O.; no invoking in C.H.], signs their foreheads and kisses them with: The Lord be with you. The baptized answer: And with thy spirit. So each separately. [He does not anoint them after the prayer.]

(2) In Eg. C.O. 46 (Tattam, pp. 60, 62) the baptized are clothed and brought into the church. The bishop lays his hand on them with affection, and says a prayer which is the germ of Test.: Lord God, as Thou hast made these worthy to receive the forgiveness of their sins in the coming world [=Test. and H., "through the laver of the second birth"], make them worthy to be filled with Thy Holy Spirit, and send upon them Thy grace, that they may serve Thee according to Thy will, for Thine is the glory, the Father, Son, and Holy Ghost in the Holy Church now and always and for ever and ever. [Test. substitutes its favourite doxology (see Note on p. 159), and omits "in the Holy Church" (see H., below). Note how Test. interpolates into this prayer its favourite phrases, dwells on the work of the Holy Spirit, darkness of unbelief, God's love of man.] Eg. C.O. continuing, directs the bishop to anoint the baptized with the oil of thanksgiving, and to put his hand on his head, saying: I anoint thee with the holy anointing oil, from God the Father Almighty and Jesus Christ and the Holy Ghost. He seals him on the forehead, kisses him and says: The Lord be, etc. The sealed answers: And with, etc. So for each.

(3) In Hauler 111 the baptized wipe themselves dry (contrast C.H.), are now clothed, and go into the church. The bishop lays a hand (or hands?) on them and invokes (cf. Test.), saying: Lord God, who hast made them worthy to merit (mereri) forgiveness of sins by the laver of the regeneration of the Holy Spirit, send upon them Thy grace that they may serve Thee according to Thy will, for to Thee is the glory, Father, Son, and Holy Spirit in the Holy Church (cf. Eg. C.O.), now and for ever and ever. Amen. Then the bishop pours the hallowed oil, and laying (a hand?) on the head of the baptized, says: I anoint thee with holy oil in (cf. Test.) the Lord the Father Almighty and Jesus Christ and the Holy Ghost. He

seals him on the forehead, kisses him, and says: The Lord be, etc. The sealed answers: And with, etc. So for each. [The Test. "God of the meek" is the Compiler's interpolation.]

We see that in Test., Eg. C.O., and H. there is a double anointing after baptism, but not in C.H. All these Church Orders mention the laying on of hands as distinct from the anointing. Tèrtullian (*de Bapt.* 7, 8; Migne, vol. i. col. 1315, 1316) mentions both: "Then, having come out of the laver, we are anointed with the blessed unction.... After that a hand is imposed, calling on and inviting the Holy Spirit by a benediction." Cf. his later work, *De resurrectione carnis* (§ 8; Migne, ii. 852): "The flesh is washed ... the flesh is anointed ... the flesh is signed ... the flesh is overshadowed by the laying on of the hand ... the flesh feeds on the body and blood of Christ." St. Cyril of Jerusalem does not mention the laying on of hands nor yet a second unction. To come to later times, the East Syrians (Nestorians) alone of Christians have always retained the laying on of the hand as a deliberate act in confirmation; in their ritual the anointing after baptism is not expressly mentioned, though it is the custom of some at least of their priests to anoint at the time of laying on the hand. The Latin Church lays on the hand indirectly by touching the baptized in the act of anointing. But the Orthodox Easterns anoint in practice with a spoon (though this is not mentioned in the Ritual), and have no laying on of hands in confirmation.

CHAPTER 10

THE BAPTISMAL EUCHARIST. At first sight it seems as if we had in Test. two separate compilers, to one of whom the Liturgy in I. 23 is due, and to another the supplementary account in the present chapter. But this is not the case. The other Church Orders have all the same peculiarity; and Achelis (*Die Canones Hippolyti* 192) points out that Justin Martyr (*Apol.* i. 65–67) similarly gives two descriptions, one of the Baptismal Eucharist and the other of the ordinary Sunday rite. The usage of baptism before the Eucharist is natural; though the East Syrians (Nestorians) reverse the order and have baptism *after* the Eucharist. But they do not in practice communicate the newly baptized *at baptism.*

BAPTISMAL EUCHARIST IN OTHER CHURCH ORDERS. (1) In C.H. 141–149 the baptized pray with all the people, who kiss them; then the deacon [begins to sacrifice],[1] the bishop brings down "reliquias mysteriales" [of the body and blood of our Lord].[1] Then he communicates the people, the presbyters bearing other cups of milk and honey, to teach the communicants that they are born again as infants. If there are no presbyters, the deacons bear the cups. The bishop says: This is the body of Christ, and This is the blood of Christ; to each they answer: Amen. Then they take milk and honey (cf. Tertullian, *de Cor. Mil.* 3, Migne ii. 99). Now, being perfect Christians, they are to persevere in good works.

(2) In Eg. C.O. 46 (Tattam, pp. 62–66) the people all pray together, and all the baptized, and say the Peace with their mouths. The deacons (Lagarde, "deacon") *bring the Eucharist to the bishop* (note Test. and the parallels, and Note, p. 222), who gives thanks over the bread because it is the type of the body of Christ, and over the cup because it is (the type of?) the blood of Christ. Milk and honey are mixed [not so C.H.], and Exod. iii. 8 is referred to: " this is the body of Christ which was given for us, that those who believe on Him should be nourished by it as infants" (cf. C.H.). . . . The bishop divides and gives the bread, saying: This is the bread of heaven, the body of Christ. The communicant answers, Amen. If there are not more presbyters, the deacon takes the cup and gives them the blood of Christ Jesus our Lord, and the milk and honey. He who gives the cup says: This is the blood of Christ Jesus our Lord. Answer, Amen. [Test. altogether and deliberately omits the milk and honey. See pp. 24, 171, 173, 176, 223, 224.] Then they are to hasten to do good works, making progress *in the service of God* (cf. Test.). The teaching of the resurrection is then referred to, but the passage is not clear. The bishop is to declare anything else that is fitting to the baptized. "This is the white stone," etc. (see p. 224).

(3) In Hauler 111–113 the newly baptized pray with all the people, not praying before with the faithful unless they have done (as commanded). Then they pray and give the Peace, and the oblation is to be *offered* (offeratur) by the *deacons to the bishop* (see p. 222), and he gives thanks [over] the bread as for an example (exemplum), which the Greek (*sic*) calls an antitype, of the body of Christ, [and over] the cup mixed with wine for an antitype, which the Greek calls a similitude (cf. Test.) of the blood which was shed for all who believed in Him; milk and honey ("melle"—error) mixed together for a complete symbol (ad plenitudinem; cf. Test. I. 23, p. 69) of the promise to the fathers, which He said [was] a land flowing with milk and

---
[1] Achelis' brackets.

honey, which Christ also gives as His flesh, through which the babes (parvuli) who believe are nourished, [Christ] in the delight (suavitate) of the word making the bitter things of the heart sweet, and [making] water for an offering for a sign of the laver, so that also the inner man, which is animal, may follow [*sic*? but ungrammatical] like things, as also the body (aquam vero in oblationem in indicium lavacri ut et interior homo quod est animale similia consequantur sicut et corpus). [This passage is extremely obscure both in H. and Test., and is clearly original in neither. The "animale" would represent ψυχικόν; Rahmani's "spiritualis" is clearly wrong.] H. continues: The bishop is to give the reason of all these things to those who partake; breaking the bread, he gives to each a portion, saying: The heavenly bread in Christ Jesus. The recipient answers: Amen. If there are not enough presbyters, the deacons are to hold the cups, and stand by with honesty and moderation, one holding the water, the second the milk [mixed with honey, see above], and the third the wine [mixed with water, see above]. The communicant to taste of each, the administrator saying thrice: In God the Father Almighty. Answer: Amen. Then: And [in] the Lord Jesus Christ and the Holy Ghost and the Holy Church. Answer: Amen. So for each one. Then every one is to hasten to do good work (operam).

OBLATION OFFERED BY THE DEACON. The Syriac word will do for "offered" or "brought near." Eg. C.O. favours the latter meaning, H. the former; the meaning in C.H. is doubtful. The word "to offer" (offerre), for the deacons bringing the elements to the bishop to consecrate, is uncommon. It is used generally for the act of consecrating the Eucharist, as at the Council of Arles, A.D. 314, which forbade deacons to "offer" (can. 15), that is, clearly (cf. canon 19) to celebrate the Eucharist. For this sense see also the eighteenth canon of Nicaea, which denies that deacons can offer (προσφέρειν); and A.C. viii. 27 (Lagarde, 266[12]), "the deacon . . . does not offer" (οὐ προσφέρει). It seems, however, sometimes to be used in the sense of administering the elements; see Hefele, *Councils*, i. 427, Eng. trans.

THE EUCHARISTIC TYPE. See p. 172. The expression occurs also in the Eg. C.O. and H. parallels to this chapter.

DEACONS WAVING [FANS?], see Note on p. 167.

WORDS OF ADMINISTRATION. In Test. these are only given for the Eucharistic Bread (see I. 23, Note, p. 170). Bishop J. Wordsworth, indeed, suggests (*Rev. int. de théol.* 1900, p. 472) that here we have two formulae, the first part being said over the bread, the second over the cup; he compares with the second half the Mystagogia expression (I. 28): "whose body being broken becometh our salvation, and [His] blood and spirit [our] life and holiness, and the water our cleansing" (p. 86). But the Abyssinian Anaphora of our Lord, which is derived from Test., has: "The body of Jesus Christ *which is of* the Holy Ghost, to hallow soul and spirit" (Brightman, L.E.W. 240 note; Ludolf does not give the Communion). It is more probable that the words "which is of"—that is, three letters in the Syriac, *DMN*—should have dropped out of the Syriac text, than that the Anaphora of our Lord should have inserted them to make sense. The Abyssinian "Anaphora of the Elders" has as the words of administration: The holy body of Emmanuel our very God, which He took of the Lady of us all (Brightman, L.E.W. 241 note). Mark the Hermit (*c. Nestorian.* 24, qu. by Brightman, L.E.W. p. civ., Addenda) at Ancyra, *cir.* 430 A.D., gives words of administration in one kind: "For thou hearest the priest (say): The Holy Body of Jesus Christ, unto eternal life." In A.C. viii. 12 (Lagarde, 259^{25} ff.) we have the double formula: The body of Christ. Answer: Amen. The blood of Christ, the cup of life. Answer: Amen. And similarly in the other Church Orders noted above.

THE ADMINISTRATORS. In Justin Martyr, *Apol.* i. 65, the deacons administer both the bread and the cup. And this is probably the meaning of Test., but Copto-arab. has omitted the words (see also page 234). In the Church Orders and later liturgies the practice varies. In C.H. 146, 147, the bishop administers in both kinds, and so in Ar. D. 38, Tertull. *de Cor.* 3. But in C.H. 214, 216, the bishop or presbyter may give leave to the deacon to administer. In Eg. C.O. and H. the bishop administers the bread, and the presbyters the cup (H., "cups"), or if there are not enough presbyters, then the deacons. There is no direction in Eth. C.O. (Ludolf). In A.C. viii. 12 (Lagarde, 259^{25} ff.) the bishop gives the bread, the deacon the cup. So in the Egyptian Liturgy derived from A.C. (Sah. Eccl. Can. 66; Tattam, p. 124; Brightman, L.E.W. 462). In the modern Abyssinian the priest gives the bread, the deacon the cup. The matter is not clear in St. Mark's Liturgy and in the modern Coptic. — The prohibition against deacons communicating presbyters is found in the eighteenth canon of Nicaea, which also forbids deacons to receive before bishops; the deacons are to receive after the presbyters, a bishop or presbyter administering to them; deacons also are not to sit among the presbyters; this is said to be against the *canons*. The Council of Arles (can. 15, 18) also forbade deacons to put themselves forward. See pp. 190, 234.

It is noteworthy that in this matter Test. shows an earlier characteristic than C.H. or Eg. C.O. This, however, is a part of the honour given in Test. to deacons.

SPILLING THE CHALICE. The other Church Orders have injunctions somewhat similar to Test. C.H. 209 say that the administrators and recipients of the mystery are to see that nothing fall to the ground lest an evil spirit get possession of it. Eg. C.O. 59 (Tattam, p. 78) says that every one is to take care that no unbeliever or mouse (Arab., a fly) or other creature eat of the Eucharist, or that any other thing have fallen into it which has strayed, for it is the body of Christ. So H. 117[16], but it has "or lest any of it fall (cadeat for cadat) and perish." C.H. 207 speak of a fly or any thing falling into the cup. Eg. C.O. 60 (Tattam, p. 80) enjoins care about spilling the cup. lest a strange spirit lick it up (so H. 117[24]).— Copto-arab. adds a sentence about portions of the bread falling to the ground. Cf. Tertullian, de Cor. Mil. 3 (Migne ii. 99).

TEACHING OF THE RESURRECTION AFTER BAPTISM. We note that the clause "the resurrection of the flesh" is not in the Test. Baptismal Creed (II. 8) as it is in Hauler. The present passage leads us to suppose that it was purposely omitted. The postponement of teaching on the resurrection till after baptism seems to be a peculiarity of Test. St. Cyril taught his catechumens about it before baptism (Cat. Lect. xv.).

THE NEW DECREE OR STONE. The parallel passage of Eg. C.O. 46 (Tattam, p. 66) has: "This is the white stone ($\dot{\eta}$ $\psi\tilde{\eta}\varphi o\varsigma$ $\dot{\eta}$ $\lambda\epsilon\upsilon\kappa\dot{\eta}$, Lagarde) about which John said that a new name is written on it, which no one knoweth but he who shall receive the stone." The passage is not in C.H., and H. breaks off before this. This is clearly a quotation from Rev. ii. 17 and an instructive early exegesis of that verse (for the "new name," cf. Isa. lxii. 2; Rev. iii. 12, xix. 12). Probably the Test. writer also wrote $\alpha\mathring{\upsilon}\tau\eta$ $\dot{\epsilon}\sigma\tau\iota\nu$ $\dot{\eta}$ ψ. $\dot{\eta}$ λ., and James of Edessa (who did not verify his quotations carefully, as we see elsewhere in Test.) misread $\lambda\epsilon\upsilon\kappa\dot{\eta}$, white, into $\kappa\alpha\iota\nu\dot{\eta}$, new (from the next line), and then translated $\dot{\eta}$ ψ. $\dot{\eta}$ $\kappa\alpha\iota\nu\dot{\eta}$, the new decree (Syr. PSQA). This Syriac word is used for a translation of $\psi\tilde{\eta}\varphi o\varsigma$ (which has also the sense of "decree") in Syriac editions of Cyril of Alexandria and Athanasius (Payne-Smith, Thesaurus Syriacus, 3198), and it is noteworthy that the Syriac translator of the Apocalypse (perhaps Thomas of Harkel, A.D. 622) renders $\psi\tilde{\eta}\varphi o\varsigma$ by hûshbânâ (computation), though he retains the adjective "white."

It would thus appear that *two* Syriac writers of the seventh century, Thomas and James, did not understand the ψῆφος of Rev. ii. 17 to mean " a stone."—Achelis (*Die Can. Hipp.* 285) gives a Hippolytean fragment (but he brackets this passage as interpolated), which says of asceticism: " This is the precious stone (lapis pretiosus) which, as John bears witness, no one knows except he who has received it."—What is the antecedent of "this" in Test. and Eg. C.O.? The doctrine of the resurrection, or baptism, or the Eucharist? In Test. apparently the resurrection; in Eg. C.O. probably the complete course of Christian doctrine, including the resurrection; in the Hippolytean fragment, self-denial. In the Revelation we have no clue; the interpretation of that passage by later writers may be seen in Alford's commentary, which mentions also a Rabbinical tradition that there fell together with the manna precious stones (lapides pretiosi; cf. Hipp. fragm. above) and pearls.[1] In any case we must in Test. supply " it," *i.e.* the ψῆφος, after " receive," not " the Eucharist" as Rahmani conjectures.—In this passage Copto-arab. has made an alteration. It reads: " Let no one know the *mysteries* of the kingdom of heaven before holy baptism is received. This is the *offering* which has a new name, which none can know unless he has deserved the baptism of the Gospel."

OPENING THE DISC. This perhaps argues the use of a veil or cover. For the veil, see Brightman's Glossary, L.E.W. 591*a*, where it is explained that covers of metal or the like are sometimes used in the East. The West Syrians (Jacobites) and Greeks use πίναξ, the word transliterated in Test., for a disc or paten (Br., L.E.W. 584*b*). The second word used by James of Edessa (*KPPTA*) is used by St. Ephrem for a paten (Payne Smith, *Thesaurus Syriacus*, 1793).

DEACONS BAPTIZING. Contrast A.C. viii. 27 (Lagarde, 266[12]): " The deacon . . . does not baptize." In Spain, at the beginning of the fourth century, the Council of Elvira (can. 77) allows deacons to baptize if there is no priest in the place; and (can. 38) permits laymen to baptize in case of necessity. Eg. C.O. 46 (Tattam, p. 58) is indefinite; it merely speaks of him " who bestows it" (baptism). This one would suppose to be the presbyter; but the deacon is not forbidden to baptize.

CHAPTER 11

THE SERVICE TO CARRY TO A WIDOW, ETC. So in A.C. iii. 13 (Lagarde, 107[20]) διακονία is alms given to a widow. The whole

[1] Dr. Milligan (*Commentary on the Revelation*) understands by the stone, the plate on the high priest's mitre.

passage (which is not in Eg. C.O.; H. is deficient here) should be closely compared with C.H. 160–163. C.H. say that the alms is to be given the same day, or if anything of necessity remain, then on the next morning, and if anything again remain, on the third day. The man at whose house it is kept is not to deduct anything (?), but "let pity alone (and that complete) bring to the man who shows it the reckoned reward" [*i.e.* the bearer of the alms is to be actuated only by pity, and that will be his reward; this seems to be the sense of a not very easy passage: "ab eo autem in cujus domo asservatur, nihil computetur ex iis rebus; sola misericordia eaque tota afferat ei qui eam exhibet, computatam mercedem"]. "Let the distributer obtain nothing, for the bread of the poor delays too long in his house through negligence." C.H. 164–168 then go on to say that an Agapé, if there is one, is to be on Sunday at lamp lighting, the bishop being present, the deacon to rise to light the lamp, the bishop to pray, psalms to be sung, and the people to be dismissed before dark (see below). This last part has been turned by Test. into a vigil before Good Friday. This explains why II. 11*b* and 12 come between II. 11*a* and 13, which refer to the Agapé.—It appears that the passage about the alms is not original to either C.H. or Test., as it is extremely obscure in both, though its general sense is plain. Probably it belongs to the "Lost Church Order," was early corrupted, and was omitted by Eg. C.O. because it was not understood.

THE MAUNDY THURSDAY EUCHARIST. This, in Test., is an exception (p. 163). Rahmani (p. 200) conjectures that this is an Agapé only. The phrase "he who suffered," etc., is extremely obscure. It seems to be the work of the Test. Compiler, but to have become corrupt either before or after the time of James of Edessa. Copto-arab., either misunderstanding the text or reading it differently, has: "On Thursday let the priest offer in the evening bread and the cup mixed with wine and water to fulfil the mystery of Pascha. Let him do the same on the Saturday." Here Copto-arab. has taken "in the last week of Pascha" to be "to fulfil the mystery of Pascha." The words "in the evening" of Copto-arab. are probably original, and have dropped out by homoioteleuton; James having, we may suppose, written "bramshâ bkhamshâ bshabâ," *in the evening on Thursday.* But how does Copto-arab. get "to fulfil the mystery" out of "in the last week"? Possibly (if he translated from the Greek and not from the Syriac) by confusing τελευτάω, *to fulfil*, and τελευταῖος, *last*, and σύμβολον, *a symbol*, and σάββατον, *a week*.

As the first clause of the sentence seems thus to have been early corrupted, it is not improbable that the text of the obscure second clause is also corrupt. Copto-arab. clearly did not understand it. If, however, we are to take the clause as it stands, it may be mentioned that the last two verbs must be either "hath offered" (past) or "draweth near" (present), or the first may be the one and the second the other. Bishop Wordsworth (*Ministry of Grace*, 372), renders "He who suffered instead of that which He offered, Himself is the offerer"; but the Syriac will necessitate the past tense for the last words: "Himself [it is] who *hath offered*. Bishop Wordsworth understands that the writer "agreed with St. Augustine in thinking the sacrifice of the Eucharist to be especially that of the mystical body of Christ, his Church, and that he held the Maundy Thursday celebration to be especially one in which Christ is the priest who offers His people to God." The Syriac past tense of the last verb (if indeed the meaning "hath offered" is correct) appears to militate against this view. Perhaps it should be, however, "He who suffered instead of that which He offered (the Church), Himself [it is] who draweth near." But the more probable explanation is that the text is corrupt, especially as the beginning of the chapter is obscure and the last clause hopeless.

PSALMS AND CANTICLES BY THE LIGHT OF THE LAMP(?), lit., by the flame (or brightness) of the Lamp. The above seems to be the sense of the Syriac, though Rahmani renders "at the lamp lighting" (ad accensionem lucernae), which certainly agrees with the "psalm at the lighting up of the lamps," at daily evening service in A.C. viii. 34 (Lag. 271^{22}), and in Silvia (see p. 238).—For the antiphonal singing, see p. 181. The present passage perhaps means that the boys are to sing psalms and hymns and that then the people are to sing a chant all together, and answer Hallelujah to all three (cf. II. 12).—Dr. Wordsworth (*Ministry of Grace*, 386) suggests a possible connexion between this "offering of a lamp" by the deacon and the Paschal taper. Cf. I. 19, Note on "Light for a type" (p. 150 f.).

CHAPTER 12

PASCHA ENDING ON SATURDAY AT MIDNIGHT. See Note on "Day and Night" in I. 21 (p. 159), and on II. 19 (p. 232).

PENTECOST. This means the fifty days before Whitsunday. Cf. Note on Pascha in II. 8 (p. 218). This was the usual meaning of the term in Christian antiquity, and Pentecost was a season of rejoicing when kneeling was not permitted (cf. Tertullian, *de Cor. Mil.* 3, Migne, ii. 99). The Council of Nicaea (can. 20) ordered all to stand for prayer on Sunday and "on the days of Pentecost." On the other hand, the Council of Elvira (can. 43) talks of the "*day* of Pentecost."

SUNDAY A DAY OF REFRESHMENT. Cf. A.C. viii. 32 (Lagarde, 269²¹ff.), where work is not to be done on Saturdays and Sundays, or in Holy Week or Easter Week.

WHITE BAPTISMAL ROBES. The reference is perhaps to Rev. vii. 13, 14, which ancient commentators referred to the baptism of martyrs in their own blood (see Alford's Commentary, *in loc.*).—In II. 9, where the parallels mention the "clothing" (but not in white), Test. says nothing about it.—For another mention of white robes, see I. 34, p. 99.

CHAPTER 13

THE AGAPÉ IN OTHER CHURCH ORDERS, as far as they illustrate Test. (1) In C.H. 170-177 catechumens receive the bread of exorcism (?), but are not to sit at the Agapé (cf. Didaché ix. 5 ?). [Christians] are to eat and drink to satiety, but not to drunkenness. "Let no one talk much or cry out, lest they laugh at you; and let them not be a scandal to men, so that your host is turned into ridicule.... But let each one pray that the saints may enter under his roof, for our Saviour says, Ye are the salt of the earth." When the bishop speaks, sitting, the rest will have gain, nor will he himself be without gain.

(2) In Eg. C.O. 47-50 (Tattam, pp. 66-70) there is a section on fasting, from which Test. has borrowed a sentence about the bishop eating with the people. "Let them receive from the hand of the bishop a portion of the same bread, before each one shall divide the bread which is for him, for this is a blessing (εὐλογία, Lagarde) and is not an Eucharist, like the body of the Lord." People are to "say grace" before they drink ("take the cup"). Catechumens are to receive the bread of exorcism and a cup. They are not to come into the Lord's Supper [*i.e.* the Agapé] with a faithful person.... "When ye eat and drink in tranquillity (Arab., in purity or modesty), drink not that ye may be drunken, that men may deride you, and he who has called you be sorrowful for your dissoluteness (Lagarde, τῇ παραβάσει ὑμῶν). But that he may pray the saints to go in to him. For He hath said: Ye are the salt of the earth." [Can Test. have misunderstood τῇ παραβάσει ὑμῶν, and read τῇ προσαναβάσει ὑμῶν, "so let them *enter* that . . . ?

Rahmani suggests that James of Edessa found εὔχομαι in his text, and read it "pray" when he should have read "*boast that the saints enter*," etc. But the parallels forbid this.] Eg. C.O. continues: "When you have been called to eat, eat only what suffices you, that he who has called you may do what he pleases with what remains, so that they may remain over for the saints, and that he may rejoice at your entering in to him." [This is not in C.H.; Test. has modified it. The words "what suffices" (τὰ καθήκοντα) get into "sufficienter" in H. (see below), and so into "abundantly" in Test.] The eaters are to eat in peace and not in strife, to answer the bishop when questioned; then to be silent with attention (Lagarde, παρατηροῦνται) until they are again questioned. [Test. has altered παρατηρ. to "choose" (cf. C.H. 102).] Eg. C.O. then goes on to allow a presbyter or deacon to preside if the bishop is absent.

(3) Hauler 113, 114, says after a lacuna, "you who are present, and so feast." Catechumens are to receive the bread of exorcism, and each one is *to offer a cup;* they are not to be at the Lord's Supper (Agapé), . . . (and so on as in Eg. C.O., not Test.). Eaters and drinkers to eat and drink honestly and not to drunkenness, and not so that any one should laugh at (you) or the host be grieved at your inquietude, but that he may pray to be made worthy that the saints may enter in to him. "For, Ye are the salt of the earth, He says." If an offering is made to all in common, called in Greek apoforetum, receive it from him, but, that all may taste, taste *sufficiently,* that also there may be left (somewhat), and that he who called you may send (it) to whom he will, as of the *relics of the saints* (tanquam de reliquiis sanctorum), and rejoice *in trustfulness* (gaudeat in fiducia). [Note that H., Eg. C.O., and Test. are all involved here; the original must have been early corrupted.] The guests are to eat in silence, not striving with words, but (hearing?) what the bishop exhorts; and if he questions about anything he is to be answered; and when the bishop speaks a [or, the] word, all modestly *praising him* (cf. Test.) to be silent till again questioned; and so on as Eg. C.O.

The idea in Test. of "eating abundantly" at the Agapé (cf. H., above) is found elsewhere. Thus Didaché x. 1: "After ye are satisfied (ἐμπλησθῆναι), thus give ye thanks." So Tertullian, *Apol.* 39 (Migne, i. 540): "They are satisfied (saturantur)."

The expression in Eg. C.O., "This is a blessing (εὐλογία)," needs some comment. The name εὐλογία (see Brightman, L.E.W. 577, 597, and Keating, *The Agapé and the Eucharist,* p. 130) was used for the bread offered at the offertory in the

Eucharist, probably as being a gift of the people. The offerings were originally made for the purposes of the Agapé as well as for the Eucharist. The name εὐλογία was afterwards used for bread formally blessed (though not consecrated) and distributed at the end of the Liturgy. This custom, which is still common in both East and West, is thought by Dr. Keating to have dated from the time when the Agapé died out. The "bread of exorcism" mentioned above seems to have been something of the same sort as the εὐλογία. In Test. II. 19 the catechumens are to receive εὐλογίαι.

We notice that in all these Church Orders the Agapé and Eucharist are quite distinct. In Eg. C.O. and H. the Agapé is called "the Lord's Supper." C.H. 172 speak of "the Lord's Agapae." For fuller information on this point, as on the whole subject of the Agapé, reference may be made to Dr. J. F. Keating's learned book mentioned above, and published since these notes were written. Chancellor Keating gives succinctly all that is known on the subject, and traces the influence of the heathen and Jewish love meals on the Christian Agapé. He holds that the Eucharist and Agapé were at first celebrated together, but that by Pliny's time (112 A.D.) they were separated, at least in parts of the Church; and that later the separation became universal.

CHAPTER 14

FIRST FRUITS. (1) C.H. 186, 187, say that one who has first fruits is to bring them to the bishop *into the church;* so the first fruits of the threshing floor, and of wine presses, oil, honey, milk, wool, and merchandise, with first fruits of trees.

(2) Eg. C.O. 53 (Tattam, p. 72) merely says: Let every one hasten to take to the bishop at all times the first fruit of the fruits (Arab., the first ripe dates), and the first of the produce (Arab., of all kinds of grain).

(3) H. 115^9 says that all are to hasten to offer the first fruits to the bishop.

(4) A.C. viii. 29 (Lagarde, 267^8 ff.) say that first fruits are to be brought to the bishop *and presbyters and deacons* for their support, and tithes for the support of the rest of the clerks and virgins and widows and the poor.

CHAPTER 15

PROPERTY. Test. has interpolated this section (apparently the work of the Compiler) between the two on first fruits

(14 and 16), which are consecutive in Eg. C.O. and C.H. and H. It arises out of the question of offerings to the bishop. See II. 23.

Chapter 16

BLESSING OF THE FIRST FRUITS. (1) In C.H. 188–194 the priest (sacerdos) says the thanksgiving [the offerer standing outside the veil].[1] The thanksgiving is quite different from Eg. C.O., H., and Test. The bishop is then directed to bless *all vegetables* of the earth, and all produce (poma) of trees and all " fruits of the earth of cucumber fields," and those who bring them.

(2) In Eg. C.O. 53, 54 (Tattam, pp. 72, 74), the bishop receives the fruits with thanksgiving, and blesses them and *names the name* of the offerer (cf. Test. prayer). The prayer is nearly that of Test., and runs: We give thanks to Thee, O Lord God, and we present to Thee the first fruit of the fruits which Thou hast given unto us to partake of them, which Thou hast perfected by Thy word, and Thou hast commanded the earth to produce every fruit for use and for gladness and food for the race of men and of all creatures. We bless Thee, O God, for these and all other things by which Thou hast benefited us. Thou hast adorned all creation with the various fruits, through Thy holy Son Jesus Christ, our Lord, by whom glory be to Thee and Him and the Holy Ghost, for ever and ever. Amen.—Eg. C.O. names as to be blessed: the vine, fig, pomegranate, olive, prune, apple, peach, cherry, almond (Arab., apricot); as not to be blessed: garlic, the onion, melon, cucumber, melon-cucumber, immature date, or any other pot herb. They may offer of flowers, the rose and the lily (*sic*, singular as Test.), but not the rest. . . .

(3) Hauler 115[12] has almost exactly the same prayer as Eg. C.O. It adds to the Eg. C.O. fruits, as to be blessed, the pear, mulberry, and damson. It does not mention the immature date, but says "no other vegetable" is to be blessed. Sometimes flowers are offered. "Let, then, the rose and the lily (singular) be offered, but not others." . . .

(4) In the A.C. prayer for blessing fruits (viii. 40, Lagarde, 274[4]ff.) we have the sentence: "who hast perfected all things by Thy word, and commandedst the earth to produce different fruits for our joy and nourishment."

[1] Achelis' bracket.

Chapter 17

OF EATING. This chapter corresponds to the words in Eg. C.O. 54 and H. 116[6], following those which have been quoted in the last chapter. Eg. C.O. says: "Everything which they shall eat they shall give thanks to God for. And when they shall taste, then they shall give glory to Him." H. says: "In all things which are received let them give thanks to the holy God, receiving them to His glory." The last clause about things strangled is an addition of Test.; the rule is implied in the second canon of the Council of Gangra (end of fourth century?), and still holds among Eastern Christians. Note that Test. omits the "blood" of Acts xv. 29. St. Augustine (*c. Faustum*, xxxii. 13) says that the rule was only observed in his time by few people. See Hefele, *Councils*, ii. 328, Eng. trans.

Chapter 18

LECTIONS AT PASCHA. These are exceptional; see p. 181. This chapter is peculiar to Test. In Eg. C.O. and H., Pascha is treated directly after what was said above, but they go on to our II. 20. C.H. also go on to the Holy Week fast, but with passages which are not in Test. For "day and night," see Note on I. 21 (p. 159).

Chapter 19

THE PASCHAL VIGIL. This chapter is peculiar to Test. For the deacons and subdeacons keeping order, cf. A.C. viii. 11 (Lagarde, 248[1]ff.), where the deacons keep order among the men and women (children specially mentioned), "to see lest any beckon, whisper, or nod"; deacons stand at the men's doors, subdeacons at the women's. Deacons keeping order is also mentioned twice in A.C. ii. 57 (Lagarde, 85[4], 86[23]); but in that chapter there is a different arrangement (Lagarde, 86[3]), the doorkeepers (πυλωροί) watching the men's entrances, the deacons the women's, and the tabernacle is referred to as a type. See also Test. I. 34, 36.

SATURDAY NIGHT. This must mean *our* Saturday night, not our Friday night. See pp. 159, 164.

CATECHUMENS RECEIVING EULOGIAE. Cf. II. 13 (Note on C.H., Eg. C.O., and H., p. 228 f.).

WIDOWS AND PRESBYTERESSES. See Note on p. 199; for the food in the temple, see the next page.

CHAPTER 20

THE FAST BEFORE EASTER. The rule in this chapter about fasting before communion applies to the Lenten fast. For the general rule, see Note on p. 239. The fast before Easter in Test. is an absolute fast of two days. It ends at the midnight between Saturday and Sunday (II. 12), and therefore the widows who "stay till dawn in the temple" take food with them.

The other Church Orders. (1) In C.H. 150–152 (bracketed by Achelis) the newly baptized and others who fast with them are to taste nothing before they take of the body of Christ, for that would be reckoned not as a fast but as a sin (cf. Test.). After the Offering they may eat as they please. In § 195, C.H. say that the week when the Jews keep Pascha is to be observed by all with the greatest zeal, and they are to take care especially that on those days they remain fasting from all desire (cupiditate), etc. Then follows the passage already quoted above in I. 28, Note (p. 184); and in §§ 197, 198, we read that the food suitable for Pascha is bread with only salt and water (cf. Test.). *Any* sick person, or one in the country far away (cf. Eg. C.O.), is to fast after Pentecost. See also Note to II. 6 (p. 211 f.).

(2) Eg. C.O. 55 (Tattam, pp. 74, 76) says in its title that no one is to take anything at Pascha before the time when the fast is completed (Tattam, "before the time in which it ought to be eaten"). It continues: "They shall not compute this fast thus, if they have celebrated Pascha before the time when the fast is completed [reference to Quartodeciman practice?]. But if any one is ill and cannot fast two days, he is to fast on the Saturday on account of the affliction [Lagarde, διὰ τὴν ἀνάγκην; see H. below], contenting himself with bread and salt and water." [In Test. this refers to pregnant women only.] Sailors at sea, and not knowing the proper day, are to fast after Pentecost [cf. C.H.; Test. has not got this].

(3) Hauler 116[9] says that no one is to partake [of food?] in Pascha before the Offering takes place; for if so the fast is not imputed to him. But if any one is pregnant and ill and cannot fast two days, she is to fast on Saturday of necessity (propter necessitatem), being content with (contenens) bread and water. Travellers by sea or a person in any necessity to fast after Pentecost. [This is much more like Test. than the other two are.]

We see that Eg. C.O., H., and Test. prescribe only a one or

two days' fast before Easter, but it is, except in cases of sickness, absolute; C.H. perhaps prescribes the whole of Holy Week, but it is only a partial fast. See further on II. 8 (p. 218). Copto-arab. says: If a pregnant woman is sick and cannot observe the Quadragesimal fast [note this], she is to fast on the Wednesday and Friday.

HAND LAID ON CATECHUMENS. See p. 182.

DEACONS AND DEACONESSES CARRYING THE EUCHARIST. Copto-arab. says: If a believer, man or woman, cannot, through sickness, come to church, let the presbyter or deacon carry the mysteries to them. It then supersedes Test. about deaconesses carrying the Eucharist.—In Justin Martyr the deacons take the Eucharist to the absent (*Apol.* i. 65).—The provision in Test. for the deaconess carrying the sacrament to the sick women is remarkable, as in II. 8 *widows* do the part usually ascribed to the deaconesses at baptism. But no doubt here this duty is given to the latter to make a parallel with the function of the deacons in this respect.

SICK PRESBYTERS. In C.H. 215, if a presbyter is sick, a *deacon* is to carry the mysteries to him, but the presbyter alone is to receive them, *i.e.* he is to administer the Eucharist to himself; cf. Test. II. 10. Here, in Test., a presbyter is to carry the sacrament to a sick presbyter.

CHAPTER 21

BISHOP AND DEACONS VISITING THE SICK. (1) In C.H. 199, 200, the deacon goes round with the bishop and points out the sick. "For it is a great thing for a sick man to be visited by the high priest; he recovers from his sickness when the bishop comes to him, especially if he prays over him, for the shadow of Peter healed a sick man."

(2) Eg. C.O. 56 (Tattam, p. 76) agrees with the first part of the above. But in the latter part it is shorter: "For the sick are consoled when they see their high priest visiting them, and they are remembered."

(3) Hauler 116[21] says that each deacon *with the subdeacons* is to observe (or pay respect to) the bishop (ad episcopum observent); to tell him of the sick, that he may visit them if he see fit. "For the sick man is much delighted when the high priest remembers him."

We note that Test. only says, "let *them* take it up." Clearly, if we compare I. 34, 40, deacons are meant, and perhaps subdeacons and widows also. It is noteworthy that Test., Eg. C.O., and H. have no reference to the gift of healing or the "shadow of Peter" as C.H. have—a mark of early date in the last. Yet Test. I. 47 refers to the gift of healing, though generally and without detail.—The phrase "especially when he is faithful" is peculiar to Test. For the name "high priest," see p. 160.

CHAPTER 22

ANTIPHONAL SINGING. See Note on I. 26 (p. 181). This chapter is peculiar to Test.

CHAPTER 23

BURIAL. The Church Orders from this point differ somewhat in arrangement and order. C.H. 220, 221, say that dying people are not to be cast out to sleep in the cemetery, but among the *poor*. He who has a house of his own is not to be taken when sick into God's house, but is only to pray, and then to return to his own house. Eg. C.O. 61 (Tattam, p. 80) says they are not to burden a man to bury men in the cemeteries, for this is the work of *all the poor*. They are to give wages to the grave digger and a gift to the keepers [of the cemetery], and "to those in that place who have had the care of it." The bishop is to support them, so that no one may press upon them among those who go to those places. This is not in Hauler at all.

The words of Test., "those who provide for each one," seem to point to a guild or society of burial authorities. The clauses about leaving property (cf. II. 15) and embalming and enshrouding are peculiar to Test. Embalming was common in Egypt up to at least the fifth century (Brightman in J.T.S. i. 262). No prayers are given in Test. for funerals. Sarapion (§ 18) gives a prayer asking for the refreshment ($\dot{a}\nu\dot{a}\pi a v\sigma\iota\varsigma$) of the soul of the departed and for his future resurrection. The churchyard keeper mentioned in Test. and Eg. C.O. is probably the $\kappa o\pi\iota\dot{a}\tau\eta\varsigma$ of Epiphanius and the Fossarius or Fossor of the Church of Cirta (Wordsworth, *Ministry of Grace*, p. 195); the officers were skilled artisans, carvers, etc., not mere grave diggers. The mention of deacons in Test. in connexion with burial is a mark of early date (cf. I. 34). The early deacons had special duties to the dead. But gradually they gave up much of their work to subdeacons and, in the West, to doorkeepers. For *Oblations for the departed*, cf. Tertull. *de Cor.* 3 (Migne, ii. 99), Cypr. *Ep.* i. 2, C.H. 169 (?); and see Dr. Swete in J.T.S. iii. 167.

Chapter 24

Hours of Prayer in the Church Orders and other Authorities. The reference in this chapter is apparently to private prayers, whether in the church or at home. At least there is no form of prayer laid down for these hours.

(1) C.H. 223–225, 233–238, say that Christians are to pray at dawn, washing their hands always when they pray, and to do the same before every several work (cf. Test.; and C.H. 241, where a Christian is told to wash his hands whenever he prays). Then follows (226–232) a passage about assemblies in the church "for the word of God," *i.e.* instruction. C.H. continue: They are to pray at the third hour because our Lord was crucified then; at the sixth hour because all creation was disturbed by the Jews' wicked deed; at the ninth hour because Christ then prayed and gave up the ghost; at sunset because it is the end of the day (cf. Test.); then at lamp lighting because David said, "I speak by night"; and at midnight because of David, Paul, and Silas [these two hours bracketed by Achelis].

(2) Eg. C.O. 57, 62 (Tattam, pp. 76, 80–86), is much longer than C.H. or Test. Believers on waking to pray before working, and so to approach their works. They are to go to church if there be instruction. On rising they are to wash their hands and then proceed to their works [repetition; and direction about going to church for instruction repeated more fully, as C.H.]. The prayer at the third hour is only in a house or chamber, not in the church; then Christ was nailed to the wood (cf. Test.); the shewbread, the lamb, the bread from heaven are mentioned. At the sixth hour Christ was crucified, and the day was divided and there was great darkness (cf. Test.). "Let them pray at that time with a fervent prayer, helping them by the voice of Him who prayed, causing all creation to be dark, by reason of the unbelief of the Jews" [cf. Test.; the passage in both is obscure, showing that it is original in neither; in Test. it is barely intelligible]. At the ninth hour there is to be a great prayer and praise; "like the souls of the righteous they shall bless the Lord God of truth; He who remembered the saints sent His Son, who is His Word, to them, who enlightened them; then the side of Christ was pierced and blood and water came out." [This is clearly the original of Test., which however is shorter; it is evolved out of Christ's prayer in C.H.] "The rest of the day it was light till evening; therefore thou also if thou hast slept (at that hour),

thou shalt remember another day and make the type of the resurrection" (see below).

(3) Hauler 119 begins a fragment thus: "God who lieth not, who remembereth His saints, and sent out His Word, illuminating them. Therefore at that hour Christ was pierced in (His) side, and poured out water and blood, and illuminating the rest of the day brought (them) to the evening. Pray also before going to bed. At midnight wash the hands and pray."

In Eg. C.O. and H. the sunset prayer is omitted. But as we find it in C.H., and also (see below) in A.C., St. Jerome, and Silvia, distinct from that of the ninth hour, it is probable that Test. purposely altered the phrase in Eg. C.O. and H. about our Lord illuminating the rest of the day (which is much involved, and which Test. probably did not well understand), and made a separate hour of prayer out of it. In the Test. midnight prayer the words "because of the resurrection" are an addition, as is the second reference to the dawn. In the latter, note the obvious anachronism about the apostles singing psalms. For the "beginning of another day," see Note on "Day and night" in I. 21 (p. 159).

(4) In A.C. viii. 33 (Lagarde, 270^{18} ff.) the hours are dawn, the third, sixth, ninth, evening, cockcrow; prayers to be said publicly or privately; the evening and dawn congregations are to be convened by the bishop. The reasons for these hours are not the same as in Test., but are similar in kind. If they cannot go to church *because of the unbelievers*, the bishop is to assemble them at home (κατ' οἶκον)—apparently if the ungodly have taken possession of the church. If there cannot be a congregation, each one, or two or three, are to pray, etc., in private. The appointed service in A.C. viii. is only for evening and dawn, in that order.

(5) St. Jerome, *Ep.* 27, speaking of Paula's convent at Bethlehem at the end of the fourth century (see Dict. Chr. Biog. iv. 218; and Wordsworth, *Ministry of Grace*, 347), mentions the hours of prayer as the morning, the third, sixth, and ninth hours, evening, midnight. But here he carries us a step further, for he is speaking of community prayers at these hours; they say the Psalter together in order. In *Ep.* 7, *ad Laetam*, he names these hours as times for private devotion, substituting "in the night" for "midnight"; and "lamp lighting" and "evening" are synonymous. Cassian (*Inst.* iii. 3, quoted by Wordsworth) says the full order of hour services at Bethlehem was only established during his stay there, A.D. 390–403.

(6) Silvia (Duchesne, *Origines*, pp. 471–473; Wordsworth, *Ministry of Grace*, 348) describes service at Jerusalem at dawn, the sixth, ninth, and tenth hours. The last is equivalent to the "lamp lighting" (it was winter)—"an immense illumination." Many psalms, hymns, litanies, and prayers, but no lections. Solitaries and virgins, with some presbyters and deacons, also keep vigil from before cockcrow to dawn.

For the absence of fixed, formal, public daily prayers in Test., see Note to I. 32 (p. 189).

PRAYERS OF MARRIED MEN. C.H. 242 say that married men are to pray whenever they wish to rise from the side of their wives. .For marriage does not stain. Eg. C.O. 62 (Tattam, p. 86) says that a married man is to pray with his wife; if she is still heathen, he is to withdraw and pray alone and return to his place. A married man is not to refrain from prayer, for he is not defiled; those who have washed need not wash again, for they are purified and clean. So H. 119[14] exactly. Test. has omitted the caution about marriage not defiling.

THE BENEDICITE OMNIA OPERA. The reference is fuller in Test. than in the other Church Orders. C.H. 244 say: "Pray at midnight; our fathers said that at that time all creation was prepared for the service of the divine glory and the orders of the angels and the souls of the just blessed God." Eg. C.O. says: "The stars and the trees and the waters are as all the host of angels who stand around; serving with the souls of the just, praising God Almighty at that time" [during the night]. So H. 120[7] very closely. C.H., Eg. C.O., and H. then go on with a paragraph about the coming of the bridegroom, which is not in Test.

CHAPTER 25

MUTUAL INSTRUCTION. The opening sentence is from Eg. C.O. 62 (Tattam, pp. 88, 90). "All ye believers, if ye fulfil these things, and remember to teach one another and to instruct the catechumens to perform them, nothing shall try you, and ye shall not mourn for ever." Hauler 120[22] has a very similar passage, but it reads: "Ye will not be able to be tempted or to perish (cf. Test.), as ye ever have Christ *in memory*" [note how Test. has characteristically turned this]. C.H. 246–251 have a much shorter form than the above: "Let us with the catechumens teach one another about the service of God; then the demons cannot sadden us, when in every prayer we *remember Christ*." They then refer to the sign of the Cross and the Paschal Lamb, as also do Eg. C.O. and H., but Test. omits these.

FASTING COMMUNION AND RESERVATION. The rule in Test. apparently involves private reservation for daily communion, as daily Eucharists are not allowed (I. 22). It implies a general rule for fasting communion, though this is not explicitly stated as in C.H. 205 ; the rule for fasting communion, indeed, had some exceptions; thus in the neighbourhood of Alexandria and in the Thebaid they communicated on Saturdays not fasting, apparently after an agapé (Socrates, *H.E.* v. 22 ; see Brightman, L.E.W. 509, note 27). And in A.D. 397 the third Council of Carthage (can. 29, not given by Hefele) excuses fasting communion on Maundy Thursday. The practice of private reservation in the third and fourth centuries is well known; the Eucharist was carried by travellers and others, and regarded as an antidote. [References besides the Church Orders are: Tertullian, *ad Uxorem*, ii. 5 (Migne, i. 1408); St. Ambrose, *Oratio in obitum fratris*, i. 43 ; St. Basil, *Ep.* 93 ; see Brightman, *ubi supra;* Wordsworth, *Ministry of Grace*, 320.] It seems probable that, as the sacrament was thus carried about by private individuals, reservation must have been in one kind. Bishop Wordsworth (*Ministry of Grace*, 380) draws attention to the old (but not original) Roman method of communion on Good Friday in the eighth or ninth century, with the bread consecrated the day before, and the unconsecrated chalice into which a portion of the consecrated bread was placed without any words being said over it.

The other Church Orders are as follows: (1) C.H. 205 say explicitly that none of the faithful are to taste anything unless they have first taken of the mysteries, especially on the days of the sacred fast. There is no idea of an antidote here.

(2) Eg. C.O. 58 (Tattam, p. 78) says conversely that every believer is to hasten to partake of the Eucharist before he tastes anything else. If they believe in it, if any one have given them deadly poison it will not hurt them [cf. St. Mark xvi. 18].

(3) Hauler 117[10] has the same.—Thus Test., Eg. C.O., and H. agree in the reference to the antidote.

CONCLUDING SENTENCE. The Test. Compiler's material ends with " prevail against you." Here C.H., Eg. C.O., and H. conclude with admonitions to keep the rules laid down [the passage C.H. 255–257 about the night of the resurrection is bracketed as an interpolation by Achelis]. C.H. has no "apocryphal pretence," Eg. C.O. 62 (Tattam, p. 92) refers to the rules as traditions of the apostles. "For thus many heresies (cf. Test.) increase, because those who preside are not willing to learn the doctrines of the Apostles." H. 121 breaks off at the beginning of the conclusion. Test. proceeds with the fiction of our Lord's words: "Lo, then, I have taught you," and in the next chapter introduces once more the word "Testament" as in I. 17, 18.

Chapter 27

THE MESSENGERS TO THE DIOCESES. For "dioceses" ($\pi\alpha\rho o\iota\kappa\iota\alpha\iota$), see p. 188. One may conjecture that the names Dositheus, Silas, Magnus, and Aquila are local names of the Test. Compiler's own country. If we are to seek for historical characters bearing these names, one may suggest for two of them Silas and Aquila of Pontus, St. Paul's companions; for though St. Paul is not mentioned in Test. by name, this would be part of the dramatic fiction, and not from opposition to the Apostle, whose writings are quoted constantly. Silas might be mentioned (if Zahn's conjecture as to authorship have any elements of truth in it; see p. 45) out of compliment to the Audian bishop Silvanus (bishop among the Goths in Moesia), who died before 377; or because a "Silvanus" carried St. Peter's First Epistle to Asia Minor (1 Pet. v. 12), if that country be the place of writing (see Introduction, p. 45). Bishop J. Wordsworth (C.Q.R. April, 1900) suggests for "Aquila" the legendary brother of Clement. In A.C. vii. 46, Aquila (St. Paul's companion) and Nicetas are said to be bishops of Asia Minor ($\tau\tilde{\omega}\nu$ $\kappa\alpha\tau\grave{\alpha}$ 'A$\sigma\acute{\iota}\alpha\nu$ $\pi\alpha\rho o\iota\kappa\iota\tilde{\omega}\nu$). Bishop J. Wordsworth suggests that Dositheus was the Samaritan heresiarch; this is hardly likely. Possibly a bishop of Seleucia (in Syria?) who confuted Sabellianism is referred to (Dict. Chr. Biog. i. 905). Or Dorotheus, Bishop of Tyre at the end of the third century, may be meant (*ibid.* 899); he wrote much on ecclesiastical history, and Lagarde publishes at the end of his "Apostolic Constitutions" (p. 282 ff.) a fragment purporting to be by him and Hippolytus, "Bishop of Rome," on the districts where the "disciples of the Lord" preached the Gospel. About Magnus no probable conjecture appears to have been made. But it must be added that none of these guesses are very likely, and one is inclined to suppose either that the names are purely imaginary, or else, as has been said, that they are local names, contemporary with the Compiler.

THE TRANSLATOR, JAMES OF EDESSA. The note ascribing the translation to James is apparently in both M. and B.

James was a notable character of the seventh century. He was appointed Monophysite (West Syrian, or Jacobite) Bishop of Edessa, or Ur-hai, in Mesopotamia, in A.D. 651, but after a short episcopate of about four years he retired from his see on account of internal troubles in his diocese and province, and devoted himself to literary work. He was invited back to his see on the death of his successor, and was reinstated in it; but died only four months after his reinstatement, in A.D. 708 or 710. The *Testament* must have been translated by him during his retirement, perhaps at Tel 'Ada, where he spent nine years, and where he afterwards died. This place is described as being between Beroea and Edessa, and would therefore be south-west of the latter city. James, who had travelled much and had visited Alexandria, knew Greek well, though Syriac was his native tongue; and he translated many Greek works into Syriac. He was also a great liturgical writer, a historian, a commentator on the Scriptures, and a grammarian. He is thought to have introduced the Greek vowel signs into Syriac. He was a great letter writer, and one of his epistles, to the presbyter Thomas, has already been noticed (see Notes on the Benediction before the Sursum Corda and the Benedictus, I. 23, pp. 169, 177). For a fairly full account of his life and writings, see Mr. C. J. Ball's article in Dict. Chr. Biog. iii. 332 (JACOBUS EDESSENUS).

ADDITIONAL NOTE

ON THE TESTAMENT AND THE CREED OF CONSTANTINOPLE

THERE is some trace of a creed of an Eastern type in the *Testament* other than the baptismal creed, which is of a Western type (see p. 217). Thus we find "suffered and was buried" twice (pp. 85, 110); the Holy Ghost is called "Paraclete" (p. 78), "the Lord" (*ib.*), "Maker of life" ($\zeta\omega o\pi o\iota\acute{o}\varsigma$, p. 108), "Consubstantial with the Father" (*ib.*); and we have "crucified for us" (p. 87; so Eg. C.O., see p. 217), but in Test. without "under Pontius Pilate." None of these expressions occur in the Nicene Creed; but all except "Paraclete" and "Consubstantial" (of the Holy Ghost) in that of Constantinople. Thus it might be thought that the *Testament* is necessarily later than 381. But the creed put forth by the Council of Constantinople was not really a new one. Already, in 374, Epiphanius in his *Ancoratus* had published a very similar, though longer, creed, and this contains all the above articles, except "Consubstantial" and "Paraclete," which last is found in Epiphanius' *Second Formula* (also of date 374). Epiphanius was bishop of Salamis (Constantia) in Cyprus, and it is probable that the formulary in his *Ancoratus* was the baptismal creed of his Church; it was in existence before him. Dr. Hort has shown that it represents the old baptismal creed of Jerusalem, with additions from the Nicene Creed and from St. Athanasius and St. Cyril of Jerusalem (Dict. Chr. Biog. iii. 122*b*). With regard to the twice occurring "suffered and was buried," it should be noticed that it is the combination of the two articles which is worthy of remark, and the combination occurs in Epiphanius as well as at Constantinople. The article "suffered" is Nicene; and "was buried" is found in early Western forms—such as the profession of faith of Marcellus of Ancyra and the Old Roman Form (Dict. Chr. Biog. i. 708), both of which are before 341. No doubt the words of St. Paul in 1 Cor. xv. 4 assured for this article an early and wide popularity.—In addition to the authorities for $\zeta\omega o\pi o\iota o\varsigma$ given on p. 201, we should probably add the Eg. C.O. baptismal creed, which has "the Quickener" (p. 218, cf. p. 214).

We cannot, then, base on the above phrases an argument for a date for the *Testament* later than 381. It may be added that the Confession of Charisius, a presbyter of Philadelphia, which was read at Ephesus in 431, concludes thus: " . . . . the Spirit of truth, the Paraclete, Consubstantial with the Father and the Son, and in the holy catholic Church, in the resurrection of the dead, in life eternal" (Dict. Chr. Biog. i. 702*a*).

See also pp. 40, 201, and Dr. Swainson's article (THE CREED) in Dict. Chr. Biog. i. 695 ff., and Hefele, *Councils*, ii. 349 (Eng. trans.).

APPENDICES

APPENDICES

APPENDIX I

THE ABYSSINIAN ANAPHORA OF OUR LORD

Translated from the Latin of Ludolf, given in his *Commentarius ad suam historiam aethiopicam*, pp. 341–345.

EUCHARISTIC PRAYER OF OUR LORD AND SAVIOUR
JESUS CHRIST

WE give thanks to Thee, O God the Holy One, the End [or, Aim] of our souls, Giver of our life, the incorruptible Treasure, the Father of Thy Only-begotten Son, our Saviour, who hath proclaimed Thy will. For Thou hast willed that we should be saved through Thee. Our heart giveth devout (devotas) thanks to Thee, O Lord. Thou art the Power (virtus) of the Father and the Grace of the nations, Knowledge of uprightness, the Wisdom of them that err, the Healer of souls, the Exaltation (magnitudo) of the meek; Thou art our Refuge (arx, asylum), the Staff of the just, the Hope of the exiles, the safe Haven of those who are buffeted as in the sea, the Light of the perfect, the Son of the living God. Shine upon us with Thine immovable grace, with the foundation and strengthening of trustfulness (fiduciae); with the wisdom and efficacy of inflexible faith and of unchangeable hope. Bestow the intelligence of the Spirit on our humility, so that we may ever in uprightness be Thy pure servants, O Lord, and that all nations may praise Thee.

The deacon saith:

For the most blessed and holy Patriarch Abba NN., and Abbuna the most reverend our Metropolitan Abba NN., who praise Thee with their prayers and their intercessions.

Stephen the protomartyr. Zacharias the priest, and John

the Baptist. For all saints and martyrs who have fallen asleep in the faith of Christ. Matthew and Mark, Luke and John, the four Evangelists. Mary the mother (genetrix) of God. Simon Peter and Andrew, James and John, Philip and Bartholomew, Thomas and Matthew, Thaddaeus and Nathanael, James the son of Alphaeus and Matthias, the twelve apostles; and James the Apostle, brother of our Lord, Bishop of Jerusalem, the house of the Sanctuary; Paul and Timothy, Silas and Barnabas, Titus, Philemon, Clement, the Seventy-two disciples and their five hundred companions; the Three hundred and eighteen orthodox fathers. May the prayers of all of them be fulfilled [in] us.

With them visit us, and remember the apostolic Church which is over all congregations in peace, which was brought forth (parta) by (per) the precious blood of Christ. And remember all patriarchs, archbishops, bishops, presbyters, and deacons who guide (dirigunt) the way of the word in truth.

The people answer:

Have mercy, O Lord, on the souls of Thy servants and Thy handmaidens who have eaten Thy body and have drunk Thy blood, who have fallen asleep in Thy faith.

The priest saith:

Yea, O Lord, we render thanks to Thee and bless Thee, and ever ask Thee, O God, Father of the heights, who rulest the treasuries of light, visit Jerusalem from heaven; O Lord of Powers, of archangels, and Strength of dominions (virtus dominantium), Glory of thrones, Raiment (amiculum) of luminaries, Joy of delights, King of kings, Father who holdest all things [as it were] in (Thy) hand and governest. And by Thy counsel Thy Son Jesus the Only-begotten was crucified for our sins. (Thou) who by the Word of Thy covenant hast made all things, being well pleased in Him, and didst send Him into the womb (uterum) of a virgin; He was conceived in the womb (ventre); He was made flesh; and His birth was known (cognita fuit) by the Holy Spirit, when He was born of the Virgin that He might fulfil Thy will and constitute a holy people for Thee. He stretched out His hands to suffering, He suffered that He might save them that suffer, them who put their trust in Thee. He was betrayed of His own will to torture that He might save those who are tortured and strengthen them that totter (nutantes), find those who are lost, and give life to the dead, and take away death and rend the bonds of Satan, and fulfil the will of His Father; that He might tread down Sheol and open the gates of life; that He might give light to the righteous, might ratify a treaty, might remove darkness, nurture the babes, and reveal His resurrection.

In that night in which they betrayed Him He took bread into His hands holy blessed and without spot, He gave thanks, He blessed, He brake and gave to His disciples, saying: Take, eat, this bread is My body which is broken for you for the forgiveness of sins; and when ye shall have done this, make (facitote) a commemoration of Me. Likewise also the cup of wine after they had supped, mixing, giving thanks, blessing and sanctifying, Thou didst give to them, Thy true blood which was shed for our sins.

Now, therefore, O Lord, we remember Thy death and resurrection, we trust in Thee, and offer to Thee bread and the cup, giving thanks to Thee, to Thee alone who [art] the Saviour, God from eternity, since Thou hast commanded us to stand before Thee and to serve Thee as (instar) priests. Therefore we also Thy servants, O Lord, ask Thee, O Lord, and beseech Thee to send the Holy Spirit and power (virtutem) upon this bread and upon this cup, [that] He may make (it) the body and blood of our Lord and Saviour Jesus Christ, world without end.[1]

Furthermore, we offer to Thee this thanksgiving, O Eternal Trinity, O Lord, the Father of Jesus Christ whom every creature and (every) soul venerate.[2] We give Thee this (istud) gift; not food nor drink do we offer to Thy holiness. Cause that it may not happen (cedat) to us for condemnation and the reproach (obtrectationem) of the enemy, nor for destruction, but (for) the medicine of our bodies and for the strength of our spirit. Yea, O our God, grant (largire) us for the sake of Thy Name that we may flee from all thoughts which displease Thee. O Lord, grant (da) to us that every counsel of death may be driven away from us, who in Thy Name have been inscribed on the inner veil of Thy most high sanctuary. Let death hear Thy Name and be amazed; let the depths be rent, the enemy be trodden down; let the malignant spirit tremble; let the dragon draw back; let unbelief be cast far off (elongetur), and the apostate be afflicted; let anger grow weak; let envy work nothing; let the obstinate be reproved, and all the avaricious be rooted out; let vexation (molestia) be taken away; let the deceiver be overthrown, and let all kinds of sorceries (veneficiorum) languish. Grant, O Lord, to the innermost eyes of our

---

[1] Ludolf here notes that in the printed Liturgy the people say: O Lord, have mercy on us (twice), O Lord, be propitious to us.
[2] Ludolf suggests that this passage is corrupt. Perhaps there is a lacuna.

heart to gaze on Thee, to praise and laud Thee, remembering Thee, and to serve Thee, for Thou alone art their portion, the Son and Word of God to whom all things are subject. Perfect and strengthen those to whom Thou hast by [Thy] grace revealed [Thyself]; heal those who are in grace; keep those who by the power (virtute) of the tongue celebrate the faith, and guide those who have become learned in the sound of the tongue (voce linguae). Ever save those who do Thy will. Visit the widows. Sustain the orphans. Sustain those who have fallen asleep in the faith.

Grant to us also, O Lord, a portion with all Thy saints; grant to us strength to please Thee as they pleased Thee. Feed Thy people in uprightness and holiness; O Lord, give to us all who receive Thy holy things a union of minds [that] we may be filled with the Holy Ghost and with the strength of the true faith; that we may give thanks to Thee for ever, and to Thy beloved Son Jesus Christ, for Thine is the honour and glory, world without end.

O Helmsman of souls, Guide of the just and Glory of the saints, give to us, O Lord, understanding eyes[1] which may alway look to Thee, and ears also which may hear Thy word only, after that now our soul is filled (saturata) with Thy grace. Make in us a clean heart, O God, so that we may always observe (consideremus) Thy greatness, who art good and lovest man, our God; make (habe) our soul grateful[2] (gratam), and grant to us a constant mind, who have received Thy body and Thy own blood; we (are) Thy humble servants, for Thy kingdom, O Lord, is illustrious and glorious, O Father, Son, and Holy Ghost, now and for ever, and world without end. Amen.

Notes on the Anaphora of our Lord

1. It is taken with a few alterations from the *Testament*. It is not clear from Ludolf whether it is in actual use in Abyssinia as an alternative liturgy for certain days, or if it is obsolete. In any case it is later than the *Testament*, and Ludolf only gives the Anaphora. On the analogy of other Eastern rites, we may conclude that the pre-anaphoral portion of the Liturgy would be the same as in other Abyssinian liturgies, and that it would include the *Testament* Litany (see Note on I. 35, 36, p. 193 f.) as modified and still used in Abyssinia.

2. It is probably translated into Ethiopic from the Greek,

---

[1] Lit.: eyes of knowledge.   [2] Or: well pleasing (to Thee).

not from Syriac: (*a*) because it seems to be earlier than James of Edessa; (*b*) because the Syriac would not have been current in Egypt or Abyssinia. Therefore it is possible that where it differs from the *Testament* it reflects the Greek more faithfully than the Syriac. Some of the differences *may* be due to James of Edessa's translation of the *Testament* into Syriac.

3. The Sursum Corda no doubt immediately preceded the Eucharistic prayer; but as the Communion is absent from Ludolf, it is impossible to say whether the Sancta Sanctis followed the Sursum Corda as in Test., or if it came later as in other liturgies.

4. *First paragraph.* An. of our Lord omits the clause of Test. (p. 72) " whom in the latter times . . . Saviour " (homoiotel.?). It is in Eth. C.O.

It also omits the clause of Test. (*ib.*) " our mind, our soul . . . for ever and ever. Amen." All this, to the mention of the Incarnation, is not in Eth. C.O. Could the above clause have been interpolated in Test. by James of Edessa ? (Rahmani remarks on the *Amen* being out of place in Test.)

exiles = Test. (*ib.*) " those who are persecuted." (Persecution being a thing of the past.)

Shine upon us = Test. " make to arise." The Syriac word is used esp. of the sun (like ἀνατέλλω, which was probably the Greek word used), and may be translated " make to shine."

5. *Diptychs* not in Test. This is a characteristic of the later Egyptian rite: the intercession ¦and diptychs are inserted in the middle of the Eucharistic thanksgiving in this place. An. of O.L. shows the germ of what is found in St. Mark, Modern Coptic, and Modern Abyssinian; in these the priest adds a long intercession. The diptychs in An. of O.L., recited by the deacon, are almost word for word the same as the beginning of the modern Abyssinian intercession (Brightman, L.E.W. 228); but the people's response is not in the latter.

Seventy-two disciples (so Modern Abyssinian and often in Syriac literature) = LXX St. Luke x. 1. See p. 192.

five hundred companions, 1 Cor. xv. 6 ?

Three hundred and eighteen orthodox fathers, of Nicaea.

guide the way of the word in truth, paraphrase of ὀρθοτομοῦντα τὸν λόγον τῆς ἀληθείας, 2 Tim. ii. 15, but here applied to all the clergy, not to bishops only, as in Test. I. 35 and elsewhere (see p. 193).

6. *The priest saith* (p. 246). Note the grouping here as in the first paragraph, " Glory *of* thrones, Raiment *of* luminaries," etc., instead of a long list of unconnected substantives as in Test.

250   APPENDIX I

by Thy counsel; this in Test. (p. 72) goes with what precedes.

gates of life = Test. (p. 73), " way of life " (the latter is common in O.T., esp. Jer. xxi. 8, opp. " way of death," and Ps. xvi. 11, Prov. vi. 23, xv. 24; the phrase "gates of life" comes probably from a confusion with Ps. cxviii. 19).

ratify a treaty (p. 247) = Test. (*ib.*), " fix the boundary." Eth. C.O. has " establish a covenant." Probably this is the meaning also in Test.

his hands holy blessed and without spot. So many later liturgies; *e.g.* modern Abyss. (Brightman, L.E.W. 232); not in Test. [Cyr. Jer. xx. 5 has " Christ received the nails in His undefiled hands and feet." Cf. p. 171.]

bread, not in Test.

make a commemoration of Me = Test. (p. 73), " ye make My resurrection " (emendation in An. of O.L. in order to bring in our Lord's words; it also has the reference to 1 Cor. xi. 26).

An. of O.L., like Test., omits our Lord's words over the cup, though Eth. C.O. has them. But "after they had supped," " giving thanks," " blessing and sanctifying," are not in Test.; and An. of O.L. suddenly changes the address from the Father to the Son [sign of antiquity].

Thy true blood (verum sanguinem tuum), probably a protest against, and correction of, the Test. (p. 73), " type of the blood." Cf. also " Thy own blood " in Post-Communion prayer of An. of O.L. (p. 248), which is not in the corresponding passage of Test.

our sins, not in Test.

7. *Oblation and Invocation* (p. 247).

we trust in thee, not in Test. or Eth. C.O.

An. of O.L. here rather clumsily interpolates an Invocation of its own, in the later style; like the Eth. C.O., it asks for the Holy Ghost; but unlike it, it specifies the transforming of the elements. It then adds the Test. Epiclesis (p. 74) as an addition, addressing it, as Test., to the Holy Trinity. It corrects the order of the Persons (Jesus Christ, the Father, the Holy Ghost) into " Father of Jesus Christ," omitting " the Holy Ghost " [perhaps because the Third Person is mentioned in the interpolated Epiclesis] and " fleeing into itself." It inserts " we give Thee this gift " [which comes strangely out of place *after* the interpolated Epiclesis], and also adds a negative, " *not* food *nor* drink do we offer to Thy holiness," *i.e.* " not common food " [cf. Just. Mart. *Apol.* i. 66 : " For not as common bread or common drink," etc.].

See Note on the Invocation, p. 173 ff.

of the enemy and *of our bodies,* not in Test.

counsel of death = Test. (p. 74), "*proud conception.*"

who in Thy Name have been inscribed. In Test. (*ib.*) it is the name which is inscribed. The oratorical passage which follows is grammatically altered.

sorceries = Test. (*ib.*, see footnote), "that begetteth bitterness."

8. *The Intercession* (p. 248) comes here as in Test., but in St. Mark, Modern Coptic, and Modern Abyssinian it does not come here, but is joined on to the Diptychs (see above). In An. of O.L. the references to revelations and gifts of healing, etc., are altered, and the phrase "power of tongues" is given a more modern turn.

9. *The Communion* is not given by Ludolf. Brightman (L.E.W. 240, note) gives from the Anaphora of our Lord: "The body of Jesus Christ which is of the Holy Ghost to hallow soul and spirit." See Test. II. 10 and Note there (p. 223).

10. *Post-Communion*, "O Helmsman of souls" (p. 248). That this is meant for a post-communion is seen by the past tense ("who have received Thy body"), whereas in the preceding paragraph we have the present, "who receive Thy holy things." So in Test. (p. 77).

APPENDIX II

THE LAST CHAPTER OF THE ARABIC DIDASCALIA

From the German of Funk, *Apost. Konst.* p. 234 ff.

§ 39. THE MYSTAGOGIA OF JESUS CHRIST, OUR GOD

THE faithful shall lift it upon high before the holy Liturgy, the Testament that He hath taught to the holy Apostles.

He who was from the beginning, and who is present and who is to come, He who died and was buried and rose again and was crowned with glory by the Father; He who hath loosed the bond of death, and who rose again from the dead; and not only art Thou Man, but Thou hast become Man without change; He who by the Holy Spirit took possession of the body of Adam and made him living; He who put on the Adam of death and made him awake, and with the body hath ascended up into heaven; He who overcame death and burst its bonds by His death, and shamed the Devil who this long time was set as lord and king over us, after he had discovered His entrance and His power, and He had burst his bonds; as his [death's] face was full of darkness, he grew fearful and was agitated when he saw the Only-begotten Son of God put on a body from a Virgin and come down to Hades. And He is the indivisible Counsel and the one Shepherd with the Father, the Maker of heaven with the Father, the Crown of angels, the Order of the highest angels, the Will of hosts, the Spirit of the glory, the Master of the eternal kingdom, the Prince of the pure, the incomprehensible Intellect of the Father. He is the Wisdom of the Father, He is the Power, He is the Right, He the Intelligence, He is the Counsel, He is the Hand, He is the Arm of the Father. We believe and confess that He is the Light of our redemption, the Helper, Teacher, Rewarder; who taketh us up; who hath won the victory thereby; our Fortress, our Shepherd, our Support, the Founder of life, our Medicine, our Food, our Judge. The confession which we confess is this: that He suffered and was born without being created; that He died while He was living, Son of the living, Son of the Father, the indivisible. Who while He was without sin took upon Him our sins; who came forth from the bosom of the Father; who distributed His redeeming body and His life-giving blood, (being) the spirit of life and purity; who made us pure through the water of baptism; who maketh glad the hearts of those who fear Him, since He is with them at all times; who hath removed us from all onsets of Satan; who hath renewed our souls, since we all exist in Him. He is God before all times, and He was with God the eternal, the everlasting. When He saw that the world was ruined through the chains of sin, and through the ignorance and the blindness that worked the error of those hellish thoughts (?), and when He desired to heal the human race, He made the Virgin's body His goal, and He placed Himself in union with it, and He healed all our senses, and He made all the adversaries' hosts to disappear, and He put on a weak body; He who is incomprehensible made the mortal body incorruptible. And therefore He appeared in the body of Adam, in order to make manifest a likeness (Bild) of incorruption in the body of Adam; He who put on an incorruptible likeness and died in that likeness, and through the Gospel freed those who had fallen into ruin and gave them holy commandments; He who is the Word of the kingdom of heaven in this Gospel. And the Devil's bonds are broken off from men, that we by His death might have a title to freedom from death, and wake up in the real world. He who is the Christ, the Son of God, hath become man, and hath taken to Him our mortal nature, which belongeth to Adam and his race. He is the first who became man, and He is the God whom the prophets began to recognise, who is proclaimed to us by the Apostles, and whom all men confess, and by God is crowned with glory, and is celebrated by the angels, and for us was crucified, whose cross is our life; who is our Support and our Saviour, the hidden Mystery, the indescribable Joy, who at all times standeth on the highest grade of the perfection which is beloved, which is inseparable from God, whose worth (Wert) cannot be uttered by these lips, the hidden mystery which the faithful know that they know though it is invisible. He is the Crucified, it is He who hath been extolled, as crowned with glory; it is He in whom we, the perfectly faithful ones, believe; and we free our pure souls from the senses, so that it is as if in truth they were not there at all, and thereby we are strong. Keep away from all transitory things, and become deaf with these pure ears, that ye may find what is well-pleasing to God, and that ye may learn to know the secret of your redemption. Ye, men and women, who boast that ye belong to Christ, must become one with the inner man, ye in whom Christ hath confirmed His covenant, and into whom He hath put His Spirit. And He hath also descended to Hades after He died, and hath made them all to live. And when Death saw Him who had come down to him, he was struck, and thought that he had found in Him a food after his desire. But when he saw the beauty of His Divinity in Him, he cried aloud and said: Who is He that conquereth me and is not like the men who are with me? Who is He that rescueth (lit., reneweth) from destruction the body which I killed? Who is He that is born without sin and destroyed sin, being Himself without sin? Who is He that put on the carnal man, being Himself from heaven? Who is He that is a stranger to my law? Who is He that robbed me of the nations which belonged to me? Who is He that giveth food through the strength of fire and death, while He hath gained the victory over them? Who is He whom the bonds of darkness could not bind? Who is He in this new apparition, whose power preventeth my doing what I will? Who is this new one, wrapped in a shroud, who is without sin? Who is He that destroyeth the treasurer of darkness by His glory, and who doth not let the souls come to me which have been delivered up to me, but causeth them to rise upwards? Who is this glory that is one and the same with the Imperishable One, and which doth not let me destroy him? Who is He whom I cannot touch? Who is He, surrounded by this light, which doth not diminish? Who is He that hath deposed me, lest I should destroy those belonging to Him who are worth nothing? It is the Christ who was crucified, on account of whom those that are on the left go to the right, and who hath raised those that were below so that they are now above, and hath made those that were behind to be before. He is raised from the dead, and hath conquered Hades, and hath by His death destroyed Death. And after His resurrection on the third day He thanked the Word of God the Father, while He said: I thank Thee, O King, for the speech (Rede) through which the whole creation hath come into existence from Thy side. That is the word that through the Spirit is in Us, which speaketh with Thee alone.

The Didascalia is ended, the doctrine of our Fathers the Apostles, consisting of thirty-nine chapters.

INDEX OF QUOTATIONS FROM AND REFERENCES TO THE BIBLE IN THE TESTAMENT OF OUR LORD

OLD TESTAMENT AND APOCRYPHA

Reference	Page	Reference	Page
Genesis iii. 8–10	70	Isaiah ix. 6	83
Exodus xix. 6	73	xi. 2	50
Leviticus xxii. 25	70	xxvi. 18	53
Numbers xi. 17-29	91	xlvii. 1	56
Deuteronomy xxix. 4	69, 89	li. 9	85
2 Samuel xiv. 7	83	liii. 1	85
xxi. 17	83	lx. 20	83
Job v. 9	104	lxv. 24	82
Psalm iv. 3	79	Jeremiah xvi. 17	70
xvi. 3	79	xxi. 8	73 (cf. 250)
li. 10	77	xxix. 11	72
12	66	xxxiii. 22	61
lxix. 5	70	Micah v. 3	56
lxxxii. 6	83	Zechariah xi. 15-17	54
lxxxvi. 11	66	2 Esdras v. 8	53
cxlvi. 3, 4	54	vi. 21	53
Proverbs xxix. 3	117	Song of the Three Children 35-65	137
Ecclesiastes xii. 2	83		

NEW TESTAMENT

Reference	Page	Reference	Page
St. Matthew[1] iv. 23	78	St. Matthew xviii. 20	68, 106
v. 13	113, 131	xxi. 9	75
16	59	xxiv. 7	51
24	70	8	59
vi. 9 ff.	76	13	54
19	80	15	57
25 ff.	92	24	56
vii. 6	61, 93	xxv. 12	102
13	54	21	95
18	138	xxvi. 27, 28	73
x. 22	54	41	51, 58
xii. 4	68	St. Mark xiii. 3, 4	50
xiii. 25	93	xiii. 8	59
xvi. 16	72	13	54
24	58, 81, 87, 106	27	55
xviii. 10	107	xvi. 18	78
16	107	St. Luke iii. 14	118

---

[1] In the case of parallel passages occurring in more than one of the Synoptists, the reference to St. Matthew alone is ordinarily given.

INDEX OF QUOTATIONS, ETC.

Reference	Page
St. Luke ix. 23	58
x. 19	83
20	64
xvi. 8	50
xx. 36	61
xxi. 25	53
xxiv. 51	138
St. John v. 24	86
viii. 12	93
x. 34	83
xii. 36	50
xiv. 2	50
3	97
17	78
20	137
27	138
xvii. 12	51
20	50, 91
xx. 17	59
22	50
xxi. 18	73
Acts i. 7	51
i. 14	60
24	67
ix. 15	51
xiii. 2	64
37	88
xv. 29	133
xx. 28	64
29	130
xxvi. 7	67
Romans viii. 15	89
viii. 22	123
ix. 21	108
xii. 11	102, 104, 106
xiii. 13	93
xiv. 10	93
xv. 6	104, 122
33	138
xvi. 16	92
20	74
25, 26	87
1 Corinthians i. 27	108
ii. 6, 7	79
7	87
9	89
10-14	62
15	94
vii. 40	117
xi. 10	71
24, 25, 26	73
xii. 1-10	114
8	74
9	74, 78
10	74
xiv. 16	75
26, 30	74
xv. 50-54	122
1 Corinthians xvi. 13	87
2 Corinthians i. 3	66
v. 10	93
xii. 2	62
xiii. 11	138
Galatians iv. 6	89
v. 22	69
vi. 14	62
Ephesians i. 18	75, 106
ii. 20	102
iv. 22	95
v. 2	67, 121
8	50
19	63
Philippians ii. 7	86
ii. 13	66
20	68, 106, 109
iii. 10	50
iv. 9	138
Colossians i. 12	75
i. 16	122
iii. 14	103
16	63
1 Thessalonians v. 5	50
v. 17	58, 106
20	71
2 Thessalonians ii. 3	51
ii. 4	51, 56
7	59
9	56
1 Timothy ii. 9	119
ii. 12	107
iii. 2, 3	64, 65
12	97
13	112
16	87
v. 5	60
10	106
17	63
2 Timothy ii. 15	100, 112
ii. 20, 21	51
21	108
iii. 2	54
Titus i. 6	64, 65
i. 8	64, 104
ii. 14	121
iii. 5	127
Hebrews ii. 14	88
vii. 3	91
xi. 5, 8	66
xiii. 2	128
St. James i. 17	71, 80, 107, 121
i. 22	54
iii. 10	88
1 Peter i. 12	80
i. 17	76
ii. 9	73
v. 7	59

INDEX OF QUOTATIONS, ETC.

	PAGE		PAGE
2 Peter i. 4	83	Revelation v. 8	107
ii. 4	95	vii. 15	67
13	96	xii. 9	56
1 John i. 1	49	xiii. 8	64
ii. 6	97	17	56
iii. 2	138	xiv. 13	58
iv. 1	55	15	58
St. Jude 12	96	xvi. 19	56
Revelation i. 3	61	xvii. 8	64
i. 8	85	xxi. 6	91
ii. 17	129	12	64
iv. 11	66	xxii. 13	91

INDEX OF SUBJECTS AND AUTHORS

ABGARUS, 185.
Abyssinian Church, 5; its liturgy, 34, 43, 167, 169, 172, 177, 178, 223, 249 f.; used milk and honey at baptism, 44; its litany, 43, 193 f. See Anaphora of our Lord.
Achelis, Professor, 9, 10, 28, 29, 151, 155, 157, 159, 203, 208, 213, 215–217, 220 f., 225, 231, 233, 239.
Acolytes, at Rome, 192; none in the East, *ib.*
Acts and Martyrdom of Matthew, 199.
Adai (Addai), Preaching of, 158.
Adai (Addai) and Mari, Liturgy of, its date, 35; omits Words of Institution, 35, 171; its Invocation, 35, 175; benediction before Sursum Corda in, 169; deacon "completing" in, 194.
"Adam" used for man, 85, 86, 184.
Administration of Eucharist, 76, 128, 177 f., 220–224, 251.
Admonition, see Deacon.
Africa, 56; name of metropolitan not used in, in fourth century, 37.
Agapé, the, 29, 31, 96, 130 f., 134, 189, 226, 228–230.
Agde, Council of, 210.
Alaric, 145.
Alford, Dean, 225, 228.
Alms (διακονία) to be delivered promptly, 129, 225 f.
Altar, the, 63, 64, 68, 70, 78, 92, 149 f.
Ambrose, St., 239.
Ambrosian Liturgy, 169.
Ambrosiaster, 173, 202, 218.
Amen of communicants, 21, 76 f., 128, 178, 221 f.
Anachronisms of the *Testament*, 27; of Codex C., 51, 143.
Anaphora of our Lord (Abyssinian), 21, 34 f., 74, 165, 167, 170, 172 f., 176, 192, 223, 245–251.
Ancyra, Council of, 37, 154, 182.

Angelic hierarchy, 23, 72, 85, 96, 122, 124, 137, 170 f., 184, 246, 249, 252.
Angels visiting man, 23, 68, 71, 99.
Anointing, see Baptism, and Oil.
Antichrist, 42, 51 ff., 56–58, 141, 144, 146.
Antidote (the Eucharist), 137, 239.
Antioch, Council of, in Encaeniis, 153.
Antioch, Liturgy of, see Chrysostom.
Antiphonal singing, 129, 135, 180 f., 227.
Antithesis, fondness of, 22, 86, 122, 123, 182–184, 252 f.
Apocalypse and *Testament* compared, 148.
Apocalypse of John (Apocryphal), 58.
Apocalyptic prelude, whether independent, 141–144; its connecting link with the Church Order, 147.
Apollinarians, 17, 36.
Apollinarius, his heresy and characteristic phrases, 16 ff., 35, 43, 44, 183–185.
"Apostle," the (St. Paul), the liturgical Epistle, 164, 181, 204.
Apostles, 21, 27, 63, 69, 81, 87, 100, 102, 110, 136; festivals of, in A.C., 32.
Apostolic Canons, their date, 13, 153; on marriage of the clergy, 153; forbid digamy to the clergy, *ib.*; allow bishops to eat meat, 163; on Lent, 218; on Wednesday and Friday fasts, 163.
Apostolic Church Order, 9; its scope and date, 11, 12, 29; its influence on the *Testament*, 11, 45, 145; its Montanistic characteristics, 12, 45; its place of origin, 12; on the order of the Apostles, 12, 144; slights women's ministry, 148, 198; division of presbyters in, 150, 200; dislikes marriage of bishops and presbyters, 153 ff., 186; allows deacons' marriage, 190; widows in, 191 f., 198; number of presbyters

and deacons in, 192, 200; on the position of readers, 203 f.; on women's veils, 210; manuscripts of, 143.
Apostolic Constitutions, their scope and date, 11, 13, 29, 32; theology of, 19, 24, 44; on our Lord's human soul, 19; subordinationism in, 19; festivals in, 32, 39; fasts in, 39, 163; probably later than the *Testament*, 32, 33; no metropolitans in, 37; stations of penitents in, 38; ascetics in, 38; the "Lifegiver" in, 40, 184; church buildings in, 149; bishop's throne in, 150; on marriage of clergy, 153; on qualifications and choice of a bishop, 153; on enthronisation of a bishop, 160; on laying on of hand or hands, 161; lavabo in, 155; day for ordinations in, 155; bishop's ordination prayer in, 158; the three bishops in, 32, 156; form of doxologies in, 160; appoint Saturday and Sunday for divine service, 163; allow wine to bishops, 163; liturgy in, 33, 167; Eucharistic Intercession in, 33, 167; Sanctus in, 170; position of Benedictus in, 177; on the ceremonial law, 177; Words of Institution in, 171 f.; Invocation in, 33, 176; blessing of oil and water in, 179; use of the name "Paraclete" in, 179; singers in, 38, 180 f.; on preaching, 182; on benedictions, 182; dismissal of penitents, etc., in, 33, 182; antithesis in, 184; on ordination of a presbyter, the other presbyters not acting, 186 f.; daily service in, 189, 227; number of presbyters in, 192; on the office of a deacon, 193; on deacons visiting the sick, 190 f.; on deacons keeping order, 232; litany in, 33, 193 f.; on confessors, 197; on widows and deaconesses and presbyteresses, 33, 44, 197–199; use the name "Lifegiver," 184, 201; on the position and ordination of readers and subdeacons, 33, 202 f., 205; on the promotion of readers and deacons, 202; on virgins, 205; on charismata, 33, 205 f.; on "newcomers," 207; forbidden trades in, 209; on soldiers, 33, 209; on length of catechumenate, 210; kiss of peace in, 210; veiling of women in, 210; on teaching and dismissal of catechumens, 33, 211; on baptism and anointing, 33, 215 f.; on Lent and Holy Week, 39, 44, 218; forbid deacons to baptize, 225; words of administration of Eucharist in, 223; psalmody in, 227; on days of rest, 228; on first fruits, 230 f.; on hours of prayer, 237.
"Appointment" of clergy (κατάστασις), 90, 97, 104, 105, 108, 111, 112, 153, 186.
Aquila, 138, 240.
Arabic Didascalia, last five chapters of, 10, 12; date, 33, 34; probably later than Test., 33 f., 154 f., 158, 161 f., 167, 176, 183; trace of a primacy in, 37, 155; church buildings in, 148 ff.; baptistery, diaconicum, lectern, bishop's house in, *ib.*; screen in, 151; allows bishop's marriage, but prefers celibacy, 154; bishop's ordination prayer in, 155 f., 158; omits revelations, 156; on days for the Eucharist, 163; on bishops' fasts and the three "Entrances," 162; daily communion of bishops in, 164; description of Eucharist in, 166 f.; incense in, 167; allows widows to be inside the sanctuary, 167 f.; developed Intercession in, 167, 176; Mystagogia in, 34, 88, 182 ff., 252–254; identifies widows and deaconesses, 167, 200; theology of, 34; psalmody, etc., in, 167; on readers of lections, 204.
Arabic translation of *Testament*, see Copto-arabic.
Arcadius, 145.
Archdeacons, none in the *Testament*, 36, 152 (see Deacon, chief); at Alexandria read Gospel, 204; the name, 152.
Arendzen, Dr., 7, 11, 143, 145, 146, 188, 192, 198.
Arianism combated in the *Testament*, 16 ff., 35, 40, 160.
Arians, 36.
Arles, Council of, 38, 208, 223.
Armenia, 57.
Armenian Church, its liturgy, 169, 177; its churches, 151.
Ascension, the, 27, 32, 126, 138, 217 f.
Asceticism, 15, 21, 24, 94.
Ascetics, 38; see Solitaries.
Asia Minor, 12; considered as place of writing of Test., 45, 159, 240; chorepiscopi in, 37.
Astronomers and astrologers not to be catechumens, 118 (cf. 123), 209.
Athanasius, St., 17, 29, 224, 242; on Lent, 218; on doxologies, 160; on veils, 151; as leader of the deacons, 152.

INDEX OF SUBJECTS AND AUTHORS

Audians, 45, 240.
Augustine, St., 38, 168, 216, 227, 232.

BABES, 73, 76, 125, 178, 213 f.
Babylon, 56.
Ball, Rev. C. J., 241.
Bangor, Antiphonary of, 201.
Baptism, time for, 121; order of, 125 ff., 213 ff.; water must be flowing at, *ib.*; responses at, *ib.*; renunciations and submissions at, 33, 126, 213 ff.; anointing before and after, 126 f., 213 ff. (see Confirmation); Eucharist after, 128, 220 ff.; formula absent, 214, 216; action split up, 216. See Creed.
Baptism of blood, 120, 211.
Baptistery, 21, 34, 63 f., 149.
Basil, St., 17, 38, 164, 239; Liturgy of (so-called), 169, 177.
Bathing at Pascha, 109, 121, 201 f.
Batiffol, P., 25.
Beginning of the day, 136, 159, 161, 164.
Benedicite Omnia Opera, 137, 238.
Benediction, two forms of, before Sursum Corda, 44, 169. See also Laying on of the hand, and Seal.
Benedictus qui venit, 42, 44, 75, 167, 177.
Bilingual countries, 43. See Interpreters.
Bishop, the throne of, 63, 149; house of, 64; offers the oblations, 63; qualifications of, 64, 153; marriage of, 65, 153 ff.; ordination of, 65 ff., 155 ff.; age of, 65; no enthronisation mentioned in *Testament*, 160; as high priest, 135, 160, 234 f.; concurrence of other bishops at ordination of, 30, 65, 155 f.; whether one or several bishops say the words, 30, 155 f.; ordination on Sunday, 65, 155; hours of prayer of, 68, 161; fasts of, 22, 68, 162 f.; food of, 68, 69, 162 f.; teaching and preaching of, 69, 84-90, 130, 164, 182; daily communion of, in Arab. Didasc., 164; dividing the word of truth, 100, 193; exorcising, 121-124, 212; breathes on catechumens, 124, 212; at Agapé, 130 f., 228 f.; receiving first fruits, 131 f., 231; visiting sick, 135, 234; providing for sexton, 136, 235; provides for the marriage of catechumens, 116; provides for virgins, 134. See Shepherd.
Bithynia, 57.

Blessings, see Eulogiae, and Benediction.
Bona, 180.
Book of Deer, 138.
Boys, see Singers.
Bread, blessing of, for the sick, 179. See Eulogiae.
Bread of exorcism, 228 f.
Brightman, Rev. F. E., 11, 13, 14, 19, 28, 38, 151, 153, 160, 164-167, 169-173, 175-179, 193 f., 204, 213, 223, 225, 229, 235, 239, 249-251.
Bryennios, Archbishop, 11.
Bunsen, C. J., 11, 12.
Burial of the dead, 98, 135, 235.
Burkitt, F. C., 215.
Byzantine rite (early), 169.

CALLISTUS, Pope, 154.
Canons of Hippolytus, scope of, 8, 9; date of, 28; not the original of these Church Orders, 8, 9; sanctuary veil in, 151; their silence about celibacy of the clergy, 153; bishops chosen by people in, 153; bishop's ordination prayer in, 28, 156, 157; on laying on of hand or hands, 161; on bishops as chief priests, 160; enthronisation of bishops in, 160; communion of bishops in, 163; liturgy described in, 165; vestments in, 163, 178; antithesis in, 184; presbyters not said to act with bishop in ordaining a presbyter, 186; ordination prayer of a presbyter same as for bishops, 28, 186 f.; restricts deacons, 195; ordination of deacon in, 196; on confessors, 196; on widows, 197; absence of deaconesses in, 200; on the position of a reader, 203 f.; no subdeacons (?) in, 203; on virgins, 205; on charismata, 205; on "newcomers," 207; forbidden trades in, 208; on soldiers, 208; length of catechumenate in, 210; on separation of sexes, 210; on dismissal of catechumens, 211; on martyred catechumens, 211; on competentes and their exorcism, 211 f.; on baptism and confirmation, 213, 219; creed in, 217; baptismal Eucharist in, 220; on administrators of Eucharist, 223; on care of the Eucharistic species, 224; on almsgiving, 226; Agapé in, 228, 230; first fruits in, 230 f.; on fasting communion, 233, 239; on the Lenten fast, 233; on bishops visiting sick, 234; on sick

INDEX OF SUBJECTS AND AUTHORS 261

presbyters, 234 ; on the dying, 235 ; on hours of prayer, 236 ; on married men's prayers, 238 ; conclusion of, 239.
Canticles, 63, 81, 129, 133, 179–181.
Cantors, see Singers.
Cappadocia, 56.
Carthage, Third Council of, 239.
Cassian, 237.
Catechumens, 29, 38 ; house of, 63, 149 ; dismissed with "laying on of the hand," 84, 120 f., 134, 182, 211 f. ; celibacy of, 116, 207 ; not to offer loaf for Eucharist, 70 ; or to be at the Agapé, 130, 228 f. ; intercession for, 101 ; rules for reception and marriage of, 115 ff., 207 ; length of instruction of, 119, 210 ; who to be admitted and who refused, 115 ff., 207 ff. ; exorcism of, 121 ff., 212 f. ; if martyred before baptism, 120, 211 ; called "Christians," 207, 210 ; to pray apart, 119, 210 ; to be examined, 120 f., 211.
Celibates, Celibacy, see Bishop, marriage of, Asceticism, Catechumens, and Virgins.
Ceremonial Law of the Jews, 177.
Chalcedon, Oecumenical Council of, 179.
Characteristic phrases in *Testament*, 21 ff.
Characteristics of *Testament*, 20 ff., 143.
Charisius, 242.
Charismata, 15, 33, 76, 78, 114, 169, 205 f.
Chief deacon, see Deacon.
Children of light, see Light.
Choirs, see Singers.
Chorepiscopi, 37, 45.
Chrism, 216. See Baptism.
Christmas, see Epiphany.
Chrysostom, St., encourages monasticism, 38 ; Eucharistic Intercession in writings of, 176 ; benediction before Sursum Corda in, 169 ; Sanctus in, 170 ; Words of Institution in, 171 ; Invocation in, 175 ; on the Lord's Prayer, 178 ; on preaching, 182 ; Liturgy of (so-called), 169, 173, 177.
Church, double meaning of, 149 ; buildings of, 36, 62–64, 148–153.
Churchyards, 135 f. ; keeper of, 136, 235.
Cilicia, 56.
Cirta, Church of, 235.
Clement of Rome, St., 7, 49, 114, 115, 138, 141, 144, 159 f., 188.

Clement, Pseudo-, Ancient Homily by, 182.
Clergy, list and number of, 99, 191 ; college of, 15, 64.
"Commemoration," 63, 101, 151.
Communicants, prayer of, 33, 76, 178.
Communion of clergy, 76, 177 ; of people, 76, 128, 178, 221 ff. ; of the sick, 134 ; a "new food," 134.
Competentes, 120 ff., 211 f.
Concelebration, 70, 165.
Concubines, 118, 208 f.
Confessors, 29 ; in the litany, 100 ; not to be ordained unless appointed bishops, 105, 196 f. ; relative position of, 203.
Confirmation, 127, 219 f.
Confusion of Persons, 20, 39, 91, 187, 247, 250.
Constantine, 36 ; his churches at Jerusalem, 43, 150.
Constantinople, penitents at, 38 ; first Oecumenical Council of, 40 ; Creed of, 20, 40, 78, 85, 201, 241 f.
Constitutiones per Hippolytum, 10, 29 ; bishop's ordination prayer in, 157 f. ; appointment of readers in, 33, 204.
Consubstantial, 20, 40, 108, 201, 241 f.
Coptic Liturgy, 5, 34, 167, 169, 172, 178, 223, 249.
Copto-arabic translation of *Testament*, 6, 42, 43, 49, 51–54, 56, 58–60, 68, 90, 136, 143, 145, 156, 160, 162 f., 165, 167, 169, 188–192, 194 f., 197 f., 201, 202, 205, 209, 211, 223 f., 225–227.
Cornelius, his list of clergy at Rome in 251 A.D., 192.
Courtyard, the, 62 f.
Creed at baptism, 31, 44, 126, 217 f., 224 ; at Jerusalem and Rome, 215, 242.
Cross, taking up the, 15, 58, 62, 71, 81, 87, 91, 106 ; festival of the, 40, 43.
Cup of the Eucharist, see Mixed Chalice ; spilling the cup, brings judgment, 128, 224.
Cyprian, St., 216 ; on readers, 203 ; on hours of service, 168 ; on "hearers," 37 ; on oblations for the dead, 235.
Cyril of Alexandria, St., 224.
Cyril of Jerusalem, St., 14, 242, 250 ; Liturgy in, 167 f. ; Sanctus in, 171 ; on the Eucharistic type, 173 ; Eucharistic Intercession in, 168, 176 ; Lord's Prayer in, 178 ; Sancta Sanctis in, 168, 170 ; no Fraction

INDEX OF SUBJECTS AND AUTHORS

in, 179; does not mention Words of Institution in the Liturgy, 170 f.; reference to Oblation, 171; Invocation in, 168, 171, 174; speaks slightingly of apocryphal books on Antichrist, 144; on the "Seal," 213; on baptism, 215; creed in, 215 f.; oil of exorcism in, 216; on confirmation, 220; on the teaching of the resurrection, 224.

DAILY service, 95 ff., 189.
Date of *Testament*, 25-42; of Trèves fragment, 141 ff.
David de Bernham, Bishop of St. Andrews, his pontifical, 180.
Dawn, order of service at, 164 f.
Day, see Beginning of the day.
Deaconesses, 33, 64, 70, 76, 101, 106, 135, 169, 192, 198-200, 205, 216, 234.
Deacons, praise of, 21, 190; menial duties of, 37, 191; the chief deacon, 36, 63 f., 152, 191; house of, 62, 64; position of, in church, 70; admonition, or ectene, or litany of, 33, 70, 99-102, 103, 121, 169, 192-194; as singers, 81; visiting the sick and needy, 94, 98, 190 f., 234; communion of, 76; qualifications of, 97; marriage of, 97, 190; admonish catechumens, 98; burial duties of, 98, 99, 235; as almoners, 98, 99; keep order in the church, 98, 102, 133, 232; as "counsellors of the clergy and mysteries of the Church," 31, 98, 190; as ministers of the bishop, 98, 104, 193, 195 f.; as guest masters, 64, 99; number of, 99, 191 f.; as the eye of the Church, 99, 193; disciplinary duties of, 102, 103, 194, 232; admonish penitents, 103; discretion of, 194; ordination of, 104, 196; not appointed to the priesthood, 104, 195 f.; at baptism, 125 f., 213-215; at the baptismal Eucharist, 128, 221 f.; as administrators of the Eucharist, 129, 223; baptizing in case of necessity, 129, 225; carrying the Eucharist to the sick, 134, 234; but not to presbyters, 129, 134, 234; prayed for in the litany, 100; offering a lamp, 129; "offering" the Oblation, 222; waving fans, 128 (?), 167, 222.
Death, Address of, 87, 88, 183, 185 f., 254.
Decius, see Dexius.
De Lagarde, see Lagarde.

Demoniacs, 33, 117, 121, 124, 212.
Departed, the faithful, prayers for, 74, 101, 132, 135, 177, 235; oblations for, 235.
Descent into hell, see Harrowing of Hades.
"Detailed Creed," the, 18.
De Virginitate, Tract, 189.
Dexius, 141.
Diaconicum, 62? 64, 149.
Didaché, 11, 13, 143, 163, 177 f., 212, 215, 228 f.
Didascalia, 12, 13, 199. See Arabic Didascalia, Ethiopic Didascalia, Apostolic Constitutions, Verona Fragments.
Didymus, 160.
Digamy, 15; forbidden to clergy, 153; of women, 198.
Diocese (παροικία), 92, 138, 188, 240.
Diocletian persecution, 204.
Dionysius of Alexandria, 28.
Diptychs, 167, 245 f., 249.
Disc (= paten), 129, 225.
Doorkeepers, 192, 232, 235.
Dorotheus, 240.
Dositheus, 138, 240.
Doxologies to prayers, 39, 159 f.
Doxology of the Lord's Prayer, 178.
Dreams, see Interpreters.
Duchesne, Abbé, 28, 218, 238.

EAST, the, 57; of a church, 63, 108, 149 f.
East Syrians (Nestorians), their churches, 151 f.; their baptism, 216, 220; their confirmation, 220; their liturgies, 35 (see Adai, Nestorius, Theodore); their Lent, 218; their chorepiscopi, 37; forbid bishops to eat meat, 163; their hymns of praise, 179; apply the Sursum Corda, 180; their choirs, 181; their lections, 204; their repetitions, 173.
Easter, see Pascha.
Easter Even, 22, 121, 133, 212, 226, 233.
Eastern Church (Orthodox), 151, 220, 225.
Ectene, see Deacon.
Edessene Canons, 14.
Egypt, interpreters in, 43; considered as place of writing of *Testament*, 44, 163, 169.
Egyptian Church Order, scope of, 9; date of, 29; does not touch on Arianism, 29; on the choice of bishops by the people, 153; says nothing of clerical celibacy, 153;

INDEX OF SUBJECTS AND AUTHORS 263

omits bishop's ordination prayer, 156 f.; has same form for bishops and presbyters, 29; on the laying on of hand or hands, 161; on the kiss of peace, 160; description of liturgy in, 165; fraction in, 179; on the ordination of presbyters, 186 f.; restricts deacons, 190, 195; on confessors, 196 f.; on widows, 197 f., 203; no deaconesses in, 200; on the position of the reader, 203; on virgins, 205; on charismata, 205; on "newcomers," 207; forbidden trades in, 208 f.; on soldiers, *ib.*; length of catechumenate in, 210; on separation of sexes, 210; dismissal of catechumens in, 211; on competentes and their exorcism, 211 f.; on baptism and confirmation, 214, 216; creed in, 217 f., 242; on the Eucharistic type, 222; baptismal Eucharist in, 221; administrators of Eucharist in, 223 f.; on care of the Eucharistic species, 224 f.; the "white stone" in, 224 f.; Agapé in, 228 f.; on first fruits, 230 f.; on the fast before Easter, 233; on bishops visiting the sick, 234; on burial of the dead, 235; on hours of prayer, 236 f.; on married men's prayers, 238; on fasting communion, 233, 239; on mutual instruction, 238; Greek original of, 29, 44; reputed authorship of, 141; conclusion of, 239.

Egyptian Heptateuch, 12, 13, 29, 147, 153. See the preceding and following.

Egyptian Liturgy derived from Ap. Const., 167, 170, 176, 223.

Elvira, Council of, 38, 164, 194, 202, 210, 212, 225, 228.

Embalming, 135, 235.

Emperors, Empire, see State.

Entrances to church and baptistery and exits, 62, 63, 148 f.

"Entrances," the eighteen exalted, 22, 68, 162.

Ephesus, Oecumenical Council of, 152, 242; Robber Synod of, 191.

Ephrem Syrus, St., 178, 184, 225.

Epiclesis, see Invocation.

Epiphanius, on presbyteresses, 39, 199; on fasts, 163; on sextons, 235; uses "the Lord," "the Lifegiver" of the Holy Ghost, 40, 201, 241 f.

Epiphany, 32, 39, 40, 90, 109.

Ethiopic Church Order, scope of, 9; date of, 30; bishop's ordination prayer in, 157 f.; on choice of bishops by the people, 153; says nothing about clerical celibacy, 153; on laying on of hand or hands, 161; liturgy in, 30, 165; absence of Eucharistic intercession in, 166, 176; meaning of "Remembering therefore" in, 173; position of Sancta Sanctis in, 170; Words of Institution in, 171 f.; Invocation in, 175 f.; ordination prayer for presbyters in, 30, 187; restricts deacons, 190, 195; on widows, readers, and subdeacons, 203; its liturgy a source of Test., 30, 44.

Ethiopic Didascalia, 12; allows bishops to be married, 154; incense in, 167; on deacons, 195 f.; on baptism of women, 216.

Ethiopic Statutes, see Ethiopic Church Order.

Ethiopic translation of the *Testament*, 6, 43, 170, 173.

Eucharist, days for, 69, 163; on Saturday, 69, 163 f.; hour for, 78, 163, 168; liturgy in the *Testament*, 69 ff.; in other Church Orders, 165 ff.; after baptism, 128 f., 220 ff.; administration and administrators of, 128 f., 222 ff. See also Communion, Type, Offering.

Eulogiae, 130, 133, 228-230.

Eusebius of Caesarea, 28, 150, 185, 192.

Eustathians, 154.

Eutychianism, 180. See Monophysitism.

Entychius, 192.

Exorcism, see Catechumens; oil of, 125 f., 213-216.

Exorcists, house of, 63; number of, at Rome, 192; in A.C., 205 f.

FALLEN, intercession for the, 101.

Fans, 128 (?), 167.

Fasts, 16, 21, 39, 44; of bishops, 22, 68; of presbyters, 92; before Easter, 39, 121, 134, 163, 233; before communion, 76, 134, 137, 233, 239; Eucharist on fast days, 69,163 f.; fast days in the week, 16, 44, 163.

Feast kept after bishop's ordination, 22, 67.

Festivals, in *Testament*, 39, 40; in Ap. Const., 32, 39.

Ffoulkes, Dr., 171, 174.

First fruits, 31, 131-133, 230 f.

Forbidden trades, 117 f., 208 f.

Forecourt, see Courtyard.

Forgery, question of, 26 ff.

Fraction, absence of, in *Testament*, 179; found in other authorities, *ib.*
Funerals, see Burial of the Dead; feasts at, 189.
Funk, Dr., 10, 13, 19, 25, 28, 29, 149 f., 166, 252.

GALLICAN Statutes, 14, 161, 186, 196.
Games, participants in, not to be catechumens, 117, 208.
Gamurrini, J. F., 14.
Gangra, Council of, 153 f., 232.
Geyer, Dr., 14.
Gifts, see Charismata.
Gloria in excelsis, 189.
Good Friday, 39, 121, 211 f., 226, 239.
Gospel, by whom read, 84, 119; in instruction of catechumens, 95, 119, 121, 211.
Grace at meals, 133, 232.
Grammarians, 117, 208 f.
Graveyard, gravediggers, see Churchyard.
Gregory of Nyssa, St., 38.
Guest house, the, 64, 99, 153.
Gwilliam, Rev. G. H., 177.

HABITATIONS, eternal, heavenly, 22, 50, 66, 81, 96, 103, 112, 122, 127.
Hammond, Rev. C. H., 169 f.
Haneberg, Dr. von, 9.
Harklean Version of Bible, 68.
Harnack, Dr., 25, 29, 30, 141, 144.
Harrowing of Hades, 74, 85, 87, 88, 185, 254.
Hauler, Dr., see Verona fragments.
Hearing (= becoming a catechumen), 106.
Hefele, Bp., 14, 37, 153 f., 175, 198 f., 202, 204, 209, 222, 232, 239, 242.
Hermas, 188.
Hermits, see Solitaries.
High priest, see Bishop.
Hippo, Council of (A.D. 393), 39, 175.
Hippolytus, 13, 28, 154, 157, 225, 240. See Canons of Hippolytus, and Constitutiones per Hippolytum.
Holy Ghost, personality and divinity of the, 20, 35, 40, 158,176; procession of the, 41.
Holy week, 39, 218, 232, 234.
Homoousion, see Consubstantial.
Horner, Rev. G., 10.
Hort, Dr., 242.
Hosanna, 167, 177.
Hours of prayer, 29, 31, 68, 109, 136 f., 236-238.

Huntsmen, public, not to be catechumens, 117, 208.
Hymns, see Canticles.

ICONOSTASIS, the, 151.
Idols, priests and makers of, to be rejected, 117.
Ignatius, Pseudo-, 14, 19, 175, 218.
Ignatius, St., on the Holy Trinity, 175; said to have introduced antiphonal singing, 181; on presbyters, 192; on the ignorance of the devil, 185.
Ignorance of angels and demons about the Incarnation, 86, 185.
Imposition of the hand, see Laying on of the hand.
Incense, 34, 166 f.
Incorruptibility, 23, 65, 72, 80, 86, 88, 95, 123.
Infants, see Babes; baptism of, 125, 213 f.; communion of, 76.
Instrumental music, absence of, 181.
Intercession at Eucharist, 74 f., 246 ff.; developed, 33, 34, 167, 176, 251.
Interpreters, 43, 44, 204; of dreams, to be rejected, 118.
Invocation, in Eucharist, 24, 33, 35, 74, 166-168, 174-176, 247, 250; in confirmation, 127, 216, 219 f.
Irenaeus, St., on Invocation, 174. See Pfaffian fragment.
Isidore of Pelusium, 204.

JACOBITES, see West Syrians.
James, Dr. M. R., 6, 58, 141 f., 146.
James, St., Liturgy of, 169, 171, 177.
James of Edessa, 5, 6, 7, 24, 26, 42, 64, 138, 142 f., 145, 151 f., 155, 159, 169, 177, 185, 193, 200, 212, 224-226, 229, 240 f., 249.
Jerome, St., 38, 210, 237.
Jerusalem, 43, 138; considered as place of writing of *Testament*, 43. See also Silvia, Constantine, Cyril.
Jews, not mentioned in *Testament*, 43; their choirs, 181; their Pascha, 233.
Judaea, 57.
Julian the Apostate, 36, 41, 42.
Justification, 23, 58.
Justin Martyr, St., 153, 160, 170, 204, 216, 220, 223, 234, 250.
Justinian, 154.

KEATING, Dr. J. F., 229 f.
Kiss of peace, see Peace.
Kneeling at prayer, 100, 121, 129 f., 227 f.
Kyrie Eleison, 152, 181, 193.

INDEX OF SUBJECTS AND AUTHORS 265

LAGARDE, Dr. de, 4, 6, 9, 11, 13, 49, 50, 53-55, 58, 97, 98, 104, 113, 117, 125, 131, 145 f., 150, 155, 158-161, 163, 167, 170-172, 176 f., 179 f., 186-190, 192-195, 197-199, 202-205, 207, 209-212, 215 f., 218, 221-225, 230-233, 237, 240.
Lamp, offering of the, 129, 150, 227.
Laodicea (in Phrygia), Council of, date, 37, 154, 191; metropolitans at, 37 ; forbids women to be near the altar, 168 f.; on singers, 38, 180 ; on the use of the stole, 37, 180, 191 ; on widows "who sit in front," 39, 198 f.; on the choice of bishops, 153 ; on subdeacons, 202.
Laodicea (in Syria), 16, 43.
Late comers, prayers for, 102, 103, 193 f. ; typical of Day of Judgment, 22, 102.
Lavabo, see Washing of hands.
Laver of regeneration, baptism the, 127, 219.
Laying on of the hand, singular or plural, 161 ; as benediction, 182.
Laymen, intercession for, 101 ; baptizing, 225.
Lectern, 63 f., 152.
Lections, 63 f.; at Eucharist, 84, 181 f.; at Pascha, 125, 129, 133, 232 ; readers of, 84, 167, 203 f.
Lent, see Pascha.
Licinius, 208.
Lifegiver, the, 20, 40, 108, 201, 214, 218, 241 f.
Light, 15, 21, 50 f., 58, 60, 63, 66, 71, 72, 77, 79, 80, 82, 83, 85, 86, 88, 91, 93 05, 97, 100, 103-105, 107, 111, 120-123, 138; how typical, 150 f.
Lightfoot, Bishop, 11, 19.
Linen, pure, 63, 151.
Litany, see Deacon.
Liturgy, see Eucharist.
Lord, the (the Holy Ghost), 20, 40, 78, 179, 201, 241.
Lord's Prayer, absence of, in *Testament* and other liturgies, 178 ; allusions to, 76, 77, 178 ; doxology of, 178 ; in Didaché, *ib.*; in A.C. at baptism, 215.
Lost Church Order, 8, 157 f., 226.
Love feasts, see Agapé.
Ludolf, Job, 9, 30, 31, 155-157, 159, 165, 167, 187, 195-197, 223, 245, 247-249, 251.
Lycaonia, 56, 57.
Lycia, 56.

MACEDONIAN heresy, 35, 41, 176.
M'Lean, N., 142.

Magicians not to be catechumens, 118 (cf. 123).
Magnus, 138, 240.
Maker of life, see Lifegiver.
Manuscripts of *Testament*, 5-7.
Maranatha, 177.
Marcellus of Ancyra, 242.
Marcionites, 164, 185.
Mark, St., Liturgy of, 169, 172, 177, 223, 249.
Mark the Hermit, 223.
Marriage after ordination, 154. See Bishops, Presbyters.
Married men's prayers, 136 f., 238.
Martyred catechumens, 120, 211.
Martyrs, festivals of, in A.C., 32.
Maundy Thursday, 121, 129, 201 f., 211, 226 f., 239.
Meat forbidden to bishops, 68, 163.
Metropolitans, absence of, 37.
Military service forbidden, see Soldiers.
Milk and honey at baptism, 24, 44, 221 f.
Milligan, Prof., 225.
Mithras, 151.
Mixed chalice, 73, 128, 221 f., 247.
Monarchical and indissoluble Church, 16, 65, 156.
Monasticism, absence of, 38.
Monophysitism and Monophysites, 5, 17, 43. See West Syrians.
Monstrous births, 53.
Montanistic influence on *Testament*, 15, 16, 44, 45, 144, 186, 194, 197, 200.
Morin, Dom G., 15, 28.
Mozarabic rite, 170.
Muratorian fragment, 149.
Mystagogia, 17, 20, 34, 69, 84-90, 182-186, 252 ff.; when said, 90, 184.

NAMING, of subdeacons and readers, 112, 202 f.; of the offerer of first fruits, 132, 231 ; of offerers for the Eucharist, etc., 63, 152.
Necromancers, see Magicians.
Neocaesarea, Council of, 37, 154, 192.
Nestorianism, 35, 180.
Nestorians, see East Syrians.
Nestorius, Liturgy of (so-called), influenced by Byzantine rite, 171 ; benediction before Sursum Corda in, 169 ; Words of Institution in, 171 f.; Invocation in, 176.
."New-comers," 115 ff., 207-209.
New stone or decree, the, 129, 224.
New [Testament], the, 119, 182, 210 f.
Newly baptized, the, 76, 128, 130, 134.

266   INDEX OF SUBJECTS AND AUTHORS

Nicaea, First Oecumenical Council of, 32, 37, 156, 196, 208, 218, 222, 223, 228, 249; Creed of, 40, 241 f.
Nicetas, 240.
Nicetas of Romatiana, 217.
Nicodemus, Gospel of, 185.
Numbers of chapters in Codex S., 189.

OBLATION, the, at the Eucharist, 33, 73, 165–168, 170–174. See Offerings.
Offering, by deacons, 128, 222; house of, 64, 152. See Eucharist.
Offerings, 62–64. See First fruits.
Oil, blessing of, 77, 78, 179; of anointing, 125 ff., 213 ff.; of exorcism, 125 f., 213 ff.; a type, 22, 78.
Old age and the presbyterate, 91, 110, 187 f., 202.
Omissions in the *Testament*, 23 f., 171, 173, 176, 221, 223, 224.
Order of the dawn service, 164 f.
Orientation of churches, 150.
Orthodox, see Eastern Church.
Oxyrhynchus Logia, 212.

PALESTINE considered as the place of writing of *Testament*, 43.
Palm Sunday, 40.
Parabolani, 191.
Paraclete, 15, 78, 179, 241 f.
Parents or kinsfolk to be sponsors for babes at baptism, 125, 214.
Parish, see Diocese.
Paronomasia, 42, 62, 91, 110, 122, 187 f., 202.
Pascha, 32, 39 f., 90, 109, 129 f., 133, 232 f.; forty days of, 39, 44, 124, 218.
Paschal taper, 227.
Paula, 237.
Payne-Smith, Dean, 49, 184, 210, 224 f.
Peace, kiss of, 68, 70, 92, 119, 128, 160, 168, 210.
Penitents 87 f., 103, 194; no stations of, 37, 38, 194.
Pentecost, 32, 39, 40, 90, 109, 130, 162, 218, 227 f.
Persecutions, 27, 35, 36, 41, 72, 96, 101, 249.
Person (theological), 180.
Personification of abstracts, 22 (where see references), 31, 183, 196.
Peter, shadow of, 234 f.
Pfaffian fragment, 172, 174.
Phials, the holy, 107, 200.
Phoenicia, 57.
Phrygia, 15, 199.
Pilgrimage of Silvia, see Silvia.
Pisidia, 57.

Place of writing of *Testament*, 42–45.
Platt, see Ethiopic Didascalia.
Pliny, letter to Trajan, 168, 181, 230; on the evil eye, 146 f.
Pneumatomachi, see Macedonian heresy.
Polycarp, 198.
Pontus, 57.
Porches, 62, 63, 149 f.
Post-baptismal sin, 24, 194.
Prayer "completed," 84, 102, 193 f.; extempore (?), 164, 193 f.
Prayers to the Son, 20, 39, 179.
Preaching, 133, 182. See Bishop.
Pre-anaphoral prayers, 78–84, 179 f.
"Presbyter" and "Priest," 177 f.
Presbyterate, spirit of the, 91, 100, 187, 195 f.
Presbyteresses, 15, 38, 39, 44, 101, 110, 134, 198–200, 202.
Presbyters, position and division of, in church, 63, 70, 150, 200; house of, 64; communion of, 76; as singers, 81; qualifications of, 90; marriage of, 186; ordination of, other presbyters assisting, 90–92, 186–188; duties and fasts of, 92–95, 162, 188; teaching of, 93; visiting the sick, 94, 188; food of, 92, 95, 188; to celebrate the Eucharist like bishops, 95; daily prayers of, 95 ff., 189; carry Eucharist to sick priests, 134, 234; number of, 99, 191 f., 200; in baptism, 125 f., 213–215; when sick, 134, 234; prayed for in litany, 100; the twelve, with phials, 107, 200.
President (=bishop), 150, 204.
"Priesthood" in Syriac, 178.
Prisoners, 81, 132.
Promotion of clergy, 112, 202; of catechumens, 120.
Property of Christians, 131 f., 135, 230 f.; of widows, 107.
Prophecy, gift of, 15, 97, 186.
Prophetesses, absence of, 16.
Prophets, 15, 22, 63, 69, 81, 84, 87, 100, 104, 110, 116, 127, 136, 181, 204; number of, 149.
Prudentius, 192.
Psalmists, see Singers.
Psalm-singing, 63, 81, 129, 135, 136, 167, 181, 189, 226.
Pseudo-Ambrose, see Ambrosiaster.
Pseudo-Clement, see Clement.
Pseudo-Ignatius, see Ignatius.
Pshiṭta version of the Bible, 51, 64, 69, 75, 104, 106, 112, 122, 138, 147, 155, 159, 168, 193, 212.

INDEX OF SUBJECTS AND AUTHORS 267

Psychic man, the, 31, 128, 222.
Pusey, P. E., 177.

QUALIFICATIONS of clergy, see Bishop, Presbyters, Deacons.
Quartodecimans, 45, 218, 233.
Quotations from the Bible, 23, 24, 255.

RAHMANI, Mgr., 4, 6, 11, 25, 55, 70, 72, 73, 85, 86, 87, 88, 90, 93, 103, 116, 126 f., 136 f., 146, 148, 149, 152, 155 f., 167, 170, 173, 183–185, 187 f., 191, 200 f., 208, 222, 226 f., 229.
Readers, position of, in church, 70; communion of, 76; intercession for, 101; numbers of, at Rome in 251 A.D., 192; promotion of, 112, 202; appointment of, on Sunday, 112; not in Test. by laying on of hands, 33, 112, 205; naming of, 202 f.; reading lections, 84, 203 f.; experience required in, 204 f.; relative position of, 203 f.; associated with chief deacon in writing and reciting names of offerers, 63, 204; keep order in the church, 133; in Sarapion, 204.
Renunciations in baptism, 33, 126, 213–215.
Repetitions, 173.
Reservation of Eucharist, 137, 164, 239.
Responses at baptism, 125 f., 213 ff.
"Rest," 23, 62, 101, 112, 132, 148, 195.
Resurrection, not taught till after baptism, 128 f., 221, 224 f.; typified by the evening, 22, 136.
Revelations, supernatural, 15, 65, 74, 92, 100, 150, 186, 198, 205 f., 251.
Riez, Council of, 37.
Roman ordinal, 186.
Rome, Lent at, 218; Good Friday communion at, 239; early service books at, 8, 169; daily service at, 189; number of clergy at, 192; position of clergy at, 203.

SAHIDIC Ecclesiastical Canons, 12 f., 167, 170, 176, 223. See Egyptian Heptateuch.
Sailors, 42, 233.
Sancta Sanctis, 71, 167 f., 170, 249.
Sanctuary, see Church, Altar, Veil.
Sanctus, absence of, in *Testament*, 170; absence of, in other liturgies, 30, 35; found in some ancient liturgies, 167 f., 170.
Sanday, Professor, 217.
Sarapion, Bishop of Thmuis, prayer-book of, 14; on the Holy Spirit, 20, 175; interpreters in, 43; doxologies in, 160; on the Sunday Eucharist, 164; liturgy of, 168; Eucharistic type in, 172 f.; Sanctus in, 168, 170; Invocation in, 25, 175; Eucharistic Intercession in, 176; Words of Institution in, 171; omits "This do," etc., 173; fraction in, 179; blessing of oil and water in, 179; ordination prayer of a presbyter in, 187; of a deacon, 196; no benediction of minor orders in, 204; oil of exorcism in, 216; no widows or deaconesses mentioned in, 200; prayers for the faithful departed in, 235.
Saturday, Eucharist on, 69, 163 f.; whether a fast or a feast, 164.
Schaff, Dr., 17.
Sea, the, travellers by, 42, 101, 233; water of, 215 f.; sea-shore, 42, 98 f.
Seal, the, 82, 124, 128, 195, 212 f., 216.
Sectarian work, *Testament* not a, 24 f., 155.
Serapion, see Sarapion.
Sermon on the Mount, application of, 92, 188.
Seventy-two disciples, 192, 249.
Sextons, 136, 235.
Shepherd, the bishop as, 23, 81, 89, 105, 120, 128, 130.
Shepherds, the clergy as, 23, 53, 54.
Sick, the, see Visiting.
Sickle of Antichrist, 58, 142, 147.
Sign of the Cross, see Seal.
Signs of the end, 50 ff.
Silas, Silvanus, 138, 240.
Silvia, Pilgrimage of, description of, 14; Christmas in, 40; Palm Sunday in, 40; "commemoration" in, 151 f., 193; incense in, 34, 167; singing boys in, 152, 181; on preaching, 182; lections in, 181; daily service in, 161, 189, 227, 238; hours of prayer in, 237 f.
Singers, 38, 81, 129, 135, 180 f., 191 f., 205.
Slaves, rules for reception of, 116, 118, 209.
Smith and Cheetham, Dictionary of Christian Antiquities, 44, 150, 152, 191 f., 200.
Smith and Wace, Dictionary of Christian Biography, 17, 41, 199, 201, 237, 240–242.
Socrates, 181, 218, 239.
Soldiers, Christians forbidden to be, 24, 33, 36, 118, 208 f.
Solitaries, 204.

268   INDEX OF SUBJECTS AND AUTHORS

Son of perdition, see Antichrist.
Sorcerers, see Magicians.
Soul of our Lord, 17, 19, 85, 87, 182, 184.
Souls have "figures," 15, 107, 200.
Sozomen, 182.
Spirit, works of the, 15.
Sponsors, at baptism, 125, 213 f.
State, references to, 35, 36, 101.
Stations, see Penitents.
Statuta ecclesiae antiqua, see Gallican Statutes.
Stephen, St., festival of, in A.C. 32.
Steps, of bishop's throne, 63. See Entrances, exalted.
Stole, use of, by chief deacon, 37, 99, 191; by cantors, etc., 180.
Strangled things not to be eaten, 133, 232.
Subdeacons, position of, in church, 70; communion of, 76; number of, 99, 191 f.; intercession for, 101; not ordained in Test. by laying on of hands, 32, 202-205; promotion of, 112, 202; not in C.H (?) or Ap. C.O., 203; appointment of, on Sunday, 111, 202; naming of, 202 f.; keeping order in church, 133, 232; visiting the sick, 234; relative position of, 203; reading lections, 204; in Sarapion, 204.
Submission, formula of, at baptism, 29, 33, 126, 213-216.
Subordinationism, 16, 19.
Sunday, day of refreshment, 130, 228; of Eucharist, 69, 163 f.; of ordination, 65, 111, 112, 155, 202.
Sursum corda, 71, 165-169, 249; applied to other offices, etc., 79, 81 f., 95, 99, 180.
Swainson, Dr., 242.
Swete, Dr., 41, 176, 201, 235.
Syria, 43, 56, 199; considered as place of writing of *Testament*, 43.
Syrian Octateuch, 5, 6, 12.
Syrians, see East Syrians, West Syrians.

TABERNACLES, see Habitations.
Tares in the wheat, 93, 188.
Tattam, Archdeacon, 9, 11, 13, 141, 153, 155, 160 f., 165, 170, 173, 176, 186-188, 191 f., 196-198, 200, 202 f., 205, 210-212, 223-225, 228, 230 f., 233 f., 236, 238 f.
Teaching of the Apostles, see Didaché.
"Temple," the, 109, 201.
Tendency of *Testament*, 19, 27.
Tertullian, on bishops as high priests, 160; on the Eucharistic type, 172;
on hours of service, 168; on the Word, 175; on readers, 203; on Pentecost, 228; passage about the souls, 15, 200; on "hearers," 37; no oil of exorcism in, 216; on confirmation, 220; on milk and honey at baptism, 221; on administrators of Eucharist, 223; on spilling the elements, 224; on the Agapé, 229; on oblations for the departed, 235; on reservation of Eucharist, 239.
Testament, the name, 3, 4, 23, 34, 49, 61, 138.
Testing spirits, 23, 55, 59, 69, 93, 120.
Thaddaeus, see Adai.
Theatrical profession forbidden to Christians, 36, 117 f., 208.
Theodore, East Syrian Liturgy of (so called), 169, 171 f., 176.
Theodoret, 152.
Theodosius II., 145.
Theology of *Testament*, 16 ff., 35. See Apollinarius.
"Third Order," the, 62, 148.
Thomas of Harkel, 224.
Throne, see Bishop.
Tithes, 230.
Toledo, First Council of, 204.
Translations of the *Testament*, 6, 43.
Travellers, intercession for, 101; by sea, 233; carry the sacrament, 239.
Treasury, the, 64, 152.
Trèves fragment of Prelude, 6, 52, 53, 57, 58, 141 f., 146 f.
Trinity, 20, 62, 65, 69, 74, 76, 124, 150, 157, 174 f., 250.
Triple division of man, 17, 182.
Trisagion, 178.
Type, the Eucharistic, 21, 73, 128, 172 f., 250.
Types, 21 f., 60, 62, 63, 64, 66, 67, 68, 69, 77, 78, 80, 86, 96, 102, 107, 133, 136, 150 f., 221 f., 232.

ÜLTZEN, Dr., 13.

VEIL, of the sanctuary, 63, 151, 167 f.; why drawn at the Eucharist, 70, 168; of the baptistery, 63; at baptism, 127; of the paten (?), 129, 225; of married women, 119, 210; of virgins, 16, 113, 205.
Verona fragments (Dr. Hauler's), description of, 10, 12, 13, 16; date of, 31, 32; not Roman or Alexandrian, 44; connecting link between the two Church Orders in, 147; ordination prayer for bishops in, 157 f.; say nothing about the celibacy of the

INDEX OF SUBJECTS AND AUTHORS 269

clergy, 153; on the choice of the bishop by the people, 153; on laying on of hand or hands, 161; on bishops as chief priests, 158, 160; liturgy in, 31, 166; Words of Institution in, 171; fraction in, 179; on the Eucharistic type, 173; Invocation in, 166, 175 f.; no Eucharistic Intercession in, 176; on presbyters assisting the bishop at a presbyter's ordination, 186; ordination prayer for presbyter in, 31, 187; for deacons, 31, 104, 196; supplies link between Ethiopic Church Order and *Testament*, 166, 196; close connection with *Testament*, 31, 44; restrict deacons, 195; on baptism and confirmation, 214 f., 219 f.; baptismal creed in, 31, 217, 224; on the Eucharistic type, 222; the baptismal Eucharist in, 221 f.; administrators of Eucharist in, 223; on care of the Eucharistic species, 224; Agapé in, 31, 229; on first fruits, 31, 230 f.; on the fast before Easter, 31, 233; on bishops visiting the sick, 234; on hours of prayer, 31, 237; on fasting communion, 239; on mutual instruction, 238 f.

Versions of the *Testament*, 6, 43.

Vessels, holy, 22, 51, 91, 108, 127.

Vestments, not mentioned in the *Testament* for the services, 37, 178; in C.H., 163, 178. See White robes.

Vigil of Easter, 125, 133, 213, 226, 232. See Easter Even.

Virgins, 76, 81, 106, 112–114, 119, 125, 134, 135, 181, 192, 204 f.; no hand to be laid on them, 113, 205; veils of female virgins, 16, 113, 205; female virgins as brides of Christ, 205.

Visiting the sick, 94, 107, 121, 134, 135, 198, 234 f.

WASHING of hands, 65, 136, 155, 167, 236.

Water, to be flowing for baptism, 125; no blessing of, for baptism, 214;
blessing of, for the sick, 78, 179; plentiful in Test., 43, 44.

West Syrians (Monophysites), 5, 37, 43, 152, 163, 225, 241; their ordinal, 156.

White robes of the newly baptized, 130, 228; of chief deacon, 99.

Widowers, bishops as, 154.

Widows, "who sit in front," 21, 38, 39, 64, 108, 111, 120, 127, 198 f.; no other professed widows in the *Testament*, 44, 199; house of, 64; included among the clergy, and within the veil at the Eucharist, 70, 167 ff.; communion of, 76; number of, 99, 191 f., 198; qualifications of, 105 f., 197 f.; monogamy of, 198; identical with presbyteresses in *Testament*, 199; to teach women, 106 f., 120, 197 f.; relation to deaconesses, 106, 198–200; their prayers are the altar of God, 107, 198; to assist deacons, 107, 200; prayer of the institution of, 108; hours of prayer of, 109; not to speak in the church, 16, 107, 198, 202; form of prayer used by, 110, 111; functions of, at baptism, 126, 216; their appointment forbidden at Laodicea, 39, 198 f.; relative position of, 203; receiving alms, 107, 129, 198, 225 f.

Wine, 68, 69, 95, 163, 188 f.

Women treated with violence, 103.

Women's ministry slighted in Apost. Ch. Order, 148, 198. See Widows.

Words of Institution, 24, 73, 170–172, 247, 250; incorporating 1 Cor. xi. 26, 73, 172, 247, 250.

Wordsworth, Bishop J., 8, 14, 16–19, 25, 28, 34, 152, 154, 156, 159, 161, 163, 168, 172 f., 175, 181–186, 189, 191 f., 194, 199 f., 203–205, 216, 222, 227, 235, 237 f., 240.

Work, Works, 22, 58, 94, 101, 104, 107, 113, 114, 119, 128, 136, 195.

ZAHN, Dr., 25, 45, 240.

www.ingramcontent.com/pod-product-compliance
Lightning Source LLC
Chambersburg PA
CBHW050341230426
43663CB00010B/1946